VIEWPOINTS ON INTERVENTIONS FOR LEARNERS WITH DISABILITIES

ADVANCES IN SPECIAL EDUCATION

Series Editor: Festus E. Obiakor and Jeffrey P. Bakken

VIEWPOINTS ON INTERVENTIONS FOR LEARNERS WITH DISABILITIES

EDITED BY

FESTUS E. OBIAKOR

Sunny Educational Consulting, Shorewood, Wisconsin, USA

JEFFREY P. BAKKEN

Bradley University, Peoria, Illinois, USA

United Kingdom – North America – Japan – India – Malaysia – China

Emerald Publishing Limited
Howard House, Wagon Lane, Bingley BD16 1WA, UK

First edition 2018

Reprints and permissions service
Contact: permissions@emeraldinsight.com

British Library Cataloguing in Publication Data
A catalogue record for this book is available from the British Library

ISBN: 978-1-78743-090-7 (Print)
ISBN: 978-1-78743-089-1 (Online)
ISBN: 978-1-78743-247-5 (Epub)

ISSN: 0270-4013 (Series)

Printed and bound by CPI Group (UK) Ltd, Croydon, CR0 4YY

ISOQAR certified
Management System,
awarded to Emerald
for adherence to
Environmental
standard
ISO 14001:2004.

Certificate Number 1985
ISO 14001

INVESTOR IN PEOPLE

Contents

About the Editors

Festus E. Obiakor, Ph.D., is the Chief Executive Manager, Sunny Educational Consulting, Shorewood, Wisconsin. He has served as Department Head and Professor, Valdosta State University, Valdosta, Georgia and The City College of New York, New York. A Teacher, Scholar, Leader, and Consultant, he has served as Distinguished Visiting Professor at a variety of universities. He is the author of more than 150 publications, including books, articles, and commentaries; and he has presented papers at many national and international conferences. He serves on the editorial boards of reputable nationally and internationally refereed journals, including *Multicultural Learning and Teaching* in which he serves as executive editor. Dr. Obiakor is a leader who has been involved in many landmark scholarly works in the fields of general and special education, with particular focus on African American and other culturally and linguistically diverse learners and he continues to prescribe multidimensional methods of assessment, teaching, and intervention for these individuals. Based on this premise, Dr. Obiakor created the comprehensive support model, an intervention model that values the collaborative, consultative, and cooperative energies of students, families, teachers/service providers, communities, and government agencies.

Dr. Jeffrey P. Bakken, Ph.D., is the Associate Provost for Research and Dean of the Graduate School at Bradley University. He has a Bachelor's Degree in Elementary Education from the University of Wisconsin-LaCrosse, and Graduate Degrees in the area of Special Education-Learning Disabilities from Purdue University. His areas of interest include the following: response to intervention, collaboration, teacher effectiveness, assessment, learning strategies, technology, smart classrooms, smart universities, and smart pedagogy. He has written more than 170 academic publications that include books, chapters, journal articles, proceedings at international conferences, audio tapes, encyclopedia articles, and has made 235 presentations at the international/national and regional/state conferences.

List of Contributors

Rita L. Bailey	Honors College, Kennesaw State University, Kennesaw, Georgia, USA
Jeffrey P. Bakken	Graduate School, Bradley University, Peoria, Illinois, USA
Erin Bone	Department of Counseling, Educational Psychology and Special Education, Michigan State University, East Lansing, Michigan, USA
Christy M. Borders	Department of Special Education, Illinois State University, Normal, Illinois, USA
Stacey Jones Bock	Department of Special Education, Illinois State University, Normal, Illinois, USA
Emily C. Bouck	Department of Counseling, Educational Psychology and Special Education, Michigan State University, East Lansing, Michigan, USA
Fredrick J. Brigham	Department of Special Education, George Mason University, Fairfax, Virginia, USA
Michele M. Brigham	Freedom High School, Loudoun County Public Schools, South Riding, Virginia, USA
Angela I. Canto	College of Education, Florida State University, Tallahassee, Florida, USA
Danielle M. Eftaxas	College of Education, Florida State University, Tallahassee, Florida, USA
Stephanie Gardiner-Walsh	Department of Special Education, Illinois State University, Normal, Illinois, USA
Karla Giese	Department of Special Education, Illinois State University, Normal, Illinois, USA
Jessica Graves	School of Education, College of Coastal Georgia, Brunswick, Georgia, USA

Stacy M. Kelly	Department of Special and Early Education, Northern Illinois University, DeKalb, Illinois, USA
Jennifer Kurth	Department of Special Education, University of Kansas, Lawrence, Kansas, USA
Carlos E. Lavin	Department of Special Education, George Mason University, Fairfax, Virginia, USA
John William McKenna	College of Education, University of Massachusetts Lowell, Lowell, Massachusetts, USA
Amanda Miller	Department of Special Education, University of Kansas, Lawrence, Kansas, USA
Sunday O. Obi	Department of Special Education, Kentucky State University, Frankfort, Kentucky, USA
Festus E. Obiakor	Sunny Educational Consulting, Shorewood, Wisconsin, USA
Kristi M. Probst	National Center on Deaf-Blindness, Western Oregon University, Monmouth, Oregon, USA
Shannon Stuart	Special Education Department, University of Wisconsin-Whitewater, Whitewater, Wisconsin, USA
Michael Wehmeyer	Department of Special Education, University of Kansas, Lawrence, Kansas, USA
Margaret P. Weiss	Division of Special Education and disAbility Research, George Mason University, Fairfax, Virginia, USA
Alison Zagona	Department of Special Education, University of New Mexico, Albuquerque, New Mexico, USA
Lindsay Zurawski	Department of Special Education, George Mason University, Fairfax, Virginia, USA

Preface

As a construct, "intervention" indicates mediation, remediation, or proactive action that can be intentional, unintentional, systemic, or individualistic. And as a topic, intervention has changed over the years from its first introduction in clinical psychotherapy, psychology, and psychiatry to affect human behavior. Today, it has become a popular topic in general and special education arenas due to advocacy, legislation, research, and new pedagogical trends. In addition, this topic can be somewhat controversial depending on the disability that a child, student, or youth might have; and it can depend on the professional dispositions of those involved in the process of working with learners with disabilities. To a large extent, in general and special education, interventions involve change-oriented pragmatic efforts to solve or ameliorate problems confronting children, youth, and adults who may or may not have exceptionalities. Despite the importance of these efforts, there is no comprehensive voluminous resource that effectively addresses differential viewpoints on interventions in the field of special education. It is in this spirit that we produce this book volume titled, *Viewpoints on Interventions for Learners with Disabilities*.

It is a common fact that there continues to be difficulty in keeping up with everything in education and also be updated in all areas related to special education. This is the more reason why we are very excited about *Viewpoints on Interventions for Learners with Disabilities*. First, this book is edited and written by leaders in the field of special education and its related fields. In other words, it is an excellent resource for regular educators, special educators, administrators, mental health clinicians, school counselors, diagnosticians, psychotherapists, and psychologists, to mention a few. And second, this book contains viewpoints and perspectives that are evidence-based, research supported, and practitioner friendly. A logical extension is that it addresses how interventions have changed over time and how they have impacted direct services for learners with disabilities.

Viewpoints on Interventions for Learners with Disabilities is a book for this day and age. As indicated, we are impressed with the scholarship and clarity of our book's contributors. In Introduction, we introduce readers to viewpoints on interventions for learners with disabilities; in Chapter 1, Weiss focuses on interventions for students with learning disabilities; in Chapter 2, Brigham et al. focus on interventions for students with emotional and behavioral disorders; in Chapter 3, Bouck and Bone focus interventions for students with intellectual disabilities; in Chapter 4, Borders et al. focus on interventions for students who are deaf and hard of hearing; in Chapter 5, Kelly focuses on interventions for students with visual impairments; in Chapter 6, Stuart focuses on interventions for students with autism; in Chapter 7, Kurth et al. focus on interventions for students with severe disabilities; in Chapter 8, Canto and Eftaxas focus on interventions for students with traumatic brain injury; in Chapter 9, Bailey focuses on interventions for students with speech or language impairments; in Chapter 10, Obi focuses on interventions for students with physical disabilities and other health impairments; and in Chapter 11, in collaboration with Graves, we go beyond tradition to discuss interventions for students with disabilities.

Finally, books of this nature will not materialize without professional collaboration, consultation, and cooperation. We thank our contributors for their dedication to excellence. This book will be an excellent resource to general and special education practitioners, educator preparation professionals, and undergraduate and graduate students. In the end, we wholeheartedly thank our wives and children for their crucial support during this worthy venture.

Festus E. Obiakor
Jeffrey P. Bakken
Series Editors

Viewpoints on Interventions for Learners with Disabilities: An Introduction

Jeffrey P. Bakken and Festus E. Obiakor

Abstract

People with disabilities have always existed in our communities and societies; however, how we treat them has always been an issue. For example, for a long time, people with physical disabilities received more attention than those with disabilities that we could hardly see (e.g., learning disabilities). Very early research focused on students with sensory impairments and then the focus shifted to students with cognitive impairments. Finally, the focus was on students with learning disabilities and emotional behavioral disorders. Early research with this last group of students focused on comparing students with and without disabilities to document deficits and characteristics of these individuals. Over time, when the characteristics were established, researchers moved their attention to interventions or ways to improve deficits in specific content areas such as reading and mathematics. This chapter is an introduction to the rest of this volume that addresses different viewpoints on interventions for students with different types of disabilities.

Keywords: Disabilities; research; research-based; interventions; outcomes

Introduction: Early Roots of Special Education

Formed by a combination of philosophical, economic, legal, sociocultural, and political factors (Fleischer & Zames, 2001; Giordano, 2007;

Viewpoints on Interventions for Learners with Disabilities
Advances in Special Education, Volume 33, 1–12
Copyright © 2018 by Emerald Publishing Limited
All rights of reproduction in any form reserved
ISSN: 0270-4013/doi:10.1108/S0270-401320180000033001

Osgood, 2007; Reynolds, 1989), the history of special education has seen continuing challenges, successes, and debates. Recent attention has focused on desired goals and outcomes, what populations should be served by special education, how research-based practices can be provided to students, and the best environment to educate students with exceptionalities.

Through the 1800s, physicians usually advised parents who gave birth to a child with a disability to let the child die or place him/her in an institution (Chesterton, 2000). Those children allowed to live were usually committed to institutions and rarely seen in public. The 1880 U.S. Federal Census offers an example of the social context of the time as it refers to a category of people as "insane, idiots, deaf-mutes, blind persons, homeless children, prisoners, paupers, and the indigent"(Ancestry.com, p. 1). Institutions were basic and less than ideal – dealing only with basic needs – and crowded with the main purpose to control people with disabilities in order to protect the public. Education was not an option for the disabled, and attendance in public schools was strictly restricted.

Initial Focus on the Sensory Disabilities

Initial efforts to deliver special education and develop specially designed instruction were focused on individuals with sensory disabilities (Best, 1930; Winzer, 1998). During the mid-sixteenth century, Pedro Ponce de Leon, a Spanish Benedictine monk, created oralism, an alternative to sign language that involved the teaching of lip-reading and speech, to teach wealthy deaf individuals to speak in order to obtain their inheritance (Buchanan, 1999; Burch & Sutherland, 2006; Lane, 1989; Winzer, 1998). The use of oralism grew and became the dominant mode of communication taught in schools for the deaf from the 1890s to the 1920s (Burch & Sutherland, 2006; Winzer, 1998). However, Michel Charles de l'Épée, a French priest, challenged the use of oralism and fostered the belief that the use of written characters and sign language was the most effective way to educate the deaf, which resulted in the use of sign language as the prevailing deaf education pedagogy during the first half of the 1800s (Winzer, 1998).

Successful instructional practices for the deaf led to efforts to develop effective specially designed approaches and techniques for blind individuals (Winzer, 1998). In 1784, Valentin Haüy, the founder of a school for the blind in Paris, devised a system of raised print and embossed books to educate blind students (see Winzer, 1998). In 1829, Louis Braille, a former student at the Paris Blind School, created a raised dot method for reading and a stylus for writing, which led to the creation of a tactile alphabet that provided blind individuals with access to reading materials and allowed them to be more fully included in French society (Koestler, 1976).

As word of the successes of these efforts to educate individuals with sensory disabilities spread outside of Europe, educators traveled to learn about these effective special education practices and to implement and expand on them in their countries (see Winzer, 1993). As a result, Dr. John D. Fischer, created the New England Asylum for the Blind in 1829, which was later renamed the Perkins Institute for the Blind now called the Perkins School for the Blind (Fleischer & Zames, 2001; Winzer, 1993). At the Perkins institute, Dr. Samuel Gridley Howe worked with Laura Bridgman, a deaf-blind student. Employing an individually designed approach based on her ability to identify letters by distinguishing shapes, Howe showed that Laura Bridgman could be educated. The groundbreaking work of Howe and Bridgman challenged the accepted beliefs that deaf-blind individuals could not learn and served as a forerunner for the ensuing accomplishments of Helen Keller and her teacher, Anne Mansfield Sullivan (Osgood, 2005; Smith, 1998).

Social Advocacy Movement

Dr. Samuel Howe was noted for his lobbying efforts to deinstitutionalize people with mental retardation and provide training for them. In 1848, he persuaded the legislature of Massachusetts to appropriate public funds to establish the first state school in the U.S. to educate persons with mental retardation. Table 1 summarizes many of the important events occurring during the social advocacy movement, which advanced the recognition of and rights for people with disabilities.

In 1946, Ambassador and Mrs. Joseph P. Kennedy (parents of U.S. President John F. Kennedy) established the Joseph P. Kennedy, Jr. Foundation in honor of their eldest son and in public recognition of the mental disability of one of their daughters. This public acknowledgment that was a surprise to the American people led many to rethink their biases concerning people with disabilities. The foundation continues today, working with and on behalf of individuals with intellectual and developmental disabilities and their families (Joseph P. Kennedy, Jr. Foundation, n.d.).

In 1961, when John F. Kennedy became the U.S. President, he organized the President's Panel on Mental Retardation, formally established the panel in 1966, and directed the members to review and report on mental retardation. The panel found that (a) the quality of care given to

Table 1: Synopsis of Events as Human Rights Began to Evolve for People with Disabilities (People who are Deaf, Blind, Intellectually Disabled, or Learning Disabled).

1817	The first permanent school for the deaf in the U.S., the Connecticut Asylum at Hartford for the Instruction of Deaf and Dumb Persons, opens.
1829	The first school in the US for children with visual disabilities, The Perkins School for the Blind (then called the New England Asylum for the Blind) opens in Massachusetts.
1840	The first American state to mandate compulsory education for children is Rhode Island.
1848	Funding for the "Massachusetts School for Idiotic and Feebleminded Youth," the first school of its kind in the U.S., is secured by Dr. Samuel Howe.
1864	The first college specifically for deaf students, Gallaudet University, is started with the help of Edward Miner Gallaudet.
1876	The first president of the organization that eventually would evolve into the American Association on Mental Retardation is Edouard Seguin.
1905	An article published by Alfred Binet and Theodore Simon describes the development of a measurement instrument that helps to identify students with intellectual disabilities: the Binet–Simon scale.
1916	Louis M. Terman and a team of Stanford graduate students completed an American version of the Binet–Simon scale. This development initiated the widespread use of intelligence testing used over the course of the next century as part of the procedure for identifying students with learning disabilities.
1918	All states in the U.S. had established compulsory education for children by this time. Education for ALL children, however, was not actually an option: Children with disabilities were not included in public schools.

Source: Adapted from McConnell (2007) and Philpot (n.d.).

people with mental retardation varied widely among state institutions, and (b) institutions were overcrowded and had inadequate budgets and staff shortages. Based on these results, the panel identified the need for staff attitudinal changes toward patients at the facilities. In addition, they recommended changes in administrative practices that were leading to widespread abuse, along with improvement in the programs available to people with mental disabilities. In response to the panel's findings, President Kennedy signed into law the Mental Retardation Facilities Construction Act. This Public Law specified that the federal government (a) make federal monies available for the construction of mental health centers and (b) provide grants to assist in the construction of public or nonprofit clinical facilities with the purpose of working with individuals with mental retardation (Public Law 88-164, Mental Retardation Facilities and Community Mental Health Construction Act, 1963). These actions led to positive systemic changes in building local and state services with the goals of (a) making institutions safe, (b) training professionals across disciplines, (c) using expertise found in universities, (d) building interdisciplinary services, and (e) supporting research in mental retardation (now called intellectual disabilities). Although it was not until later that specialized education was mandated for persons with disabilities, the social advocacy movements made progress in providing better measurable services for them.

The Emergence of Specialized Interventions

Whereas intial efforts to design and provide specially designed instruction were focused on individuals with sensory exceptionalities, the provision of special education began to expand to include individuals with cognitive disabilities. Although this period in the history of special education saw the development of specialized interventions for this group of individuals, it also was characterized by the rise of institutions and specialized schools.

Specialized Interventions for Individuals with Cognitive Disabilities

In the early 1800s, the work of Jean-Marc-Gaspard Itard with Victor, who was referred to as the wild boy of Aveyron, served as a seminal event in the field of special education (Safford & Safford, 1996). Itard developed a specially designed pedagogy that enhanced Victor's language and cognitive development, which showed that individuals previously considered uneducable could learn (see Safford & Safford, 1996). Itard's work served as a springboard for other European scholars and educators (Hinshelwood, 1900;

Ireland, 1877; Morgan, 1896) to disseminate their efforts to study and validate a collection of effective special education instructional practices. The most prominent of these efforts was Édouard Seguin's publication, *Treatise on Idiocy*, which presented a set of specialized instructional principles, techniques, and devices that provided others with a pedagogical model for teaching individuals with cognitive disabilities (Giordano, 2007).

Advocacy Groups

The rise of specialized schools and classes and the legislation in Europe led families and professionals to form advocacy groups that called for greater inclusion of individuals with exceptionalities into all aspects of society including providing them with increased educational opportunities (Yell, Rogers, & Rogers, 1998). These groups included the Council for Exceptional Children, a professional organization that was founded in 1922, and the Cuyahoga County Ohio Council for the Retarded Child, one of the initial groups of families who banded together to advocate for their children in 1933.

The Rise of Socially Constructed Disability Categories

The mandates and movements to educate students with exceptionalities contributed to a concomitant increase in the numbers of students identified and changes in the types of students with exceptionalities served by special education. While special education initially focused on serving students with sensory disabilities and then cognitive disabilities, students with socially constructed disabilities now make up the vast majority of students served by special education. These changes were fostered by the creation of such socially constructed disability categories as *emotional disturbance* and *learning disabilities* (Armstrong, 2002). In particular, the category of learning disabilities, a term initially used by Kirk and Bateman (1962), related to students who performed poorly but did not have sensory, physical, or severe cognitive disabilities. This led to a significant growth in the number of students served by special education and the thrust toward a noncategorical approach to structuring the delivery of special education services (Brownell, Sindelar, Kiely, & Danielson, 2010). Additionally, there has been a surge in the number of students receiving special education services who are identified as having an autism spectrum disorder or an attention-deficit disorder (Salend, 2011).

The Ongoing Commitment to Research-Based Practices

Consistent with the field's inception and continuing efforts to develop and disseminate empirically based interventions, the commitment to create and use research-based practices that fosters equality, quality instruction, and educational opportunities for all students continues to be a hallmark of the field of special education (Crockett, Gerber, Gersten, & Harris, 2010). The 1960s and 1970s were characterized by (a) debates over effective models (e.g., the medical model, diagnostic-prescriptive teaching model, and the behavioral model); (b) pedagogical approaches (e.g., perceptual and modality training, dietary changes, motor patterning, and aptitude-by-treatment interaction approach (Mostert & Crockett, 2000; Van Acker, 2006); and (c) the emergence of the precision teaching model that was predicated on examining teaching effectiveness and collecting data related to students' mastery of specific behavioral objectives (Brownell et al., 2010).

Early special education research focused on characteristics of individuals with disabilities. Much of the research investigated student deficits and documenting difficulties they exhibited. For example, research on students with learning disabilities often had samples of students identified with a learning disability and those not identified (normal). They would then have both groups complete an academic task (i.e., reading a passage and retelling it) and compare the results of both groups. The results would indicate that students with learning disabilities did worse than students who did not have a disability. Much of the early research focused on comparing students with and without disabilities and documenting the deficits students with disabilities were experiencing. After the deficits were substantially documented, researchers then began to focus on intervention research, which aimed at finding ways to improve deficit areas of students with disabilities

Special education research has contributed significantly to knowledge and practice not just related to individuals with disabilities but for all learners. Special educators have had the dual responsibility of (a) designing interventions that meet the feasibility criteria for general education classrooms aimed at enhancing outcomes for a range of learners and (b) developing intensive interventions for special educators to meet the individual learning and behavior needs of students with disabilities (Vaughn & Swanson, 2015). Over the past 20 years, considerable emphasis in special education has been placed on designing and implementing effective practices for enhancing outcomes for all learners, including those with disabilities, served in the general education classroom (see Vaughn & Swanson, 2015).

It is generally agreed that intervention research refers to scientifically based efforts to document specific techniques intended to improve, in some acceptable way, the functioning of individuals characterized as learning disabled (Scruggs, 1990). It seems critical that all students included in intervention research studies be shown to exhibit some deficit in the area targeted for intervention (Scruggs, 1990). A major goal of intervention research is to develop effective treatments for students with disabilities. It is important that researchers pursue criteria for determining treatment effectiveness. Skill and strategy-based training have resulted in effects that are consistently positive (Scruggs, 1990).

Once specific interventions are determined to be effective, it is assumed they will be disseminated widely for the purpose of improving practice. Initially, validated practices may be published in special education journals where they are read by university professors, classroom teachers, and undergraduate and graduate students. This is an important forum for dissemination of results (Scruggs, 1990).

Empirical investigations may first start in a laboratory setting where extraneous factors can be controlled and then after positive results would move to an actual classroom setting. In the classroom setting, actual school-based materials could be implemented with all students. Classroom-based research requires the implementation of many different interconnected experiments conducted over extended periods of time, but have the advantage of providing the most valuable information for the special education field. Both laboratory and classroom-based procedures are of critical importance in intervention research.

The Movement to Inclusive Education

Concerns about the growth and segregated nature of special education initially expressed by Lloyd Dunn (1968) and supported by the ongoing research questioning the efficacy of special education programs (McLeskey, 2007), legislative and judicial actions, the persistent problem of disproportionate representation of culturally and linguistically diverse students, and the work of advocacy groups led the field of special education to initially focus on mainstreaming, and then the implementation of inclusive education programs that educate all students together in the general education classroom (Osgood, 2005; Valle & Connor, 2010; Salend, 2011). In general, the research findings suggest that inclusive education can benefit students with and without exceptionalities when their teachers use differentiated instruction and assessment as well as curricular and teaching accommodations within the general education setting (Black-Hawkins, Florian, & Rouse, 2007; Cushing, Carter, Clark, Wallis, & Kennedy, 2009; Salend & Garrick Duhaney, 2007). Because inclusive education is a relatively new philosophy and inclusion programs are multifaceted and varied in their implementation and the services provided (Ainscow, 2008; Idol, 2006), research and models that enhance its implementation, effectiveness, and long-term impact continue to be focuses for the field (Sindelar, Shearer, Yendol-Hoppey, & Liebert, 2006).

The inclusive education movement has led researchers to continue to conduct and share research regarding the efficacy of general education placements for students with exceptionalities (McLeskey, 2007; Salend, 2011). The growing body of research has resulted in the development and validation of innovative practices that have become integral parts of general education such as universal design for learning, collaborative teaching arrangements, cooperative learning, family involvement and empowerment techniques, learning strategy instruction, positive behavioral supports, self-management strategies, and culturally responsive teaching (Gibson & Obiakor, 2018; Obiakor, 2018; Obiakor, Banks, Rotatori, & Utley, 2017; Salend, 2011). The technological advances of the late twentieth and early twenty-first centuries also have led to widespread use of a range of assistive and instructional technologies that enhance student learning and socialization, foster individualized instruction, expand access to all aspects of society, and transform views of exceptionality (Beard, Bowden Carpenter, & Johnston, 2011; Brownell et al., 2010; Blackhurst, 2005; Gibson & Obiakor, 2018).

Conclusion

This chapter sets the stage for the rest of the book chapters on viewpoints and on interventions for learners with disabilities. It also emphatically reiterates the common knowledge that people with disabilities have lived among us in our respective communities. However, the focus was on disabilities (e.g., physical disabilities) that were visible. Later, it became apparent that some disabilities could not be seen physically (e.g., learning disabilities). Over time, individuals conducted research on students with disabilities. Very early research focused on students with sensory impairments and then the focus shifted to students with cognitive impairments. Finally, the focus was on students with learning disabilities and emotional behavioral disorders. Early research with this last group of students focused on comparing students with and without disabilities to document deficits and characteristics of these individuals. Over time, when the characteristics were established, researchers moved their attention to interventions and research that focused on improving student deficits in specific content areas like reading and mathematics. Finally, there is no doubt that frantic efforts have been made to improve interventions for learners with disabilities. Our focus today should be on how to create more intervention techniques that will help people with disabilities to maximize their fullest potential. Clearly, to enhance interventions in the future, we must continue to broaden our scopes toward using evidence-based techniques, emphasizing inclusive education for learners with and without disabilities, and recognizing multicultural education as an important ingredient in special education.

References

Ainscow, M. (2008). Making sure that every child matters: Towards a methodology for enhancing equity within educational systems. In C. Forlin (Ed.), *Catering for learners with diverse needs: An Asia-Pacific focus* (pp. 11–29). Hong Kong: Hong Kong Institute of Education.

Armstrong, F. (2002). The historical development of special education: Humanitarian rationality or 'wild profusion of entangled events'? *History of Education*, 31(5), 437–456.

Beard, L. A., Bowden Carpenter, L., & Johnston, L. (2011). *Assistive technology: Access for all students* (2nd ed.). Columbus, OH: Pearson Education.

Best, H. (1930). Educational provisions for the deaf, the blind, and feeble-minded compared. *American Annals of the Deaf*, 75, 239–240.

Black-Hawkins, K., Florian, L., & Rouse, M. (2007). *Achievement and inclusion in schools*. London: Routledge.

Blackhurst, A. E. (2005). Historical perspective about technology applications for people with disabilities. In D. Edyburn, K. Higgins, & R. Boone (Eds.), *Handbook on special education technology research and practice* (pp. 3–29). Whitefish Bay, WI: Knowledge by Design.

Brownell, M. T., Sindelar, P. T., Kiely, M. T., & Danielson, L. C. (2010). Special education teacher quality and preparation: Exposing foundations, constructing a new model. *Exceptional Children*, 76, 357–377.

Buchanan, R. (1999). *Illusions of equality*. Washington, DC: Gallaudet University Press.

Burch, S., & Sutherland, I. (2006). Who's not here yet? American disability history. *Radical History Review*, 94, 127–147.

Crockett, J., Gerber, M., Gersten, R., & Harris, K. (2010 April). The contributions of research to special education's past, current, and future identity. Paper presented at the annual meeting of the Council for Exceptional Children, Nashville, TN.

Cushing, L. S., Carter, E. W., Clark, N., Wallis, T., & Kennedy, C. H. (2009). Evaluating inclusive educational practices for students with severe disabilities using the program quality measurement tool. *The Journal of Special Education*, 42, 195–208.

Dunn, L. (1968). Special education for the mildly retarded: Is much of it justifiable? *Exceptional Children*, 35, 5–22.

Fleischer, D. Z., & Zames, F. (2001). *The disability rights movement: From charity to confrontation.* Philadelphia, PA: Temple University Press.

Gibson, L., & Obiakor, F. (2018). *Computer-based technology for special and multicultural education: Enhancing 21st century learning.* San Diego, CA: Plural Publishing.

Giordano, G. (2007). *American special education: A history of early political advocacy.* New York, NY: P. Lang.

Hinshelwood, J. (1900). Congenital word-blindness. *Lancet*, 1, 1506–1508.

Idol, L. (2006). Toward inclusion of special education students in general education: A program evaluation of eight schools. *Remedial and Special Education*, 27, 77–94.

Ireland, W. W. (1877). *On idiocy and imbecility.* London: Churchill.

Joseph P. Kennedy, Jr. Foundation. (n.d.). Retrieved from http://www.jpkf.org/index.html

Kirk, S., & Bateman, B. (1962). Diagnosis and remediation of learning disabilities. *Exceptional Children*, 29, 73–78.

Koestler, F. A. (1976). *The unseen minority: A social history of blindness in America.* New York, NY: David McKay Co.

Lane, H. (1989). *When the mind hears: A history of the deaf.* New York, NY: Vintage.

McConnell, T. (2007). *History of special education.* Retrieved from http://www.xtimeline.com/timeline/Timeline-for-Special-Education.

McLeskey, J. (2007). *Reflections on inclusion: Classic articles that shaped our thinking.* Arlington, VA: Council for Exceptional Children.

Mental Retardation Facilities and Community Mental Health Construction Act of 1963 [CMHA]. (1963). P.L. 88–164. Retrieved from www.archives.nysed.gov/edpolicy/research/res_digitized.shtml

Morgan, W. P. (1896). A case of congenital word blindness. *British Medical Journal*, 2, 1378.

Mostert, M. P., & Crockett, J. B. (2000). Reclaiming the history of special education for more effective practice. *Exceptionality*, 8, 133–143.

Obiakor, F. E. (2018). *Powerful multicultural essays for innovative educators and leaders: Optimizing "hearty" conversations.* Charlotte, NC: Information Age.

Obiakor, F. E., Banks, T., Rotatori, A. F., & Utley, C. (2017). *Leadership matters in the education of students with special needs in the 21st century.* Charlotte, NC: Information Age.

Osgood, R. L. (2005). *The history of inclusion in the United States.* Washington, DC: Gallaudet University Press.

Osgood, R. L. (2007). *The history of special education: A struggle for equality in American public schools (Growing up: History of children and youth).* Westport, CT: Praeger Publishers.

Philpot, D. J. (n.d.). *History of federal statutes affecting special education.* Retrieved from www.dphilpotlaw.com/html/history_of_federal_statutes.html. Accessed on April 5, 2010.

Reynolds, M. C. (1989). An historical perspective: The delivery of special education to mildly disabled and at-risk students. *Remedial and Special Education,* 10, 7–11.

Safford, P. S., & Safford, E. J. (1996). *A history of childhood and disability.* New York, NY: Teachers College Press.

Salend, S. J. (2011). *Creating inclusive classrooms: Effective and reflective practices* (7th ed.). Columbus, OH: Pearson Education.

Salend, S. J., & Garrick Duhaney, L. M. (2007). Research related to inclusion and program Effectiveness: Yesterday, today, and tomorrow. In J. McLeskey (Ed.), *Reflections on inclusion: Classic articles that shaped our thinking* (pp. 127–129 and 147–159). Arlington, VA: Council for Exceptional Children.

Scruggs, T. E. (1990). Commentary. Foundations of intervention research. In T. E. Scruggs & B. Y. L. Wong (Eds.), *Intervention research in learning disabilities* (pp. 66–77). New York, NY: Springer.

Sindelar, P. T., Shearer, D. K., Yendol-Hoppey, D., & Liebert, T. W. (2006). The sustainability of inclusive school reform. *Exceptional Children,* 72, 317–331.

Smith, J. D. (1998). Histories of special education: Stories from our past, insights for our future introduction to the special series. *Remedial and Special Education,* 19(4), 196–200.

Valle, J., & Connor, D. (2010). *Rethinking disability: A disabilities studies approach to inclusive practices.* New York, NY: Mc-Graw Hill.

Van Acker, R. (2006). Outlook on special education practice. *Focus on Exceptional Children,* 38(6), 8–18.

Vaughn, S., & Swanson, E. A. (2015). Special education research advances knowledge in education. *Exceptional Children,* 82(1), 11–24.

Winzer, M. A. (1993). *The history of special education: From isolation to integration.* Washington, DC: Gallaudet University Press.

Winzer, M. A. (1998). A tale often told: The early progression of special education. *Remedial and Special Education,* 19(4), 212–218.

Yell, M. L., Rodgers, D., & Rodgers, E. L. (1998). The legal history of special education. *Remedial and Special Education,* 19, 219–229.

Chapter 1

Viewpoint on Interventions for Students with Learning Disabilities: Instruction Matters

Margaret P. Weiss

Abstract

Students with learning disabilities (LD) have a wide range of academic needs. Since the passing of P.L. 94-142, significant research has been done on effective interventions for this group of students. Starting with the Learning Disabilities Research Institutes through the recent Handbook of Learning Disabilities, reviews of lines of research make several broad ideas about interventions clear. Primary among these is that students with LD can learn if provided with appropriate, effective instruction. Specifics about this idea and its implications are discussed in the following chapter.

Keywords: Learning disabilities; interventions; effective instruction; evidence-based practice

Students with learning disabilities (LD) make up the largest group of individuals identified with disabilities in K-12 schools (39.2%; U.S. Department of Education, 2016). This group is also probably the most diverse in terms of academic needs and characteristics. The definition of LD, alone, provides a glimpse into the vast array of possible characteristics that these students may exhibit:

Viewpoints on Interventions for Learners with Disabilities
Advances in Special Education, Volume 33, 13–29
Copyright © 2018 by Emerald Publishing Limited
All rights of reproduction in any form reserved
ISSN: 0270-4013/doi:10.1108/S0270-401320180000033002

A. IN GENERAL – The term "specific learning disability" means a disorder in one or more of the basic psychological processes involved in understanding or in using language, spoken or written, which disorder may manifest itself in imperfect ability to listen, think, speak, read, write, spell, or do mathematical calculations.
B. DISORDERS INCLUDED – Such a term includes such conditions as perceptual disabilities, brain injury, minimal brain dysfunction, dyslexia, and developmental aphasia.
C. DISORDERS NOT INCLUDED – Such a term does not include a learning problem that is primarily the result of visual, hearing, or motor disabilities, of mental retardation, or emotional disturbance, or of environmental, cultural, or economic disadvantage (U.S. Department of Education, 2006, 34 CFR 300.8(c)(10))

How students are identified as having a learning disability is a completely different and often controversial issue that has evolved over time (Fuchs & Fuchs, 1998; Maki, Burns, & Sullivan, 2017; Williams, Miciak, McFarland, & Wexler, 2016). However, the reality is that in Mrs. Jones's fifth grade class, there may be three students with LD; one exhibits difficulty in consistently and accurately pulling multiplication facts from memory, another may not be able to automatically provide the sound related to a specific letter of the alphabet, and the third may be able to share well-formulated thoughts when speaking, but cannot put together a complete sentence or use punctuation rules correctly when writing. To meet the needs of these students and all of the others in the class is quite a task. However, given the fact that students with LD are experiencing unexpected underachievement, and this underachievement is not caused by intellectual disabilities or other economic, cultural, or socioeconomic reasons, the research the field has accumulated over time on interventions consistently indicates at least one thing: instruction matters.

State of LD

Roughly 3.4% of the school-age student population was served through Individuals with Disabilities Education Act (IDEA) as students with LD in 2014. Of these students, 69.2% spent 80% or more of their day in a regular classroom (U.S. Department of Education, 2016). Nearly 71% of students with LD exited school with a regular high school diploma in 2014; compared to 83% of the public school population (National Center for Education Statistics, 2017). However, according to the National Center for Learning Disabilities (NCLD, 2017) with data from the U.S. Census

Bureau, only 46% of working-age adults with LD are employed, compared with 71% of working-age adults without LD. In the 2014 Annual Report to Congress, results of state assessments are not disaggregated by disability area; however, the results of students with disabilities as a whole are telling. In the report, 36.1% of students with disabilities were proficient on state grade-level tests in grade 3 math. By high school, it drops to 18.7%. In reading, 32.1% of third graders with disabilities are proficient; by high school, it is 25% (U.S. Department of Education, 2016). In the *State of LD* document (2017), NCLD found that 33% of classroom teachers and other educators think "learning or attention issue is really just laziness" and 43% of parents would not want others to know that their child has a learning disability. Clearly, there is still work to be done to help students with LD achieve their goals and dreams. The path begins with effective instruction delivered to target specific student need.

Summary of Research on Interventions for Students with LD

In the late 1970s and early 1980s, after false starts with a variety of approaches such as psycholinguistic and perceptual process training programs, the U.S. Office of Education funded five research centers to pursue an evidence-based approach to instruction for students with LD (Hallahan & Mercer, 2002). These original centers were at Columbia, University of Illinois at Chicago, University of Kansas, University of Minnesota, and the University of Virginia. Each center had a specific focus (see Table 1). Columbia was led by Dale Bryant and focused on aspects of information processing with researchers such as Jeannette Fleischner, Joanna Williams, and Walter MacGinitie. The University of Illinois at Chicago group was led by Tanis Bryan and conducted research on social competence and attributions. The University of Kansas Center was directed by Don Deshler and focused on interventions for adolescents. The University of Minnesota group was directed by James Ysseldyke and focused on identification and curriculum-based assessment with the likes of Stan Deno. Finally, the University of Virginia Center, directed by Dan Hallahan, focused research on attention issues, cognitive behavior modification techniques, and strategy instruction with researchers such as John Lloyd (Hallahan & Mercer, 2002). These research teams engaged in systematic lines of research, with elementary and high school students, including interventions and analyses of skills with replication and generalization, which laid the foundation for our thinking about learning and interventions for students with LD today.

Table 1: Learning Disabilities Research Institutes.

Institute	Focus	Director
Columbia University	Memory and study skills, arithmetic, basic reading and spelling, interaction of characteristics of the text and the reader, and reading comprehension	Dale Bryant
University of Illinois at Chicago	Social competence and attributions	Tanis Bryant
University of Kansas	Adolescents with LD	Don Deshler
University of Minnesota	Identification and curriculum-based assessment	James Ysseldyke
University of Virginia	Attention issues, cognitive behavior modification, and strategies for use on academic tasks	Dan Hallahan

Source: Adapted from Hallahan and Mercer (2002).

LD Research Institutes' Findings

In an article summarizing the Institutes, Barbara Keogh (1983) drew the following conclusions: (a) they were productive and shared findings in formats for both researchers and practitioners; (b) the research was programmatic, progressing from understanding student characteristics to developing ways to intervene; (c) the research was of good overall quality; and (d) the major contribution "is the systematic study of learner and instructional variables" (p. 120). She also identified three broad generalizations that resonate in evidence-based practices (EBPs) today. The first is "the recognition of learning disabilities as a strategic, information-processing problem provided important conceptual direction to the field" (p. 122). This recognition provided an operational foundation that students with LD have functional issues, not structural issues, which can be addressed with instruction and targeted attention on teaching strategic approaches to tasks. The second generalization is that the interventions developed worked. As such, she states: "Taken as a whole, the results suggest that LD pupils can and do learn when instruction is derived from an information-processing perspective" (p. 124). These interventions were developed and tested in a thoughtful, conceptually based manner and resulted in positive outcomes for students. The final generalization Dr. Keogh identified was that, "it is clear that LD is a complex condition; that is, that social, motivational, and affective, as well as intellectual, components are involved" (p. 124). The complexity of a learning disability cannot be minimized and instructional interventions must address these complexities in order to be effective. This is clear in the multicomponent nature of current EBPs. Perhaps the statement from the article that is very simple and yet provides the most impact is: "The effect of the interventions has been documented, and the work as a whole has demonstrated impressively that LD pupils can learn" (p. 126). To put it another way, students with LD can learn if their needs are targeted and effective interventions are implemented with fidelity. Instruction matters.

Meta-analyses

In a series of meta-analyses conducted in the late 1990s, Swanson (1999), Swanson, Carson, and Sachse-Lee (1996), and Swanson and Hoskyn (1998) attempted to evaluate the impact of intervention studies on outcomes of students with LD. The focus was on group design studies and interventions that targeted a variety of domains, including reading, math, attitude, intelligence, social skills, perceptual processes, vocabulary, and creativity. In the first analysis (Swanson et al., 1996), 78 studies fit their criteria, and the authors calculated 325 effect sizes (ESs), yielding an average ES of 0.85 (ES of 0.8 and above is considered substantial; Cohen, 1988). When parsed out by a teaching strategy, eclectical strategies (not falling into any category) yielded an ES of 0.59, remedial (individual tutoring) yielded an ES of 0.68, direct instruction an ES of 0.91, and strategic (cognitive) instruction an ES of 1.07. A general conclusion was that no domain was resistant to change, particularly those whose interventions included components of strategic and direct instruction. In the later two analyses, 180 studies were included, resulting in 1,537 ESs and an average ES of 0.79. When parsed out by interventions that included components of specific models, results from studies showed that a combined model of strategic instruction and direct instruction (ES = 0.84) significantly outperformed strategy instruction alone (ES = 0.72), direct instruction alone (ES = 0.68), and neither (ES = 0.62; Swanson, 1999). Instructional components included in strategic instruction and direct instruction models are identified in Table 2. Instructional components that consistently predicted better outcomes for students with LD included the following: (1) control of task difficulty, (2) strategy cuing, (3) small interactive groups,

Table 2: Instructional Components of Strategic Instruction and Direct Instruction Models.

Strategic Instruction	Both	Direct Instruction
Advance organizer	Effective instruction includes the following: review of previous learning, statement of objective, teacher presentation of new material, guided practice, independent practice, and formative evaluation	Break tasks into small steps
Organization	Active presentation of information	Administer probes
Generative learning	Clear organization	Administer feedback frequently
Elaboration	Step-by-step progression from subtopic to subtopic	Provide diagram/picture presentation
General study strategies	Use of examples, demonstrations, and visual prompts	Allow for independent practice
Thinking about/ controlling one's thinking	Conscious assessment of student understanding and adjustment to it	Break instruction into simpler phases
Attributions		Instruct in small groups
Evaluating effectiveness of strategy		Teacher modeling
		Rapid pace
		Individualized instruction
		Teacher asking questions

Source: Adapted from Swanson and Haskyn (1998).

(4) sequencing, (5) drill-repetition-practice, (6) segmentation, (7) technology (e.g., visuals and graphic displays), (8) direct questioning/response, and (9) supplement to teacher and peer involvement (Swanson, 1999).

In examining these studies in a systematic, quantitative fashion, Swanson and colleagues reiterated the findings from the institutes: interventions can make a significant impact on the learning of students with LD. It is important to consider that these interventions addressed a variety of areas, the majority in reading, and there were varying effects. However, in these analyses, the authors were able to tease out areas where impact could be made and were also able to draw a clearer picture about the components of interventions that had an impact on the outcomes. The critical components included in combining strategic instruction and direct instruction models improved student outcomes more so than other models or the models individually. Again, students with LD can learn if their needs are targeted and effective interventions are implemented with fidelity. Instruction matters.

Recent Reviews of Sustained Research Programs

In more contemporary reviews of sustained research programs, authors in the second edition of the *Handbook of Learning Disabilities* described critical components of their instructional programs across content areas. All authors had conducted research over at least 10 years in specific content areas and all had received significant amounts of funding to do so. Lovett, Barron, and Frijters (2013) describe their research in word identification, including fluency, phonemic awareness, phonics, and decoding. In their line of research, they concluded that (a) strategy instruction and direct instruction are critical; (b) attribution and motivation training are important, particularly for older students; (c) there is a need for multi-component interventions at important points across grade levels, and (d) varying needs of students means varying instructional and remedial responses. The attention given to understanding the component skills necessary in reading, the areas of difficulty for students with LD, and then specific targets for intervention have expanded our knowledge of what to do when students fail to learn to read. There is still much to be learned about reading failure as students get older but, again, research by this group provides evidence that effective, multicomponent reading interventions can improve outcomes for students with LD.

In the area of reading comprehension, Williams and Pao (2013) and Vaughn, Swanson, and Solis (2013) synthesize their findings that explicit instruction of specific strategies that include scaffolding, questioning, organization, and peer-mediated learning improves students' outcomes. Williams and Pao (2013) originally found that teachers were often not requiring students to read expository text because of its unfamiliar structure and students' lack of experience. Instead, teachers were often accommodating by reading it aloud themselves or providing summaries of the information. By explicitly teaching text structures such as cause and effect with the previously described effective instructional components, Williams and others were able to improve the reading comprehension skills of students with LD at the elementary level. Similarly, at the adolescent level, Vaughn and colleagues implemented reciprocal teaching and Collaborative Strategic Reading (CSR). Both are multicomponent interventions that include explicit instruction and practice of strategies, scaffolding, and peer-mediated learning. They concluded that these standardized treatments had an impact on student skills, and, when students showed a need, they could be taught specific strategic approaches to reading comprehension tasks.

In math, Fuchs, Fuchs, Schumacher, and Seethaler (2013) synthesized results from multiple studies of instruction for students with LD who had difficulty with basic facts, students who had difficulty with word problems, and those who had difficulty with both. Using the example of multicomponent Pirate Math from several elementary studies, Fuchs et al., identified six principles for remediation that echo previous findings: (1) instructional explicitness, (2) instructional design to minimize learning challenge (scaffolding), (3) strong conceptual basis within instruction, (4) drill and practice, (5) cumulative review, and (6) motivators to help students regulate their behavior (p. 396). Again, when these components were included in instruction, students made gains.

As a final example, Graham, Harris, and McKeown (2013) summarized their work with writing across grade levels. They described students with LD as having "difficulty with the self-regulation of organized strategic behaviors; incomplete and even inaccurate knowledge about important academic tasks, such as writing; and low motivation" (p. 410). To address these issues, their research focused on directly teaching students both the skills and the strategies necessary to be a successful writer and the motivational means to support them. The result has been a very successful intervention model, Self-Regulated Strategy Development (SRSD), with effective writing strategies (e.g., POW-Pick my ideas, Organize my notes, and Write and say more). This intervention model includes many of the components previously described as effective, including develop and activate background knowledge, discuss it (the strategy), model it, memorize it, support it (scaffolding), and independent practice (Harris, Graham, Mason, & Friedlander, 2008).

There are many other examples in the research about how the specific interventions that include components of strategic and direct instruction impact student learning. A long line of research by Scruggs and Mastropieri (2013) on keyword mnemonics illustrates how mnemonics only work if they are explicitly taught, along with instruction on the strategy to retrieve the information (i.e., listen to the word, think of the keyword, think of the picture, and remember the definition). Or the work done by Deshler and colleagues related to content enhancement. Specifically, structuring material for students with LD in a graphic organizer is meaningless and difficult to remember if students are not specifically taught what the relationships are between the items on the organizer (explicit instruction), what the information links together to create (scaffold), and how to systematically recognize the pattern independently in new material (systematic approach to the task; Ellis & Howard, 2007). Together, these examples provide evidence to support the claim that instruction matters.

Big Ideas About Interventions for Students with LD

The reader should not draw the conclusion from this discussion that interventions for students with LD are the panacea for all problems. To the contrary, one would not take aspirin to treat an upset stomach nor should one continue to take the aspirin when the stomachache does not go away. Similarly, a teacher needs to understand the specific need of a student with LD, that is, student's characteristics, prerequisite skills, motivational factors, and current level of performance, before expending the time and energy required to implement an intervention with fidelity. That teacher also needs the opportunity to teach – the time and space to implement the intervention and monitor student progress. Without either of those, the most effective intervention will not be successful with the individual student with LD. Rather, the purpose here is to identify the big ideas behind effective interventions for students with LD that run across content specific strategies and techniques. In other words, what would one want every special educator to know about interventions? Given the review of research findings here, at least five big ideas are evident: (1) teachers need to be able to identify a systematic approach to a task and the requisite skills necessary to complete the tasks, (2) teachers must be skilled at the use of explicit instruction and strategic instructional components, (3) instruction must be scaffolded from teacher-directed to student independence, (4) instruction must include multiple opportunities for practice with specific feedback, and (5) teachers inclusion of appropriate attribution and self-regulation components will encourage student engagement.

Identification of Systematic Approach to Tasks

In the self-monitoring work completed by Hallahan and colleagues at the University of Virginia Learning Disabilities Research Institute, the goal was to increase on task behavior of students with LD. Researchers analyzed this task carefully and operationalized the concept of paying attention as it related to time on task. Students were taught to listen for the tone, ask themselves "was I paying attention?" determine their response, and mark it on their recording sheet. Before students could answer "was I paying attention?" researchers explicitly taught them what it meant to pay attention.

In the work on text structure by Williams and Pao (2013), again, researchers analyzed the task and determined that looking for clue words and key vocabulary would help students determine the specific structure. From there, they could take the next sequence of steps, using an appropriate graphic organizer. The intervention included identifying clue words, specific vocabulary related to the structure, specific questions to ask to determine the structure, and then a graphic organizer to document all of the responses. Of course, students would not learn to use these text structure guides on material if they did not understand what cause/effect meant or if they used materials that they could not understand. These are specific examples of how, in order to be effective with students with LD, interventions must include concrete, recognizable actions that can be explained, modeled, and taught and that proceed in a logical order to completion of the task. This addresses students' inability to interpret and break down tasks on their own and their documented lack of strategic approaches to academic tasks.

Explicit Instruction

As evidenced by the effectiveness of the combined strategic and direct instruction models (Swanson, 1999), students with LD need to be taught what teachers want them to learn. Language must be consistent at all times. Instruction must proceed through the sequence of objectives stated, strategy/knowledge modeled, guided practice, independent practice, and assessment. The stages of SRSD in writing are evidence of the effectiveness of this sequence (Graham et al., 2013). Currently, educators are using the term explicit instruction and many teacher education programs in special education have included the text, *Explicit Instruction*, by Archer and Hughes (2011) into their coursework. Often, general education colleagues may balk at the suggestion of using explicit instruction because they interpret it to mean standing at the front of the classroom and lecturing. However, reviewing the intervention research described previously, it is clear that explicit instruction is not equivalent to a teacher giving knowledge to a passive learner. Rather, explicit instruction includes the teaching of a strategy or plan of attack for a task, in addition to content, that is required repeatedly within a content area. Explicit instruction requires a teacher to actively engage students in guided and independent practice to assess mastery (Archer & Hughes, 2011). For example, a special educator may go through an explicit instruction lesson on how to source a document when using primary sources in a social studies course (Okolo & Ferretti, 2013). She is not attempting to teach what is in the document; rather, she is attempting to teach a strategic approach to the task and does so by stating the objective, modeling it, scaffolding their learning by engaging students in guided practice, and then introducing independent practice for use in their social studies classrooms.

Scaffolded Instruction

In the 1999 analysis, Swanson identified control of task difficulty as one of the most significant instructional factors related to effective interventions. Swanson equates control of task difficulty with scaffolding as it is the sequencing of tasks related to instruction from easy to more difficult, with teacher assistance as needed. The teacher acts as a support as she moves from modeling a task to having students participate in a similar task, providing multiple examples and nonexamples, and then to having them complete the task independently. Once the student is successful in completing the task independently, the teacher provides a more difficult task or a task that is not completely similar to the one modeled. For example, when teaching a student a strategy to identify a text structure (Scruggs & Mastropieri, 2013; Williams & Pao, 2013), a teacher would begin with text that has an evident text structure and is written at or below the students' independent reading level. The teacher would progress to higher reading levels and to texts that do not have as explicit a structure only after students show mastery of the strategy. In addition, the teacher would not introduce more than one different structure at the same time. Too often, for students with LD, the teacher moves from easy to difficult tasks too quickly or without adequate practice.

Multiple Opportunities for Practice with Feedback

In describing the six principles of effective remediation of math skills, Fuchs et al. (2013) emphasize the need for drill and practice and cumulative review. In many of the interventions described, this drill and practice comes in small group instruction or in peer-mediated instruction. In general education classrooms of 20 or more students, the student with LD who is struggling to master a concept is not going to raise his hand to answer a question or respond to a teacher unless forced to do so because she is afraid of being wrong in front of peers. Therefore, in whole group instruction, that student will not get an opportunity to practice what is being taught. Given our understanding of the characteristics of many students with LD who have difficulty processing long strings of auditory information, who have deficits in prerequisite areas, or who have attention issues, if they are not given the opportunity to practice new knowledge, they will not learn it (Hallahan, Lloyd, Kauffman, Weiss, & Martinez, 2005). Even more notable is the fact that they may have misunderstandings or misinterpret the information given and, without an opportunity to practice and receive feedback, teachers will not know it until it is too late, and they have to unteach and reteach. Providing opportunities to practice in structured situations such as peer-mediated or small groups in multicomponent interventions such as CSR (Vaughn et al., 2013) allows students to practice and receive feedback without being called out in the whole group, and it allows them multiple opportunities for that practice.

Attribution and Self-regulation Components

Students with LD often attribute their failures to internal sources and their successes to external sources (Hallahan et al., 2005). They often lack self-efficacy in areas of weakness (Graham et al., 2013), and they fail to self-regulate their use of effective strategies (Hallahan et al., 2005). Given these characteristics, including attribution training and self-regulation components in effective interventions has stretched from the LD Research Institutes to current interventions such as SRSD. In a component analysis, Graham et al. (2013) determined that "the added value of teaching self-regulation procedures specifically in the SRSD model is 0.48 standard deviation, statistically greater than no effect" (p. 427). In the Discuss It phase, teachers and students discuss writing, examine current performance, and complete goal-setting. Teachers also emphasize effort and appropriate attributions, use self-statements throughout modeling, and reinforce these as students begin to practice. Students are encouraged to include attribution statements as simple as "I can do this" and self-regulation is initially guided by checklists and acronyms –all memorized in an important stage of the instruction (Harris et al., 2008).

Viewpoint: Instruction Matters

The premise of this chapter is that, in thinking about interventions for students with LD, instruction matters. The field has invested a great deal of energy and resources in developing interventions, field testing them, conducting research on them, and disseminating them to practitioners. This has been done with the support from a variety of funding sources but, mostly, from the efforts of researchers, teachers, and students who are dedicated to finding ways to help students with LD succeed. Do we have all of the answers? Absolutely not. Is our research complete? No. Are effective interventions always implemented? Again, no. Are we achieving the outcomes we want for students with LD? Hardly. Is there a simple answer? LD are complex and so are the interventions that address them. So what does it all mean?

For Practitioners

The bottom line for teachers of students with LD is that these students can learn, and they should receive effective instruction, not merely accommodations. This is fraught with problems – – testing students on grade-level reading skills when they are two grade levels below, participating in instruction in content areas that relies on skills that students have not mastered, determining how to fit instruction into already full school days, and making sure the paperwork is complete. In the current system, we need to identify an effective way to take the long view for these students. As a former secondary special educator and learning specialist at the college level, I have seen, too often, that the diploma is the goal. Do what it takes to get the student to the diploma and the struggle is over. The problem with this is that, for the student, the diploma is a beginning, not an ending. It is the beginning of their struggle to participate in postsecondary education or function in a career. Just like their nondisabled peers, they need the skills to accomplish these goals. If students with LD are *accommodated* without receiving the instruction they need, outcomes will not improve, and these students will not receive what IDEA promised.

As a field, we need to ask *how* to give students with LD what they need, given what we know about instruction.

For Teacher Educators and Professional Development Providers

In order to get effective interventions to students with LD, teachers must be knowledgeable of effective interventions, and they must be confident and competent in their use. This is another tall order, given that teacher attrition and burnout are such problems in special education (Brunsting, Sreckovic, & Lane, 2014). Plenty of teachers come in through alternative pathways or are on emergency certificates, just to meet the demand of numbers of students. There are researchers who have done a great deal of work on ideas for the retention and training of teachers of students with disabilities (Boe, Cook, & Sunderland, 2008; McLeskey & Billingsley, 2008); however, even teachers who are fully licensed may not be as knowledgeable about or competent in implementing EBPs as one would hope. This creates a twofold problem: (1) students do not receive the instruction that they require and (2) there is no expert professional advocating on behalf of the students' instructional needs. Therefore, very little change can happen for these students and their outcomes will be sacrificed.

Teacher preparation programs must include basic principles of instructional delivery and effective interventions in their coursework, with all of the other things that must be covered. Teacher candidates need multiple opportunities for practice with specific feedback. This would include evaluating student need, targeting specific skills, choosing from known EBPs, and implementing the intervention with fidelity. There is a tremendous amount written about the research to practice gap, but there are also suggestions on how to alleviate it (e.g., McLeskey & Billingsley, 2008). These suggestions need to address how to get teachers who are already in the classroom up to speed on new and more effective interventions as well.

For Administrators

Administrators are pulled in many different directions in their quest to meet all of the expectations laid at the feet of schools. However, starting from the principle that instruction matters for students with LD will help shape broader decisions and guide an administrators' support for special educators. For example, Bettini, Cheyney, Wang, and Leko (2015) include task significance as a key component in administrators' support for special educators. They define task significance as "perceptions of the importance of one's work" and state that it is closely tied to feedback. Emphasizing that the special educators' expertise in specific interventions for students with LD, along with the importance of this instruction in improving student outcomes, will help empower teachers. Involving these teachers in decision making related to schedules and teaching opportunities and listening to what the students need (not what is in vogue) are additional ways to emphasize support for instruction. Finally, asking questions about how we know whether or not the students are making progress at regular intervals and what instruction is occurring will affirm focus on instruction as long as it is appropriate and individualized.

Conclusion

Barbara Bateman and Mary Linden (2006) outline the steps in the Individualized Education Program (IEP) process in sequence:

> The first step of the process involves evaluation of a child and decision on eligibility for FAPE. The second step is the development of an IEP based upon the child's unique needs. The third step is the determination of an appropriate placement based upon the IEP. (p. 18)

Once a student is identified as needing special education, providing the appropriate instruction should be the first priority for all involved in the writing and implementation of a student's IEP. As administrators, teachers, and parents wrestle with determining how to serve the needs of students with LD, it is critical to keep instruction at the forefront of their considerations. Placement options and service delivery models should be secondary to instruction; inappropriate instruction can occur anywhere. Each one of the described interventions was built to assist the student with LD in becoming an independent learner. They are meant to be explicitly taught and practiced to mastery so that learners can then adapt and use them in different ways in different situations. The goal is not to make the students reliant upon great teachers; rather it is to implement instruction that eventually makes the teacher unnecessary for the success of that student. Careful, systematic research has guided the field to a solid foundation of interventions. As we move forward, it is important to incorporate these into classrooms and to continue the careful research.

References

Archer, A., & Hughes, C. (2011). *Explicit instruction: Effective and efficient teaching.* New York, NY: Guilford Press.

Bateman, B. D., & Linden, M. A. (2006). *Better IEPs: How to develop legally correct and educationally useful programs* (5th ed). Verona, WI: Attainment.

Bettini, E. A., Cheyney, K., Wang, J., & Leko, C. (2015). Job design: An administrator's guide to supporting and retaining special educators. *Intervention in School and Clinic, 50,* 221–225.

Boe, E. E., Cook, L. H., & Sunderland, R. J. (2008). Teacher turnover: Examining exit attrition, teaching area transfer, and school migration. *Exceptional Children, 75,* 7–31.

Brunsting, N. C., Sreckovic, M. A., & Lane, K. L. (2014). Special education teacher burnout: A synthesis of research from 1979 to 2013. *Education and Treatment of Children, 37,* 681–712.

Cohen, J. (1988). *Statistical power analysis for the behavioral sciences* (2nd ed.). New York, NY: Academic.

Ellis, E. E., & Howard, P. W. (2007). Graphic organizers: Power tools for teaching students with learning disabilities. *Current alert series* (Issue 13). Charlottesville, VA: Division for Learning Disabilities and Division for Research of the Council for Exceptional Children. Retrieved from TeachingLD.org.

Fuchs, L. S., & Fuchs, D. (1998). Treatment validity: A unifying concept for reconceptualizing the identification of learning disabilities. *Learning Disabilities Research & Practice, 13,* 204–219.

Fuchs, L. S., Fuchs, D., Schumacher, R. F., & Seethaler, P. M. (2013). Instructional intervention for students with mathematical learning disabilities. In H. L. Swanson, K. R. Harris, & S. Graham (Eds.), *Handbook of learning disabilities* (2nd ed., pp. 388–404). New York, NY: Guilford.

Graham, S., Harris, K. R., & McKeown, D. (2013). The writing of students with learning disabilities, meta-analysis of self-regulated strategy development writing intervention studies, and future directions: Redux. In H. L. Swanson, K. R. Harris, & S. Graham (Eds.), *Handbook of learning disabilities* (2nd ed., pp. 405–438). New York, NY: Guilford.

Hallahan, D. P., Kauffman, J. M., Lloyd, J. W., Weiss, M. P., & Martinez, L. (2005). *Introduction to learning disabilities* (3rd ed.). Boston, MA: Allyn & Bacon.

Hallahan, D. P., & Mercer, C. D. (2002). Learning disabilities: Historical perspectives. In R. Bradley, L. Danielson, & D. P. Hallahan (Eds.), *Identification of learning disabilities: Research to practice* (pp. 1–65). Mahwah, NJ: Erlbaum.

Harris, K. R., Graham, S., Mason, L. H., & Friedlander, B. (2008). *Powerful writing strategies for all students.* Baltimore, MD: Brookes.

Keogh, B. K. (1983). A lesson from Gestalt psychology. *Exceptional Education Quarterly, 4,* 115–127.

Lovett, M. W., Barron, R. W., & Frijters, J. C. (2013). Word identification difficulties in children and adolescents with reading disabilities: Intervention research findings. In H. L. Swanson, K. R. Harris, & S. Graham (Eds.), *Handbook of learning disabilities* (2nd ed., pp. 329–360). New York, NY: Guilford.

Maki, K. E., Burns, M. K., & Sullivan, A. (2017). Learning disability identification consistency: The impact of methodology and student evaluation data. *School Psychology Quarterly, 32*, 254–267.

McLeskey, J., & Billingsley, B. S. (2008). How does the quality and stability of the teaching force influence the research-to-practice gap?: A perspective on the teacher shortage in special education. *Remedial and Special Education, 29*, 293–305.

National Center for Education Statistics. (2017). *The condition of education.* Washington, DC: Author.

National Center for Learning Disabilities. (2017). *The state of LD: 2017.* Retrieved from https://www.ncld.org/the-state-of-learning-disabilities-understanding-the-1-in-5

Okolo, C. M., & Ferretti, R. P. (2013). History instruction for students with learning disabilities. In H. L. Swanson, K. R. Harris, & S. Graham (Eds.), *Handbook of learning disabilities* (2nd ed., pp. 463–488). New York, NY: Guilford.

Scruggs, T. E., & Mastropieri, M. A. (2013). Science and social studies education for students with learning disabilities. In H. L. Swanson, K. R. Harris, & S. Graham (Eds.), *Handbook of learning disabilities* (2nd ed., pp. 448–462). New York, NY: Guilford.

Swanson, H. L. (1999). Instructional components that predict treatment outcomes for students with learning disabilities: Support for a combined strategy and direct instruction model. *Learning Disabilities Research and Practice, 14*, 129–140.

Swanson, H. L., Carson, C., & Sachse-Lee, C. M. (1996). A selective synthesis of intervention research for students with learning disabilities. *School Psychology Review, 25*, 370–391.

Swanson, H. L., & Hoskyn, M. (1998). Experimental intervention research on students with learning disabilities: A meta-analysis of treatment outcomes. *Review of Educational Research, 68*, 277–321.

U.S. Department of Education. (2006). *Assistance to states for the education of children with disabilities and preschool grants for children with disabilities.* Retrieved from http://idea.ed.gov/explore/view/p/,root,regs,.html

U.S. Department of Education. (2016). *38th annual report to Congress on the Implementation of the Individuals with Disabilities Education Act.* Washington, DC: Author.

Vaughn, S., Swanson, E., & Solis, M. (2013). Reading comprehension for adolescents with significant reading problems. In H. L. Swanson, K. R. Harris, & S. Graham (Eds.), *Handbook of learning disabilities* (2nd ed., pp. 375–387). New York, NY: Guilford.

Williams, J. L., Miciak, J., McFarland, L., & Wexler, J. (2016). Learning disability identification criteria and reporting in empirical research: A review of 2001–2013. *Learning Disabilities Research & Practice, 31*, 221–229.

Williams, J. P., & Pao, L. S. (2013). Developing a new intervention to teach text structure at the elementary level. In H. L. Swanson, K. R. Harris, & S. Graham (Eds.), *Handbook of learning disabilities* (2nd ed., pp. 361–374). New York, NY: Guilford.

Chapter 2

Promoting Positive Freedoms for Secondary Students with Emotional and Behavioral Disorders: The Role of Instruction

Frederick J. Brigham, John William McKenna, Carlos E. Lavin, Michele M. Brigham and Lindsay Zurawski

Abstract

Secondary-level students with emotional and behavioral disorders (EBD) have significant academic and behavioral difficulties that require expert instruction to improve school and transition outcomes. Tensions between free and appropriate public education (FAPE) and least restrictive environment (LRE) mandates occur in the planning and delivery of specialized instruction and supports to these students. In this chapter, we consider alternate conceptions of freedoms as they may relate to the provision of special education services. However, a recent Supreme Court ruling highlighted the importance of FAPE in consideration of the student's individual circumstances. This emphasis on FAPE poses a significant challenge for teachers, who may be unprepared and insufficiently supported to be effective. As a result, it may be advantageous to organize effective practices according to a taxonomy that is based on the types of performance demands that are placed on students in secondary classrooms. The taxonomy we propose provides a framework to support teacher training and decision making. We provide an overview of the performance demands placed upon students with EBD in secondary grades. Examples of

Viewpoints on Interventions for Learners with Disabilities
Advances in Special Education, Volume 33, 31–53
Copyright © 2018 by Emerald Publishing Limited
All rights of reproduction in any form reserved
ISSN: 0270-4013/doi:10.1108/S0270-401320180000033003

effective practices to improve student performance for each type of demand are provided.

***Keywords*:** Students with emotional and behavioral disorders; FAPE; secondary students; teacher training

Public school teachers are agents of the state and, by virtue of that agency, bound by restrictions and duties as is the state. The state in this case includes the federal government as well as state and local governments. It is common for philosophers, legal scholars, political activists, and others to debate the authority of the state and its agents to influence the activities of individuals. Anyone who has worked with students with emotional and/or behavioral disorders (EBD) has heard students claim that their teachers have *no right* to require them do something or to stop them from doing something. Sometimes, these assertions from students are correct. There are restrictions on the authority of school personnel to take certain actions. The principle of least restrictive environment (LRE) is based, in part, on the presumption that removing an individual from an environment shared by his or her peers is intrusive enough to require the protections of due process. Discussions of rights that focus on the limits of authorities to take actions relative to individuals or groups, however, fail to capture the full range of rights.

Power versus Duties

Garvey (1989) suggested that there are two kinds of rights embedded in the understanding of the U.S. Constitution, negative rights and positive rights. Negative rights are essentially limits on what the government can compel its citizens to do. Negative rights, therefore, are checks on authority. Garvey suggested that positive rights are a more recent development in constitutional thinking. Positive rights refer to the duties the government has toward its citizens. We suggest that Garvey's analysis provides a useful tool for framing decisions about special education services for students with EBD.

Negative Freedoms

The limitations of school officials to take certain actions are related to conceptions of negative freedoms, Garvey described negative freedoms as those restraints upon the government that prevent interference with an individual's ability to live as freely as possible. In essence, negative freedoms are "freedoms from." According to Garvey and a number of other legal scholars and philosophers, the conception of liberty in terms of negative freedoms, the freedom from government intervention was the dominant conception of liberty throughout the nineteenth and much of the twentieth century. However, Garvey suggested that after 1960,[1] considerations of freedoms began to take on a different perspective that he describes as "positive freedoms."

Positive Freedoms

Positive freedoms refer to government's obligations to provide assistance so that individuals can do things that they are unable to do on their own. The requirement that public education systems provide students with disabilities a free and appropriate public education (FAPE) is an example of such a positive freedom.

Garvey noted that the U.S. Constitution is vague with regard to which kind of freedom it endorses. Although much of the rhetoric about constitutional issues appears to have been in regard to the right to be free of government intervention (negative freedoms), "the Constitution says point blank that the government must provide certain benefits, like jury trials and compulsory due process" (Garvey, 1989, pp. 219–220). Thus, the existence of the positive freedom is embedded, at least in limited form, in the U.S. Constitution.

Interaction of Positive and Negative Freedoms

There is some degree of reciprocity between the citizen and the government, and the government can, in the interest of protecting a citizen's other freedoms, limit rights or freedoms in some way. For example, Garvey noted that trading jobs for freedom of speech is wrong. Even though an individual may willingly resign from a political activity for a job or other benefit, the suggestion is that allowing this to happen, at least in a systematic manner, is problematic. Garvey noted:

---

[1]Historians (e.g., Brinkley, 1996) often suggest that the rise of belief in government's responsibility to assist its citizens can be traced to the Roosevelt administration and the New Deal when the government became committed to providing at least minimal assistance to the poor and unemployed.

One explanation the Court has given is that your speech may benefit other people. The government harms them by getting you to trade your speech for a job. Another possibility is that speech – especially political speech – plays an important part in our ideal of human excellence. We should not let people degrade themselves into silence even if they do so willingly. (p. 219)

LRE versus FAPE

We suggest that the same logic regarding negative and positive freedoms applies to the education of individuals with EBD. Brigham, Ahn, Stride, and McKenna (2016) provided an example that contrasts these two types of freedom. They noted that some schools were willing to allow students with EBD to leave the classroom when they believed that they were unable to deal with the demands of instruction. Brigham et al. referred to this practice as "vagabond therapy" and pointed out that the pursuit of inclusion in a general education setting (a negative freedom to not be moved from one's peers) was undermining the attainment of FAPE (the positive freedom to attain an education). They asserted that LRE cannot be judged unless one has convincing evidence that FAPE is being delivered. Thus, the reason that the students were allowed to remove themselves from instruction matters. Students' pursuit of FAPE is likely to "benefit us all" because educated students will be more productive and require less support in the future. However, allowing students to excuse themselves from instruction because it serves some purpose other than providing FAPE (i.e., inflating numbers of students served in general education settings) may be questionable.[2]

Purpose of Action

Garvey's (1989) essay described the role of purpose in judging government actions that are harmful in some way. Wrongful behavior, in this

---

[2]Some may argue that students afforded this treatment may need it to avoid some sort of explosive outburst that would disrupt instruction for themselves or others, but Brigham et al. (2016) argued that too often, such treatment was provided without evidence of such need and without any formal attempt to teach students to maintain themselves in class for longer periods of time. As a result, the practice, was counter-productive in too many cases.

sense, must be intentional not accidental. Garvey provided the following illustration:

> As applied to complex actions, this is the principle of the double effect. Suppose I am an oncologist. I know that morphine will relieve the suffering of my patient, but it will also hasten her death. It is not wrong to administer the drug to relieve her present suffering. But it would be wrong if my purpose was to shorten her agony by shortening her life. My actions in the two cases are identical. The rightness and wrongness of my behavior depends on my intentions. (p. 227)

Mapping Garvey's analogy onto students with EBD yields the following logic: *I know that allowing students to excuse themselves from instruction will relieve their present discomfort, but it will limit the benefits of FAPE and enhance the appearance of LRE.* It is not wrong to allow students to excuse themselves to relieve their present discomfort. But it would be wrong if the purpose was to simply enhance the appearance of LRE or to limit FAPE. Thus, one type of freedom can conflict with another type of freedom.

Implications of the Endrew F. Case

The analogy in the preceding paragraph does not hold as directly as it may appear. In that analogy, IEP teams are left to balance the negative and positive rights with little guidance as to which type of rights to emphasize. Is it better to maintain an individual in a classroom setting that is similar to his/her peers if the outcomes are quite dissimilar to the peers or should one focus on making the outcomes more similar to peers, even if the setting becomes more dissimilar to the peers? Recent developments in case law now require schools to provide more evidence of direct benefit from education programs. Chief Justice John Roberts remarked in the opinion delivered in the *Endrew F. v. Douglas County School District* case that the standard set by the court was markedly more demanding than the "merely more than *de minimis*" test applied in previous cases. Roberts continued that for many children with disabilities, "receiving an instruction that aims so low would be tantamount to sitting idly ... awaiting the time when they were old enough to drop out" (Howe, "Opinion analysis," para 7).

The *Endrew F.* opinion suggests that the emphasis upon negative freedoms related to LRE may be shifting toward emphasis upon positive freedoms of receiving FAPE. It is doubtful that emphasis upon LRE will be or even should be eliminated, but it is clear that the responsibility for school personnel to demonstrate FAPE is on the rise. Thus, our authority to alter behavior of students with EBD is dependent upon which rights, negative or positive, that are most valued. We conclude that the authority to affect the negative freedoms of our students derives from our responsibility to promote their positive freedoms. Without demonstrable evidence of FAPE, the claims of school personnel regarding promotion of positive freedoms are doubtful, regardless of the environment in which they are carried out. In other words, making only *de minimus* progress while remaining in a general education setting is as unacceptable as it would be in a setting more dedicated to students with disabilities.

Achievement and Services Provided to Students with EBD

Students with EBD present particular problems among groups of individuals with higher-incidence disabilities. They receive lower academic grades than do many students in other disability categories (i.e., learning disabilities, attention-deficit hyperactivity disorders, and other health impairments) despite evidence that their scores on standardized assessments are comparable to other individuals with disabilities (Anderson, Kutash, & Duchnowski, 2001; Benner, Nelson, Ralston, & Mooney, 2010; Bradley, Doolittle, & Bartolotta, 2008; Sutherland & Wehby, 2001). Further, Bradley et al. (2008) reported data indicating that 97% of adolescent students with EBD were performing below grade level. This is not surprising, given that the first element of the federal definition of students who are emotionally disturbed (EBD in current discussions) describes inability to learn that cannot be explained by other factors. Thus, underachievement is a prominent preexisting condition for students with EBD.

Disappointing Outcomes.

It appears that simply *having* an IEP does not always confer sufficient benefit to many students with disabilities. Chesmore, Ou, and Reynolds (2016) examined the outcomes for students receiving special education services for at least four years in grades one through eight in the Chicago City Schools. They reported that children who had, at any time, received special education services had significantly lower rates of high school completion, as well as higher rates of crime, depression, and substance abuse. Chesmore et al. (2016) suggested that special education itself may not be the problem. Rather, they suggested that what is happening in special education may be related to the disappointing outcomes noted in their study. We agree with these authors in this conclusion. If schools were able to deliver evidence-based practices to students with EBD and we still saw disappointing outcomes, there may be more reason to question the legitimacy of special education services. However, wholesale elimination or the dramatic reduction of special education services before such a demonstration would be premature and, in our opinion, destructive to the individuals whom advocates purport to help.

Why Aren't We Doing Better?

Other studies (e.g., Morgan, Frisco, Farkas, & Hibel, 2017) have reported similar disappointing outcomes despite the existence of a robust set of evidence-based practices that reliably improve the performance of individuals with disabilities. Some authors (e.g., Boardman, Argüelles, Vaughn, Hughes, & Klingner, 2005; Burns & Ysseldyke, 2009; McKenna & Ciullo, 2016) have observed that evidence-based practices are rarely reported or observed in the classrooms of many students with disabilities. Other authors (e.g., McLeskey & Billingsley, 2008) describe the lack of adequate preparation of well-qualified teachers as well as the instability of special education teachers in teaching positions (i.e., attrition and migration), and inadequate work conditions as reasons that instructional practices often fail to reflect what is known about effectiveness. Additionally, Bradley et al. (2008) noted that students with EBD were less likely to have fully trained teachers and more likely to receive instruction from paraprofessionals than were other students.

Exacerbating the problems related to underpreparation is the pressure upon schools and teachers to make student placements as close to the regular education setting as possible regardless of the effectiveness of the placement (Brigham et al., 2016). Bradley et al. (2008) also noted that "students with EBD are likely to receive accommodations, but are unlikely to receive academic support services" (p. 9). Thus, the evidence suggests that current practices in special education for students with EBD lean heavily upon the negative freedom to be left in a setting that is similar to one's peers and provide limited attention to the positive freedom of delivering FAPE that leads to increasing the academic competence of these students.[3] The alignment of Individuals with Disabilities Improvement Act (2005) with the No Child Left Behind Act (2002) provided a strong link between FAPE and academic competence as manifested in the general education curriculum no matter how or where it is delivered (Huefner, 2008).

Providing instruction of Students with EBD in Secondary Schools

The data reviewed thus far paints a relatively bleak picture of the preparation of teachers of students with EBD and the effectiveness of the instruction that they provide. Many of the foregoing observations were made across the entire range of ages and grades of students served in the schools. Teachers of students with EBD in secondary settings face particular difficulties that may not be as prominent for teachers of younger students. Secondary teachers are required to master more specialized academic content than are teachers of younger children. This content mastery requirement co-occurs with the need to provide remediation in basic skills to students who lack such fundamental preparation. Additionally, special education teachers may be required to provide instruction in settings dedicated to serving individuals with disabilities as well as in co-teaching and/or consultative arrangements. These requirements are all in addition to carrying out behavior intervention plans and other classroom management duties.

This suggests that teachers of students with EBD are faced with significant and varied responsibilities for which they may lack both adequate preparation *before* assuming the role and adequate support *after* assuming the role. Billingsley (2004) summarized the literature regarding teacher attrition, and reported that younger and inexperienced special educators as well as uncertified teachers are more likely to leave than their older, more experienced and fully credentialed counterparts. Special education teachers of students with EBD are more likely to be younger and uncertified than are other teachers (Bradley et al., 2008). Consequently, special education teachers who serve students with EBD are more likely to leave the profession or to transfer to other roles within education. As a result,

---

[3]We note that Henderson, Klein, Gonzalez, and Bradley (2005) reported that students with EBD are more likely than students with other disabilities to be served in classrooms comprised, primarily, of students with similar disabilities. Rather than condemning the placement model, we suggest that these findings refer back to what is being done within the classrooms.

the individuals who are most likely to be teaching students with EBD are least likely to have a well-elaborated and organized understanding of their role. That is, these individuals lack the kind of expertise necessary for effective functioning in their roles (Sternberg & Horvath, 1995). Thus, teachers of students with EBD may need effective instructional supports as much as their students. In response to the need for clear support and structure for special education teachers of students with EBD, Brigham and Wiley (2017) suggested that beginning teachers be trained with a standard treatment protocol and be required to master the basics contained therein before being promoted to make complex decisions regarding individualization.

Other reviews (e.g., Benner et al., 2010; McKenna, Kim, Shin, & Pfannenstiel, 2017; Mooney, Ryan, Uhing, Reid, & Epstein, 2005; Weiss, 2015) have addressed various aspects of basic skills instruction, behavior management, and co-teaching for students with EBD. Some authors have focused upon teaching specific content domains to students with disabilities (e.g., Scruggs, Mastropieri, Brigham, & Marshak, in press; Therrien, Taylor, Watt, & Kaldenberg, 2014). We commend the interested reader to these publications for detailed descriptions of specific instructional procedures that are supported for students with disabilities. However, understanding, selecting, and justifying instructional strategies can be as challenging for teachers as is cooperation with these instructional strategies for individuals with EBD. Providing some sort of structure to justify and organize instructional interventions that are different from those provided to other students can help students with EBD understand why the strategies are needed as well as how the strategies are intended to help them.

Four Challenges for Completing a Secondary Education

We suggest that after addressing the needs for basic skills and aside from content-specific skills and knowledge, four overarching areas of concern remain for completing a secondary education. These areas are the following:

a. Discriminating essential from nonessential information.
b. Recalling target information quickly and accurately.
c. Organizing target information into a coherent representation of the to-be-learned material.
d. Expressing one's learning in forms that can be understood by others.

Considering instructional interventions from this perspective has the potential to reduce the cognitive load for both students and teachers because it provides a superordinate set of categories to organize our approach and, also, includes justification of why strategies in each area *should* be employed. The first part of this chapter discussed special educators' obligation to provide instruction (i.e., why we need to do these things). The remainder describes a way of organizing and justifying approaches to instruction (i.e., why we are going to do it this way).

It is clear that these areas are far from mutually exclusive. People who can discriminate the essential from the nonessential are more likely to recall the information, and it is clear that one can neither organize nor express understanding of things that cannot be recalled. However, there are tools that can be deployed to specifically address each of these potential problem areas. Additionally, many interventions employ tools that address more than one problem area. Teachers who understand which areas are being addressed and which areas are left unaddressed in a multistep intervention are in a better position to augment instruction with additional interventions. We next describe the problems and a general approach that is available for dealing with problems in each of these four areas.

Discriminating Essential from Nonessential Information

Learners who approach domains with which they have little experience or background knowledge are quickly overwhelmed by the amount of information that they encounter. When every new term is equally meaningful or meaningless, it is difficult to perceive any way to organize the experience. Students with EBD have poor academic development. One of the results of poor development is limited reading experience. Individuals with limited reading experience fail to perceive the structure of texts or to note various cues that authors provide to signal important elements of the text (Brigham, Berkley, Simpson, & Brigham, 2007). Graphic organizers (Novak & Gowin, 1984) are a group of techniques that can greatly enhance students' ability to discriminate important from nonessential information.

Graphic organizers visually depict interrelationships of superordinate and subordinate ideas, using spatial arrangements, geometric shapes, lines, and arrows to portray the content structure and to demonstrate key relationships between concepts (DiCecco & Gleason, 2002). A variety of graphic organizers have been developed for specific text formats (e.g., causal relationships, compare and contrast, and hierarchical organization; Ellis & Howard, 2007; Gallavan & Kottler, 2007). Hall, Kent, McCulley, Davis, and Wanzek (2013) suggested five steps for using graphic organizers during instruction:

1. Identify the structure of the text that students are reading and choose a graphic organizer that matches this text structure.[4]
2. Provide students with a brief explanation as to how this type of graphic organizer can aid in their comprehension of the text.
3. Model how to enter information into the graphic organizer, giving opportunities for student participation.
4. Transfer responsibility for the completion of the graphic organizer to students.
5. Encourage students to explain the conceptual relations represented in their graphic organizers. (p. 51)

We suggest that in addition to providing structure to the lesson, the provision of a graphic organizer helps students by encouraging them to consider how each unit of information that they encounter is related to the larger theme of their reading or other instructional medium. Additionally, a graphic organizer is a more concrete and enduring representation than is the claim on the part of the learner that she has mastered the material. Claims that one has mastered the material without some sort of validation (optimally, a test) are really nothing more than the learner's sense of familiarity or having seen the material before (Brown, Roediger, & McDaniel, 2014).

There are other supports for this area of challenge for secondary students, but, in the end, each of them will have some component for making the structure of the material more explicit and forcing decisions as to the importance of a unit of information in relation to other units of information. Information that is well structured and deeply processed is more likely to be recalled than is information receiving only superficial consideration. This is particularly true of information that can be expressed in common language; however, it is often necessary to use terminology that is unfamiliar to the learner and, because of its unfamiliarity, quite abstract (Scruggs & Mastropieri, 1989). We next describe a strong method for supporting recall of this kind of information.

---

[4]Examples of two different graphic organizers are presented in Appendix A of this document.

Recalling Target Information Quickly and Accurately

Students with learning and behavior problems have consistently demonstrated problems with recall of factual information. As a consequence of this difficulty, these students often fail academic tests, both classroom and state-level minimum competency tests, thereby, limiting their access to the general education curriculum (Scruggs & Mastropieri, 2000).

Mnemonic strategies are tools to improve recall of verbal factual information, particularly, vocabulary, through the creation of links that effectively connect familiar with unfamiliar information. Several different varieties of mnemonic strategies have been created, including the *first letter strategies* and the *keyword* method (Brigham & Brigham, 2001).

Letter Strategies. Many readers will be familiar with first-letter strategies where the first-letters of the target information are selected to create an acronym to aid in recall of the information. For example, the acronym "HOMES" is often used to prompt recall of the names of the great lakes (Huron, Ontario, Michigan, Erie, and Superior). Teachers tell us that they like this method because it is relatively easy to use as is the similar technique using sentences, where the first letters of a series of words are used to prompts recall of target information. For example, the spelling of the word geography can be prompted by the phrase, "*G*eorge's *E*lderly *O*ld *G*randfather *R*ode *A* *P*ig *H*ome *Y*esterday" or by the phrase, "*G*eorge *E*ats *O*ld *G*rey *R*ats *A*nd *P*aints *H*ouses *Y*ellow."

For this method to be effective, it is necessary that the learner already have the to-be-recalled information committed to memory. Without knowledge of the names of the great lakes, the acronym, HOMES, is of little value. The mnemonic tool, "*T*en *Z*ebras *B*ought *M*y *C*ar" provides an example of the limitation of letter mnemonics. Medical students often rely on this mnemonic to aid in the recall of the branches of the facial nerve (superior to inferior) as they exit the anterior border of the parotid gland (*T:* temporal, *Z:* zygomatic, *B:* buccal, *M:* mandibular, *C:* cervical). Few readers of the present text are likely to have studied human anatomy at a level where such information was emphasized, so the terms represented by the first letter of each word are unavailable to them. Consequently, the zebra mnemonic, like any first letter mnemonic can be very effective, but only under the circumstances where the learner already possesses the target information and needs only a small prompt to be successful. Secondary education, however, requires learners to recall associations of information that, like the branches of the facial nerve are outside of their repertoire of experience and are, therefore quite abstract and difficult to recall. *Keyword mnemonics* have great power for such tasks.

The Keyword Method. When using the keyword method, a concrete, acoustically similar word is created for the unfamiliar information to be learned. Scruggs et al. (in press) provided an example to promote recall that *Canidae* is the scientific name of the biological family of dogs. First, a familiar acoustically similar keyword is created to represent the new word (e.g., "candy"). Next, an interactive picture is created in which the keyword ("candy") is shown interacting with the meaning (dog), in this case, a picture of a dog eating or begging for candy. The last step is to teach the learners the process for retrieval. When learners are asked what does canidae mean? Learners should first think of the keyword ("candy"), think of the picture with the candy in it (a dog eating candy), and retrieve the correct answer, *dogs*.

In a recent application to teaching our own students, we (Michele Brigham and Frederick Brigham) created a keyword mnemonic to help U.S. history students recall that a *tariff* is a tax placed on a good (or product) entering the United States (or any other country). We selected "tear off" as the acoustically similar keyword, and then created an interactive image with a large tag attached to a shipping container. The keyword, "tear off" appeared on the tag as the instruction "Pay tax, then TEAR OFF and ship to USA." When students took the state end, of course, examine for U.S. history, several of them reported that a question regarding tariffs was on the test and that they used the image from class to help them remember what a tariff was.

Keyword mnemonics are associated with one of the largest positive effect sizes in all of special education literature. The technique is, admittedly, a little tricky to master. It also takes several repetitions of the associations for students to master them, but once mastered, these memories are persistent and available for the learner to use in a variety of situations. Knowing facts is important, but educational goals shoot higher than simply having a set of unrelated facts at hand. Learners must be supported in organizing their store of factual information into a meaningful whole.

Organizing Target Information

We previously described graphic organizers as a useful tool to help students discriminate meaningful from nonessential information. As the name of the tool implies, information that has been placed in a graphic organizer is far more organized and elaborated than it would be if a learner simply read about the topic or listened to a lecture or discussion of the topic. A well-organized body of knowledge needs to be internalized in a coherent fashion in order for it to function as the basis for further learning in the domain (Brigham, 2009). Although completing a graphic organizer is an important first step, it is probably insufficient to creating the kind of cognitive structures that enable individuals with learning and behavioral problems to become independent in a domain and to use their learning to address complex questions. We describe two techniques, the "Question Exploration Routine" (QER) and "Coached Elaboration" that hold promise for actively promoting organization and interrelation of ideas. Both of these techniques involve the use of structured, active questioning by teachers to promote active information processing.

The QER. The "QER" (Bulgren, Marquis, Lenz, Deshler, & Schumaker, 2011) is designed to support thinking about and answering complex questions for students with disabilities. QER employs a graphic organizer with six thinking steps posed as questions:

1. What is the critical question?
2. What are the key terms?
3. What are the supporting questions and answers?
4. What is the main idea answer?
5. How can we use the main idea?
6. Is there an overall idea? Is there a real-world use?

Teachers employing QER provide an advance organizer, give the topic of the lesson, and explicitly inform the students of the importance of target information. The teacher distributes the graphic organizer and prompts students to take notes on the organizer and participate in the discussion. The teacher and students then work together to address the questions in the graphic organizer. Finally, the students review the information they recorded and use that information to answer questions. Students tested on content where instruction employed QER performed substantially better than students receiving the same content through lectures.

Coached Elaboration. Coached elaboration (Scruggs, Mastropieri, & Sullivan, 1994; Scruggs, Mastropieri, Sullivan, & Hesser, 1993; Sullivan, Mastropieri, & Scruggs, 1995) is an extension of practices developed in educational psychology (e.g., Pressley, Johnson, & Symons, 1987) for typical learners to individuals with learning and behavioral problems. Sullivan et al. (1995) structured the elaboration process to assist learners with disabilities to create their own precise elaborations. We have found that skilled teachers, particularly skilled co-teachers, employ this technique in their day-to-day teaching. However, coached elaboration takes both practice in carrying out the steps *and* a clear understanding of when it is likely to benefit students.

Understanding when the process is likely to be beneficial to students has proven to be a difficult challenge for teachers-in-training with whom we have worked. The difficulty comes in discriminating between associations that are arbitrary (e.g., Thomas Edison invented the light bulb) and associations that can be explained logically, given sufficient prior knowledge and reasoning skills (e.g., Alexander Graham Bell invented the telephone).[5] The first step that we suggest is practice in identifying statements of fact and the logical associations and background knowledge that would be necessary for a meaningful elaboration. In cases where the association is more arbitrary, keyword mnemonics are the method of choice.

Once the target information and logically related necessary background information is selected, the coaching technique is relatively straightforward. We provide an example of the procedure in Table 1. The point of each step is for the student to produce a reasonable elaboration. If the student produces such an elaboration at any step, the coaching is ended. If not, the teacher moves to next level of coaching. The first step, Coaching One, is always the statement of a fact, followed by the general prompt, "Why would that make sense?" In Coaching Two, the teacher provides a more focused prompt to help the student produce an appropriate elaboration. The Coaching Two prompt is usually in the form of "What else do you know about___?" In Coaching Three, the teacher provides additional context for the elaboration to prompt the student to produce the link between the fact and necessary prior knowledge. In Coaching Four, the teacher presents the elaboration between the factual statement and its explanation, asking the student to verify whether or not it makes sense.

Students provided with coached elaborations performed substantially and significantly better on recall tasks than did students who were instructed through direct practice. However, the research demonstrates that students require very explicit questioning that is targeted directly to student construction of an appropriate response. Additionally, it appears that students have a great deal of difficulty implementing this strategy independently (Mastropieri et al., 1996), so teacher support is a critical element to its success.

---

[5]Edison invented lots of things. The light bulb was one of them, but he had no personal interest that drove him to making the light bulb. Bell, however, was the son of a deaf person as well as the husband of another deaf person. Knowing those facts can help make the elaboration of Bell's work on the telephone meaningful.

Table 1: Example of Coached Elaboration Steps.

Statement of Fact	Logically Related Necessary Prior Knowledge
Large, single crop bonanza farms were wiped out by the drought but smaller farms often survived.	The large farms were set up to grow only one crop, but smaller farms could be more flexible in the crops they grew.
Coaching levels[a]	
Coaching one	Large, single crop bonanza farms were wiped out by the drought, but smaller farms often survived. *Why would that make sense?*
Coaching two	*Think,* what were the large bonanza farms like?
Coaching three	*Remember,* bonanza farms were set up to grow only one kind of crop; *so why would it make sense that* the drought would affect those farmers more than those with smaller farms?
Coaching four	The large farms were set up to grow only one crop, but smaller farms, could be more flexible in the crops they grew, *so would it make sense that* the drought affected the large farms more than the small ones?

[a] The italicized parts of the coaching prompts will be the same for every example. It is the non-italicized parts that change.

Expressing One's Learning

Even if one has carried out all of the general learning tasks in the previous sections successfully, demonstrating one's knowledge by expressing it to others is a major challenge. Gage, Wilson, and MacSuga-Gage (2014) noted that writing done in educational and workplace settings requires recursive processes of planning, drafting, reviewing, revising, and editing to produce several drafts of a text. This work is cognitively demanding and requires persistence on the part of the writers. As can be expected from the foregoing discussions of academic achievement, students with EBD perform at levels that are far below those needed for adequate writing.

Mastropieri and Scruggs (2014) noted that there has been a great deal of progress in understanding how to teach strategies for planning, organizing, revising, and writing using graphic organizers and instruction in self-regulated strategy development (SRSD) for students with or at risk for EBD. However, mastering complex skills such as written expression requires a great deal of practice, and we know far less about the intensity and practice necessary for accomplishment in this domain. "The importance of providing sufficient, intensive, explicit instruction and the relevant practice necessary for developing writing competence has been underemphasized in recent literature" (Mastropieri & Scruggs, 2014, p. 80).

Most approaches to supporting development of writing skills employ a combination of graphic organizers, discussed earlier, and SRSD. In general, SRSD for writing integrates three areas: (a) six stages of explicit writing instruction across a variety of genres; (b) explicit instruction in self-regulation strategies, including goal setting, self-monitoring, and self-instruction; and (c) development of positive student attitudes and self-efficacy about writing (Regan & Mastropieri, 2009). SRSD approaches employ teacher modeling of recursive stages of instruction (develop background knowledge, discuss it, model it, memorize it, support it, and provide independent practice). These stages are used in SRSD to develop genre specific and general writing strategies. Self-regulation is emphasized through goal setting, self-instructions, self-monitoring, and self-reinforcement (Mason, Harris, & Graham, 2011). Strategies for specific tasks have been developed; however, Mason et al. (2011) suggest that a general writing strategy that can be used across several genres may be the better approach to instruction for writers who have serious difficulties. One such approach is called, POW plus TREE.

POW, A General Approach to Improving Writing Abilities. One of the most studied approaches to writing for students who have serious writing difficulties is POW (Regan & Mastropieri, 2009). POW (*P*ick my idea, *O*rganize my notes, *W*rite and say more) guides students to (a) think about, brainstorm, and pick ideas prior to writing; (b) select a planning strategy to help with organizing notes; and (c) write from a plan and remember to add new information while writing. POW can be combined with other supportive strategies to extend and improve student performance. In each extension, a different second strategy is added to POW, yielding a two-part strategy name, POW plus _____.

One strategy that research consistently supports for opinion writing is POW plus TREE. The TREE element of the strategy (*T*opic sentence, 3 or more *R*easons, *E*nding to wrap it up, *E*xamine for all parts) supports opinion-writing. Additional elements are available to augment the POW strategy. We suggest that mastering the basics through POW plus TREE would result in a substantial improvement in the writing performance of students with EBD.

Conclusion

Much of the discussion of the rights of students with EBD in special education has focused upon the negative rights associated with LRE; however, recent developments including a case decided by the U.S. Supreme Court suggest that positive rights to acquire an education are becoming more dominant. Students with EBD not only are characterized by behavioral problems but also by serious levels of academic underachievement. Thus, students with EBD are very difficult to teach. The difficulties experienced by these students are exacerbated by the tendency of schools to utilize untrained and inexperienced teachers or paraprofessionals to provide instruction. As a result, interventions may lack organization and clear justification.

We suggest that in addition to basic skills instruction and discipline-specific tasks, four major challenges face students with disabilities in completing secondary education. Considering instruction according to these four challenges: (a) discriminating essential from nonessential information, (b) recalling target information quickly and accurately, (c) organizing target information into a coherent representation of the to-be-learned material, and (d) expressing one's learning in forms that can be understood by others can provide a more effective approach to student support. We also provided examples of tools in each of these areas. Given that novice and untrained personnel are often responsible for instruction of students with EBD, it makes sense that a basic set of tools such as those suggested here would benefit the students as well as the teachers who labor to help them.

References

Anderson, J. A., Kutash, K., & Duchnowski, A. J. (2001). A comparison of the academic progress of students with EBD and students with LD. *Journal of Emotional and Behavioral Disorders*, *9*(2), 106–115. doi:10.1177/106342660100900205

Benner, G. J., Nelson, J. R., Ralston, N. C., & Mooney, P. (2010). A meta-analysis of the effects of reading instruction on the reading skills of students with or at risk of behavioral disorders. *Behavioral Disorders, 35*(2), 86–102.

Billingsley, B. S. (2004). Special education teacher retention and attrition: A critical analysis of the research literature. *The Journal of Special Education, 38*(1), 39–55. doi:10.1177/00224669040380010401

Boardman, A. G., Argüelles, M. E., Vaughn, S., Hughes, M. T., & Klingner, J. (2005). Special education teachers' views of research-based practices. *The Journal of Special Education, 39*(3), 168–180. doi:10.1177/002246690503900 30401

Bradley, R., Doolittle, J., & Bartolotta, R. (2008). Building on the data and adding to the discussion: The experiences and outcomes of students with emotional disturbance. *Journal of Behavioral Education, 17*(1), 4–23. doi:10.1007/s10864-007-9058-6

Brigham, F. J. (2009). Confusing the momentary and the monumental. *Focus on Research, 22*(2), 1–2.

Brigham, F. J., Ahn, S. Y., Stride, A. N., & McKenna, J. W. (2016). FAPE-Accompli: Misapplication of the principles of inclusion and students with EBD. In J. P. Bakken (Ed.), *General and special education inclusion in an age of change: Impact on students with disabilities* (pp. 31–47). Bingley: Emerald Group Publishing Limited.

Brigham, F. J., Berkley, S., Simpson, P., & Brigham, M. M. (2007). Comprehension strategy instruction. *Current Practice Alerts #12.* Reston, VA: Division for Learning Disabilities & Division for Research of the Council for Exceptional Children.

Brigham, F. J., & Brigham, M. M. (2001). Mnemonic instruction. *Current Practice Alerts #5.* Reston, VA: Division for Learning Disabilities & Division for Research of the Council for Exceptional Children.

Brigham, F. J., & Wiley, A. L. (2017, October). Enhancement or individualization? Reconsidering a tradition adrift. Paper presented at the annual meeting of Teacher Educators for Children with Behavioral Disorders, Tempe, AZ.

Brinkley, A. (1996). The new deal: An overview. *Social Education, 60*(5), 255.

Brown, P. C., Roediger, H. L., III, & McDaniel, M. A. (2014). *Make it stick: The science of successful learning.* Cambridge, MA: The Belknap Press of Harvard University Press.

Bulgren, J. A., Marquis, J. G., Lenz, B. K., Deshler, D. D., & Schumaker, J. B. (2011). The effectiveness of a question-exploration routine for enhancing the content learning of secondary students. *Journal of Educational Psychology, 103*(3), 578–593. doi:10.1037/a0023930

Burns, M. K., & Ysseldyke, J. E. (2009). Reported prevalence of evidence-based instructional practices in special education. *Journal of Special Education, 43*(1), 3–11. doi:10.1177/0022466908315563

Carnine, D. W., Miller, S., Bean, R. M., & Zigmond, N. (1994). Social studies: Educational tools for diverse learners. *School Psychology Review, 23*(3), 428–441.

Chesmore, A. A., Ou, S.-R., & Reynolds, A. J. (2016). Childhood placement in special education and adult well-being. *The Journal of Special Education, 50*(2), 109–120. doi:10.1177/0022466915624413

DiCecco, V. M., & Gleason, M. M. (2002). Using graphic organizers to attain relational knowledge from expository text. *Journal of Learning Disabilities, 35*(4), 306–320.

Ellis, E. S., & Howard, P. S. (2007). Graphic organizers: Power tools for teaching students with learning disabilities. *Current Practice Alerts #13.* Reston, VA: Division for Learning Disabilities & Division for Research of the Council for Exceptional Children.

Gage, N. A., Wilson, J., & MacSuga-Gage, A. S. (2014). Writing performance of students with emotional and/or behavioral disabilities. *Behavioral Disorders, 40*(1), 3–14.

Gallavan, N. P., & Kottler, E. (2007). Eight types of graphic organizers for empowering social studies students and teachers. *The Social Studies, 98*(3), 117–128. doi:10.3200/TSSS.98.3.117-128

Garvey, J. H. (1989). The powers and the duties of government. *San Diego Law Review, 26*(2), 209–228.

Hall, C., Kent, S. C., McCulley, L., Davis, A., & Wanzek, J. (2013). A new look at mnemonics and graphic organizers in the secondary social studies classroom. *Teaching Exceptional Children, 46*(1), 47–55. doi:10.1177/004005991304600106

Henderson, K., Klein, S., Gonzalez, P., & Bradley, R. (2005). Teachers of children with emotional disturbance: A national look at preparation, teaching conditions, and practices. *Behavioral Disorders, 31*(1), 6–17.

Howe, A. (2017, March 23). Opinion analysis: Court's decision rejecting low bar for students with disabilities, under the spotlight. *SCOTUSblog.* Retrieved from http://www.scotusblog.com/2017/03/opinion-analysis-courts-decision-rejecting-low-bar-students-disabilities-spotlight/

Huefner, D. S. (2008). Updating the FAPE standard under IDEA. *Journal of Law & Education, 37*(3), 367–379.

Individuals with Disabilities Improvement Act of 2004. (2005). 20 U.S.C. § 1400 *et seq.*

Mason, L. H., Harris, K. R., & Graham, S. (2011). Self-regulated strategy development for students with writing difficulties. *Theory Into Practice, 50*(1), 20–27.

Mastropieri, M. A., & Scruggs, T. E. (2014). Intensive instruction to improve writing for students with emotional and behavioral disorders. *Behavioral Disorders, 40*(1), 78–83.

Mastropieri, M. A., Scruggs, T. E., Hamilton, S. L., Wolfe, S., Whedon, C., & Canevaro, A. (1996). Promoting thinking skills of students with learning disabilities: Effects on recall and comprehension of expository prose. *Exceptionality, 6*(1), 1–11.

McKenna, J. W., & Ciullo, S. (2016). Typical reading instructional practices provided to students with emotional and behavioral disorders in a residential and day treatment setting: A mixed methods study. *Residential Treatment for Children & Youth, 33*(3–4), 225–246. doi:10.1080/0886571X.2016.1207217

McKenna, J., Kim, K., Shin, M., & Pfannenstiel, K. (2017). An evaluation of single-case reading intervention study quality for students with and at risk for emotional and behavioral disorders. *Behavior Modification*, 41(6), 868–906.

McLeskey, J., & Billingsley, B. S. (2008). How does the quality and stability of the teaching force influence the research-to-practice gap? *Remedial and Special Education*, 29(5), 293–305. doi:10.1177/0741932507312010

Mooney, P., Ryan, J. B., Uhing, B. M., Reid, R., & Epstein, M. H. (2005). A review of self-management interventions targeting academic outcomes for students with emotional and behavioral disorders. *Journal of Behavioral Education*, 14(3), 203–221. doi:10.1007/s10864-005-6298-1

Morgan, P. L., Frisco, M. L., Farkas, G., & Hibel, J. (2017). Republication of "A propensity score matching analysis of the effects of special education services". *The Journal of Special Education*, 50(4), 197–214. doi:10.1177/0022466916686105

No Child Left Behind Act of 2001. (2002). 20 U.S.C § 6301 *et seq.*

Novak, J. D., & Gowin, D. B. (1984). *Learning how to learn*. New York, NY: Cambridge University Press.

Pressley, M., Johnson, C. J., & Symons, S. (1987). Elaborating to learn and learning to elaborate. *Journal of Learning Disabilities*, 20(2), 76–91.

Regan, K., & Mastropieri, M. A. (2009). Self-regulated strategy development (SRSD) for writing. *Current Practice Alerts #17*. Reston, VA: Division for Learning Disabilities & Division for Research of the Council for Exceptional Children.

Scruggs, T. E., & Mastropieri, M. A. (1989). Reconstructive elaborations: A model for content area learning. *American Educational Research Journal*, 26(2), 311–327. doi:10.3102/00028312026002311

Scruggs, T. E., & Mastropieri, M. A. (2000). The effectiveness of mnemonic instruction for students with learning and behavior problems: An update and research synthesis. *Journal of Behavioral Education*, 10(2), 163–173. doi:10.1023/a:1016640214368

Scruggs, T. E., Mastropieri, M. A., Brigham, F. J., & Marshak, L. (2017). Science and social studies. In J. M. Kauffman, D. P. Hallahan & P. C. Pullen (Eds.), *Handbook of special education* (2nd ed., pp. 571–581). New York, NY: Taylor and Francis.

Scruggs, T. E., Mastropieri, M. A., & Sullivan, G. S. (1994). Promoting relational thinking: Elaborative interrogation for students with mild disabilities. *Exceptional Children*, 60(5), 450–457.

Scruggs, T. E., Mastropieri, M. A., Sullivan, G. S., & Hesser, L. S. (1993). Improving reasoning and recall: The differential effects of elaborative interrogation and mnemonic elaboration. *Learning Disability Quarterly*, 16(3), 233–240. doi:10.2307/1511329

Sternberg, R. J., & Horvath, J. A. (1995). A prototype view of expert teaching. *Educational Researcher*, 24(6), 9–17.

Sullivan, G. S., Mastropieri, M. A., & Scruggs, T. E. (1995). Reasoning and remembering: Coaching students with learning disabilites to think. *The Journal of Special Education*, 29(3), 310–322. doi:10.1177/002246699502900304

Sutherland, K. S., & Wehby, J. H. (2001). Exploring the relationship between increased opportunities to respond to academic requests and the academic and behavioral outcomes of students with EBD. *Remedial and Special Education, 22*(2), 113–121. doi:10.1177/074193250102200205

Therrien, W. J., Taylor, J. C., Watt, S., & Kaldenberg, E. R. (2014). Science instruction for students with emotional and behavioral disorders. *Remedial and Special Education, 35*(1), 15–27. doi:10.1177/0741932513503557

Weiss, M. P. (2015). Co-teaching: Not all special educators should dance. In B. Bateman, J. W. Lloyd, & M. Tankersley (Eds.), *Enduring issues in special education: Personal perspectives* (pp. 155–165). New York, NY: Routledge.

Appendix A. Examples of two different graphic organizers

Group and Organize Graphic Organizer

Gallavan and Kottler (2007) provided suggestions for eight different forms of graphic organizers. Each serves a different purpose. Here, we provide an adaptation of a "Gropup and Organize" graphic organizer. The purpose of this organizer is to show type, category, or classification. It is best employed with objectives that use verbs such as, arrange, categorize, classify, group, etc.

Classify the Features of the Economies of the North and the South before the American Civil War

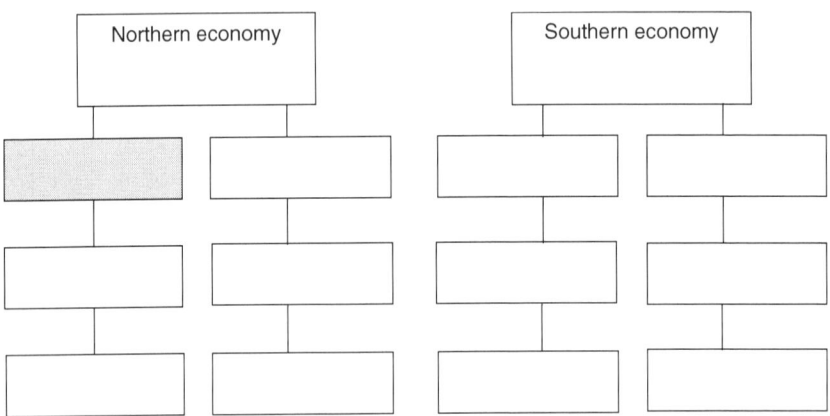

Problem-Solution-Effect Graphic Organizer. Carnine, Miller, Bean, and Zigmond (1994) provided a graphic organizer for a more interactive relationship among ideas. The problem-solution-effect organizer is intended to help students perceive multiple perspectives on an issue. It is best employed with objectives that use verbs such as, compare, contrast, evaluate, or group. The following example is adapted from Carnine et al. (1994, p. 436).

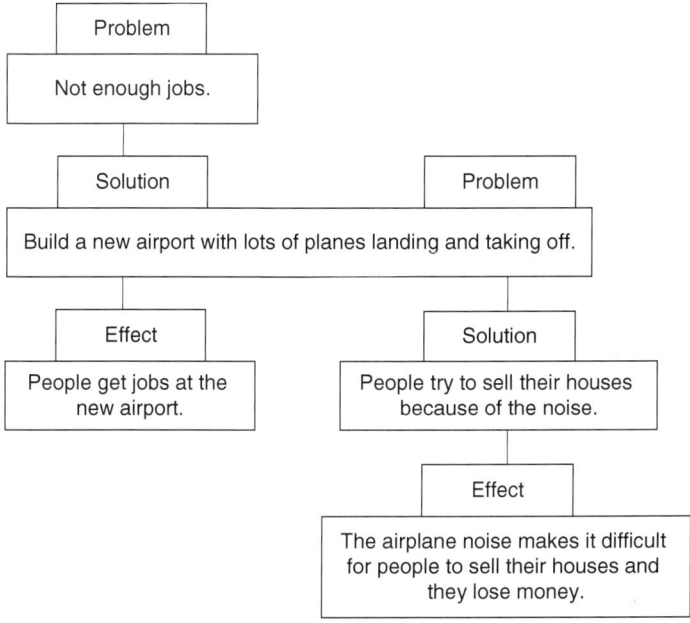

Chapter 3

Interventions for Students with Intellectual Disabilities

Emily C. Bouck and Erin Bone

Abstract

This chapter reviews the intervention research literature – particularly interventions deemed evidence-based – for students with intellectual disability across academic and life-skills instruction. Although the focus of this chapter is the spectrum of students covered under the term "intellectual disability," the majority of research on evidence-based interventions for students with intellectual disability focus on students with more moderate and severe intellectual disability, rather than students with mild intellectual disability. The majority of the interventions determined to be evidence-based within the literature for students with intellectual disability – across both academic and life skills – tend to be those that fall within the purview of systematic instruction.

Keywords: Academics; life skills; mathematics; literacy; evidence-based practices

Students with Intellectual Disability

Students with intellectual disability are a heterogeneous group. Students with intellectual disability includes students with an IQ of 70 or below, according to the school law, and 75 and below, as well as challenges with adaptive behavior (e.g., social skills and daily living skills; Bouck, 2012a)

Viewpoints on Interventions for Learners with Disabilities
Advances in Special Education, Volume 33, 55–73
Copyright © 2018 by Emerald Publishing Limited
All rights of reproduction in any form reserved
ISSN: 0270-4013/doi:10.1108/S0270-401320180000033004

according to the American Association of Intellectual and Developmental Disability. In schools, students are often referred to as having mild intellectual disability, moderate intellectual disability, severe intellectual disability, and profound intellectual disability (Schalock et al., 2010). A mild intellectual disability is classified as an individual with an IQ between 55 and 70, a moderate intellectual disability as an IQ between 40 and 55, a severe intellectual disability as an IQ between 25 and 40, and a profound intellectual disability as an IQ less than 25 (Bouck, 2012a). Hence, the population served under the Individuals with Disabilities Education Act (IDEA, 2004) is diverse, representing students with a myriad of intellectual abilities as well as adaptive behavior strengths and challenges.

Although students with mild intellectual disability compose the largest population of students with intellectual disability (American Psychiatric Association, 2000; Polloway, Lubin, Smith, & Patton, 2010), the existing research base on education and educational interventions for students with intellectual disability focus on students with moderate and severe intellectual disability. In other words, students with mild intellectual disability are neglected from the research or aggregated inappropriately with students with moderate and/or severe intellectual disability (Bouck & Satsangi, 2015; Polloway, 2004, 2005, 2006; Sabornie, Evans, & Cullinan, 2006). The less attention being given through research suggests less attention and support in practice to the education of students with mild intellectual disability (Bouck, 2004, 2007; Edgar, 1987; Fujiura, 2003; Gargiulo, 2015).

Throughout this chapter, the lack of attention to students with mild intellectual disability will be implicitly highlighted as we review the majority of research highlighting evidence-based, research-based, or even promising practices for students with intellectual disability focus on students with moderate and severe intellectual disability. This gap is critical and problematic. As Bouck and Satsangi (2015) discussed, students with mild intellectual disability do differ from those with moderate and severe disabilities and deserve attention and support for the appropriate strategies and practices relative to productive interventions.

Educating Students with Intellectual Disability

Just as students assumed under the term intellectual disability are diverse, so too are the educational – curriculum – options for this population of students. Although a range of curricular options exist to educating students with intellectual disability (Bigge, 1988; Bouck, 2005; Pugach &

Warger, 2001), the majority of the focus on curriculum for students with intellectual disability falls among two options: an academic curriculum and a life-skills curriculum (Bouck, Doughty, & Savage, 2015). An academic curriculum refers to a focus on providing students with intellectual disability access and participation in general education curriculum. In other words, instruction is focused on – or inclusive of – academic standards (Bouck, 2012b). There are multiple ways in which students with intellectual disability can participate in an academic curriculum, including learning the curriculum within a general education class with accommodations, receiving the general education curriculum with augmentation (e.g., teaching and learning assessment and outcomes are different), and through embedding academic content standards – and instruction focused on those standards – within life-skills instruction (Bouck, 2012b; Collins, Hager, & Galloway, 2011; Giangreco, Clonigner, & Iverson, 1998; Wehmeyer, Lattin, & Agran, 2001).

A life-skills curriculum – also referred to as a functional curriculum, real-life skills, or real-world curriculum – reflects instruction focused on the skills an individual needs to live, work, and participate in an inclusive society (Bouck et al., 2015). The key to true life-skills instruction involves a focus on authentic chronologically age-appropriate skills. In other words, the skills taught need to connect to a student's actual current and future life rather than arbitrary skills (Bouck et al., 2015). A life-skills curriculum includes some components of functional academics (e.g., literacy and mathematics), social skills, self-determination, communication access, daily living skills, independent living, financial skills, vocational education, and transportation (Patton, Cronin, & Jairrels, 1997).

Historically, the focus on educational programming for students with an intellectual disability was a life-skills curriculum (Cronin & Patton, 1993; Kolstoe, 1970). Yet, a shift occurred in the later decades of the 1900s toward the participation of students with intellectual disability in general education curriculum and attention transferred to teaching students with intellectual disability academic skills (Bouck et al., 2015). Current educational laws and policies (e.g., No Child Left Behind Act of 2001, 2002; IDEA, 2004) privileged an academic focus with language stipulating all students were to have access to the general education curriculum as well as be held accountable to state standards (Collins, 2013). As suggested above, the two different curriculum approaches – a life skills and an academic – do not need to be at odds. Rather, one can embed life-skills instruction into an academic focus *and* academic instruction into a life-skills focus (Bouck et al., 2015; Collins et al., 2011).

Evidence-Based or Research-Based Interventions

Regardless of the curricular orientation, educational practices for students with intellectual disability should be evidence-based or, at a minimum, research-based. Although often used synonymously, evidence-based practices and research-based practices are not the same label. The term evidence-based practice essentially means that an educational practice has sufficient high-quality, methodology sound research studies that offer data as to its effectiveness (Cook, Smith, & Tankersley, 2012; Cook, Tankersley, & Landrum, 2009). To state that an educational practice is evidence-based is to give it the highest distinction. Research-based practices are then ones that have research to support the practice, although the quality of said research has not necessarily been examined (Cook & Cook, 2013; Slavin, 2002). Research-based practices may also be referred to as data-based, scientifically based, or empirically validated practices. There are also "promising practices," which may be considered as those practices for which there is evidence, but not enough to be considered evidence-based or not meeting all the criteria set to classify a practice as evidence-based (Hudson & Test, 2011). For example, an intervention may be supported by multiple strong research studies, but all conducted by the same research team (Hudson & Test, 2011). Best practices or recommended practices are also ones distinct from both evidence-based, research-based, and best practices. Best practices are typically interventions that are recommended as good to use by others (i.e., individuals or organizations), although may not have research to support their effectiveness (Cook & Cook, 2013).

Challenges exist with discussing evidence-based and research-based interventions for students with intellectual disability. For one, as noted, the category of intellectual disability is heterogeneous. Hence, we must operationally define practices as evidence-based for whom. It is inappropriate to assume that a practice determined to be evidence-based for students with severe intellectual disability is automatically evidence-based for students with mild intellectual disability. However, some examinations of evidence-based practices are loosely focused on students with intellectual disability or even developmental disabilities or moderate/severe disabilities. And, as previously noted, the majority of examinations of evidence-based practices fail to consider students with mild intellectual disability. Likewise, although research-based and evidence-based practices date back to last decade the application of quality indicators and standards to educational interventions is slowly catching up. The focus of this chapter will attempt to be on evidence-based and research-based interventions for students with intellectual disability across academic and life-skills instruction.

Academic Interventions

Across academic instruction in general, multiple evidence-based or research-based interventions exist to support students with intellectual disability. One such intervention is embedded trial instruction used with constant time delay, although it was only evaluated relative to students with moderate and severe intellectual disability (Hudson, Browder, & Wood, 2013). Embedded trial instruction refers to the presentation of trials – or opportunities to engage in a task – multiple times across or within activities in which the task may naturally occur (see Table 1). A constant time delay intervention occurs when an educator waits a constant amount of time (e.g., 0 seconds, 10 seconds) prior to providing a prompt or assistance to a student after asking a student to complete a task (Shurr, Jimenez, & Bouck, in preparation). Another intervention that considered evidence-based interventions with regards to academic instruction for students with developmental disabilities – inclusive of students with intellectual disability – is use of task analysis or task analytic instruction (Spooner, Knight, Browder, & Smith, 2012). A task analysis essentially breaks down a chained task (i.e., complex or multistepped as opposed to discrete, which consists of one step) into the individual steps needed to complete it (Spooner et al., 2012).

It should be noted that in many research studies, as well as practical applications within classrooms, multiple interventions are used. In other words, often there is a treatment package implemented (i.e., multiple interventions), rather than one single intervention. For example, a prompting system (e.g., system of least prompts) and/or constant time delay are often implemented along with task analytic instruction. These different interventions represent systematic instruction; the interventions are consistent with principles of applied behavior analysis (Spooner et al., 2012).

Reading. Reading is a critical, complex skill, conceptualized as involving five areas: phonemic awareness, phonics instruction, fluency, vocabulary, and reading comprehension (National Reading Panel, 2000). Historically, attention to reading instruction for students with intellectual disability – particularly students with moderate and severe intellectual disability – focused on sight word recognition, rather than instruction on decoding or comprehending (Browder, Wakeman, Spooner, Ahgrim-Delzell, & Algozzine, 2006; Hudson & Test, 2011).

Table 1: Evidence-Based Academic Interventions.

Intervention	Focus	Description	Example
Embedded trial instruction	• Academics	An educator presents trials naturalistically across or within activities; behaviors or skills are taught with typical routines (McDonnell et al., 2006).	An educator presents sight words to a student across their day in the general education classroom in which the words would naturally be used (cf., McDonnell et al., 2006; Wolery, Anthony, Synder, Werts, & Katzenmayer, 1997).
Time delay	• Academics • Reading – teaching symbols	An educator waits a constant amount of time (e.g., 0 seconds, 10 seconds) prior to providing a prompt or assistance to a student after asking a student to complete a task (Shurr et al., in preparation).	An educator is teaching middle school students with mild intellectual disability to use app-based fraction pieces to solve addition of fraction problems with unlike denominators. When the problem is given, the educator waits 10 seconds before providing any assistance at each step.
Task analytic instruction	• Academics	An educator creates a series of individual steps in sequential order to complete a chained task; typically prompts are applied to each step to garner a response (Spooner et al., 2012).	An educator breaks down the task of using concrete Base 10 blocks manipulatives to solve double-digit addition problems into step-by-step procedures, teaches students these steps, and provides prompting at each step when students attempt to undertake the task.

Prompting	• Reading – sight words	Prompting includes time delay (see above) as well as the system of least prompts, which involves a hierarchy of prompts that are delivered until a student answers or answers correctly until the last prompt is delivered (e.g., full physical assistance; Doyle, Wolery, Ault, & Fast, 1988).	An educator presents a sight word (e.g., stop) and asks a student to read the word. The educator, using the system of least prompts with a 10 second time delay, waits 10 seconds. If the student does not respond, the educator prompts the student by gesturing to the word. If the student does not respond within another 10 seconds, the educator provides a verbal cue "please read the word." If the student does not respond within another 10 seconds, the educator models reading the word (e.g., stop) and presents another word.
Shared story reading	• Reading – comprehension	An educator reads a story and then provides support for a student to interact with the story (Hudson & Test, 2011).	An educator pairs picture symbols with concrete words (e.g., tractor, horse, and truck) to support students as they read a short story about farming.
In vivo instruction	• Mathematics	An educator provides instruction that occurs within a natural setting (i.e., the setting in which a task typically occurs).	An educator takes students to a grocery store every week where they purchase a list of items to make a meal, while staying within a predetermined budget.

Researchers evaluated some educational literacy interventions relative to their quality and effectiveness. For example, Browder, Ahlgrim-Delzell, Spooner, Mims, and Baker (2009) determined time delay – operationally defined to begin with a zero-time delay – to be an evidence-based practice for students with moderate-to-severe developmental disabilities relative to teaching symbols, inclusive of early literacy relative to picture and word recognition. Browder et al. (2006) found systematic instruction – particularly systematic prompting (e.g., time delay, system of least prompts) – to be an evidence-based practice for teaching students with moderate or severe intellectual disability sight words. Finally, Hudson and Test (2011) found shared story reading to have moderate-level evidence, meaning the existing research on shared story reading present an acceptable quality. Shared story reading essentially refers to when a story is read aloud and the student receives support to interact with the story. Examples of support include word–picture pairs and repeated readings (Hudson & Test, 2011).

Writing. Writing, along with reading, composes literacy. Writing is a multifaceted academic domain consisting of handwriting as well as composing text (e.g., planning, organizing, drafting, editing, and revising text; Flower & Hayes, 1981). Little research examines writing interventions for students with intellectual disability and, hence, few-to-no practices are evaluated as evidence-based for teaching writing to students with intellectual disability (Joseph & Konrad, 2009). Although not evidence-based, Cannella-Malone, Konrad, and Pennington (2015) provided interventions to support students with intellectual disability with writing. They suggested the value of using assistive technology to support students across the areas of writing, from pencil grips to help with handwriting to speech-to-text to help with text generation, and a grammar and spell check program (e.g., Grammarly) to assist with editing. Other interventions to support writing include the use of prompting, such as the system of least prompts (i.e., a prompting hierarchy starting with students being more independent and increasingly providing more dependent prompts; Collins, Branson, Hall, & Rankin, 2001). Strategy instruction as an intervention can also support students with intellectual disability in writing. Strategy instruction generally implies that a strategy is applied to the actual construction of text, from the planning to the final editing (Joseph & Konrad, 2009; Konrad & Trela, 2007; Konrad, Trela, & Test, 2006). For example, Konrad and Trela (2007) developed GO 4 IT... NOW!, a writing strategy based on self-regulated strategy development (SRSD) model. GO 4 IT... NOW! involves teaching students to write goals and objectives, while identifying a timeline and ordering one's steps. GO 4 IT...

NOW! is taught within the typical SRSD model involving activating background knowledge; introducing, modeling, memorizing, and supporting the strategy and its use, and then allowing students to be independent (Konrad & Trela, 2007).

Mathematics. Mathematics is another important and multifaceted academic domain. Mathematics is inclusive of computation and problem-solving, operations and algebra, geometry, measurement and data analysis. Historically, mathematics instruction for students with intellectual disability – particularly considering students with more moderate and severe intellectual disability – focused more on functional mathematics or the mathematics for daily living (e.g., telling time, purchasing skills; Browder, Spooner, Ahlgrim-Delzell, Harris, & Wakeman, 2008).

In term of evidence-based practices, Browder et al. (2008) suggested the research existing on mathematics instruction for students with moderate or severe intellectual disability demonstrates the effectiveness of systematic instruction as well as in vivo (i.e., in real-life settings) instruction (Courtade, Test, & Cook, 2015). Examples of systematic instruction include the system of least prompts (e.g., a prompting hierarchy which starts with the least intrusive and becomes increasingly so – such as ending with physical assistance – when students fail to respond), time delay, specific correct praise, and error correction (Browder et al., 2008). An example of in vivo instruction relative to mathematics include going to a grocery store to learn purchasing skills, including use of real money and price comparison (Browder et al., 2008).

While not yet identified as an evidence-based or promising practice for students with intellectual disability, research does exist to support the use of manipulatives in supporting students with intellectual disability in mathematics. The research on manipulatives for students with intellectual disability runs across the spectrum from students with mild-to-moderate/severe intellectual disability. The research base on manipulatives includes support for both concrete manipulatives (i.e., physical objects a student can manipulative or move to explore a mathematical topic) and digital or virtual manipulatives (i.e., online or app-based representations of concrete manipulatives), as well as manipulatives as stand-alone interventions and/or manipulatives as part of a graduated sequence of instruction (e.g., the concrete-representational-abstract approach; Bouck & Park, in press; Bouck, Working, & Bone, 2018).

Bouck, Chamberlain, and Park (2017) found middle school students with mild intellectual disability were more successful with both concrete and app-based manipulatives in solving double- or triple-digit subtraction than solving the problems without any supports. Bouck, Park, Shurr, Bassette, and Whorley (in press) found the use of virtual manipulatives as part of an instructional sequence adapted from the concrete-representational-abstract framework – the virtual-representational-abstract framework – to be effective in supporting middle school students with mild intellectual disability in learning place value, addition, subtraction, and multiplication. Root, Browder, Sanders, and Lo (2017) compared concrete and virtual manipulatives, delivered as part of an intervention package consisting of schema-based instruction (i.e., when students were taught the schema or problem structure of different types of problems), for elementary students with moderate intellectual disability and autism. The three students all preferred virtual manipulatives and two students acquired the steps of the task analysis to complete the problems with virtual manipulatives. Finally, in a study of more applied or functional mathematics, Bouck, Park, and Nickell (2017), found the concrete-representational-abstract approach – with concrete money manipulatives – to be effective in teaching middle school students with intellectual disability to solve problems involving making change with coins.

Another emerging research-supported mathematic intervention for students with intellectual disability is modified schema-based instruction (MSBI; e.g., Root et al., 2017). Researchers explored MSBI across elementary and secondary students with mild, moderate, and severe intellectual disability and autism (e.g., Ley Davis, Spooner, & Saunders, 2017; Root et al., 2017; Saunders, Browder, Root, & Brosh, 2017; Spooner, Saunders, Root, & Brosh, 2017). MSBI follows traditional schema-based instruction in which students are taught problem types, but the traditional approach is modified by providing students with preconstructed organizers as well as the use of manipulatives. MSBI also involves task analysis and prompting (Spooner et al., 2017).

Science. Although less research on science education and students with intellectual disability exists, particularly research that documents evidence-based or research-based interventions, researchers have explored interventions to support students with intellectual disability in science. Older reviews of existing literature on teaching science to students with severe disabilities determined the majority of the research focused on the life skills or functional elements of science, including health skills (Courtade, Spooner, & Browder, 2007; Spooner, Knight, Browder, Jimenez, & DiBiase, 2011). Spooner et al. (2011) labeled specific practices as evidence-based for teaching science to students with severe disabilities: task analytic instruction and time delay (refer to Table 1).

Life-Skills Interventions

Life-skills instruction in-and-of-itself has strong evidence for its use in secondary education when considering postschool and transition outcomes (Test et al., 2009). The inclusion of life skills into an educational program positively predicts such postschool outcomes as independent living, employment, and postsecondary education participation (Mazzotti, Rowe, Cameto, Test, & Morningstar, 2013).

Systematic instruction is also considered an evidence-based practice relative to life-skills instruction for students with intellectual disability (Browder, Wood, Thompson, & Ribuffo, 2014; see Table 2). Systematic instruction is inclusive of such practices as the system of least prompts, time delay, multiple exemplars (i.e., the presentation of multiple examples and nonexamples), and fading (i.e., when supports are lessened over time; Cooper, Heron, & Heward, 2007; Pennington, Courtade, Ault, & Delano, 2016). Also, similar to academic instruction, implementation of interventions in vivo or in community settings is also an evidence-based practice for life skills (Test et al., 2009). Hence, when teaching students how to greet customers at a place of employment, it is more beneficial to teach such skills within the context of an actual place of employment (Test, Spooner, Holzberg, Roberston, & Davis, 2016).

Another evidence-based intervention for teaching daily living skills to students with intellectual disability is visual activity schedules (Spriggs, Mims, van Dijk, & Knight, 2017). Although the evidence-based practice synthesis by Spriggs et al. (2017) covered a variety of skills (e.g., daily living, academics, and vocational), the majority focused on life skills. Visual activity schedules are an intervention in which visual supports (e.g., pictures) are provided sequentially as cues to support a student to complete a task. The goal of visual activity schedules is to provide sufficient visual prompts to enable an individual to independently complete the task (Koyama & Wang, 2011; Spriggs et al., 2017).

A research-supported intervention for students with intellectual disabilities relative to life skills is video-based instruction, inclusive of video modeling (i.e., an individual watches an entire video and then engages in a task) and video prompting (i.e., an individual watches each step of a task and then completes that task prior to watching the next clip; Cannella-Malone, Fleming, Chung, Wheeler, Basbagill, & Singh, 2011; Mechling, 2005). Video modeling or video prompting are typically done with computers or mobile devices, such as smartphones or tablets (Ayres, Mechling, & Sansosti, 2013). Video modeling can be used as a form of self-operated prompting systems; self-operated prompting systems

Table 2: Evidence-Based Life Skills Interventions.

Intervention	Description	Example
Systematic instruction	An educator provides instructional approaches consisting of five steps to achieve an educational outcome: (a) defines the behavior, (b) describes what an educator will do (i.e., procedures), (c) consistently applies the procedures, (d) monitors progress (i.e., collects data), and (e) makes data-based decisions (Drasgow, Wolery, Chezan, Halle, & Hajiaghamohseni, 2017; Iovannone, Dunlap, Huber, & Kincaid, 2003). Note, instructional approaches using applied behavior analysis are systematic instruction (Drasgow et al., 2017).	An educator uses a task analysis along with the system of least prompts to teach a student to use an ATM (Storey & Miner, 2011).
In vivo instruction	An educator provides instruction to students in a real-life setting where they would need or use the skills (Courtade et al., 2015).	An educator teaches students how to use public transportations using an actual bus rather than simulating the process in a classroom setting: paying, the act needed to stop a bus, and reading a bus schedule at the stop.
Visual activity schedules	An educator provides a student with a series of images used to depict a sequence of events, which provide prompts and allows time for the student to prepare for the next task (Koyama & Wang, 2011).	A sign is mounted next to the sink with pictures depicting the steps of washing hands (e.g., turn on water, wet hands, get soap, rub hands together, rinse hands, drying hands with paper towel).

generally refer to systems in which an individual can use him or herself. Once created (Mechling, Gast, & Seid, 2010), visual activity schools can also be considered a form of self-operated prompting systems.

Self-operated prompting systems (i.e., use of self-instructions) can also be delivered by pictures or audio (i.e., picture and audio prompting, respectively; Bouck, Doughty, & Savage, 2015). Self-operated prompting systems are considered a research-based intervention for students with intellectual disability (den Brok & Sterkenburg, 2015; Smith, Shepley, Alexander, & Ayres, 2015). Savage and Taber-Doughty (2017) specifically concluded that self-operated auditory prompting systems (i.e., tools that deliver audio prompts) were an evidence-based practice for students with intellectual disability.

Another form of technology – computer-based interventions – was indicated to be a promising practice for teaching life skills to students with intellectual disability (Ramdoss et al., 2012). However, the systematic review of the existing literature on computer-based interventions by Ramdoss et al. (2012) featured a software, which is now not commercially available; although effective, the options are now not attainable. While not explicitly available, apps designed to support life skills may serve as potential future option to support life-skills teaching and learning for students with intellectual disability.

Conclusion

Although this chapter attempted to address the spectrum of students with intellectual disability – across disability severity and age, the reality is the majority of the research or syntheses of research documenting evidence-based, research-based, or promising practices focuses on students with moderate and severe intellectual disability rather than mild intellectual disability. Hence, this chapter is forced to focus to a greater extent on students with moderate and severe intellectual disability. The field of special education is beginning to understand, and hence use, evidence-based practices to educate students with intellectual disability. Yet, it remains imperative that evidence-based practices are appropriately determined and then referenced in practice for those whom they have been evaluated as interventions for. In other words, many of the evidence-based practices discussed this chapter were specific to students with moderate and severe intellectual disability; it would be inappropriate to automatically assume they were evidence-based practices for students with mild intellectual disability.

Across the different instructional areas examined, a consistency emerged – systematic instructional interventions as evidence-based practices for students with moderate and severe intellectual disability. Across academic and life-skills instructional area, systematic instructional interventions were denoted as evidence-based, such as, task analytic instruction, time delay, and in vivo instruction. These interventions found to be evidence-based should be the basis for educational programming for students with intellectual disability. Researchers should also continue to examine research-based and/or promising practices to evaluate their merit as evidence-based interventions. Examples of such interventions include video modeling, use of manipulatives to support mathematics teaching and learning, and shared story reading.

References

American Psychiatric Association. (2000). *Diagnostic and statistical manual of mental disorders* (4th ed.). Washington, DC: Author.

Ayres, K. M., Mechling, L., & Sansosti, F. J. (2013). The use of mobile technologies to assist with life skills/independence of students with moderate/severe intellectual disability and/or autism spectrum disorders: Considerations for the future of school psychology. *Psychology in the Schools, 50*, 259–270. doi:10.1002/pits.21673

Bigge, J. (1988). *Curriculum based instruction for special education students.* Mountain View, CA: Mayfield.

Bouck, E. C. (2004). The state of curriculum for secondary students with mild mental retardation. *Education and Training in Developmental Disabilities, 39*, 169–176.

Bouck, E. C. (2005). Impact of factors on curriculum and instructional environments for secondary students with mild mental retardation. *Education and Training in Developmental Disabilities, 40*, 309–319.

Bouck, E. C. (2007). Lost in translation?: Educating secondary students with mild mental impairment. *Journal of Disability Policy Studies, 18*, 79–87.

Bouck, E. C. (2012a). Intellectual disability/mental retardation. In J. A. Banks (Ed.), *Encyclopedia of diversity in education* (pp. 1202–1204). Thousand Oaks, CA: Sage.

Bouck, E. C. (2012b). Secondary curriculum and transition. In P. Wehman (Ed.), *Life beyond the classroom: Transition strategies for young people with disabilities* (5th ed., pp. 215–233). Baltimore, MD: Paul H. Brookes.

Bouck, E. C., Chamberlain, C., & Park, J. (2017). Concrete and app-based manipulatives to support students with disabilities with subtraction. *Education and Training in Autism and Developmental Disabilities, 52*, 317–331.

Bouck, E. C., Doughty, T. T., & Savage, M. (2015). *Footsteps toward the future: A real-world focus for students with intellectual disability, autism spectrum disorder, and other developmental disabilities.* Arlington, VA: Council for Exceptional Children.

Bouck, E. C., & Park, J. (in press). A systematic review of the literature on mathematics manipulatives to support students with disabilities. *Education and Treatment of Children.*

Bouck, E. C., Park, J., & Nickell, B. (2017). Using the concrete-representational-abstract approach to support students with intellectual disability to solve change-making problems. *Research in Developmental Disabilities, 60,* 24–36.

Bouck, E. C., Park, J., Shurr, J., Bassette, L., & Whorley, A. (in press). Using the virtual-representational-abstract approach to support students with intellectual disability in mathematics. *Focus on Autism and Developmental Disabilities.*

Bouck, E. C., & Satsangi, R. (2015). Is there really a difference? Distinguishing mild intellectual disability from similar disability categories. *Education and Training in Autism and Developmental Disabilities, 50,* 186–198.

Bouck, E. C., Working, C., & Bone, E. (2018). Manipulative apps to support students with disabilities in mathematics. *Intervention in School and Clinic, 53,* 177–182. doi:10.1177/1053451217702115

Browder, D., Ahlgrim-Delzell, L., Spooner, F., Mims, P. J., & Baker, J. N. (2009). Using time delay to teach literacy to students with severe developmental disabilities. *Exceptional Children, 75,* 343–364.

Browder, D. M., Spooner, F., Ahlgrim-Delzell, L., Harris, A. A., & Wakeman, S. (2008). A meta-analysis on teaching mathematics to students with significant cognitive disabilities. *Exceptional Children, 74,* 407–432.

Browder, D. M., Wakeman, S. Y., Spooner, F., Ahlgrim-Delzell, L., & Algozzine, B. (2006). Research on reading instruction for individuals with significant cognitive disabilities. *Exceptional Children, 72,* 392–408.

Browder, D. M., Wood, L., Thompson, J., & Ribuffo, C. (2014). *Evidence-based practices for students with severe disabilities.* Document No. IC-3. University of Florida, Collaboration for Effective Educator, Development, Accountability, and Reform Center. Retrieved from http://ceedar. education.ufl.edu/tools/innovation-configurations/

Cannella-Malone, H. I., Fleming, C., Chung, Y.-C., Wheeler, G. M., Basbagill, A. R., & Singh, A. H. (2011). Teaching daily living skills to seven individuals with severe intellectual disabilities: A comparison of video prompting to video modeling. *Journal of Positive Behavior Interventions, 13,* 144–153. doi:10.1177/1098300710266593

Cannella-Malone, H. I., Konrad, M., & Pennington, R. C. (2015). ACCESS! Teaching writing skills to students with intellectual disability. *TEACHING Exceptional Children, 47*(5), 272–280.

Collins, B. C. (2013). What happened to functional curriculum? In W. L. Heward (Ed.), *Exceptional children: An introduction to special education* (10th ed., pp. 436–437). Upper Saddle River, NJ: Pearson.

Collins, B. C., Branson, T. A., Hall, M., & Rankin, S. W. (2001). Teaching secondary students with moderate disabilities in an inclusive academic classroom setting. *Journal of Developmental and Physical Disabilities, 13,* 41–59.

Collins, B. C., Hager, K. D., & Galloway, C. C. (2011). The addition of functional content during core content instruction with students with moderate disabilities. *Education and Training in Developmental Disabilities, 46,* 22–39.

Cook, B. C., & Cook, S. C. (2013). Unraveling evidence-based practices in special education. *The Journal of Special Education, 47,* 71–82. doi:10.1177/0022466911420877

Cook, B. G., Smith, G. J., & Tankersley, M. (2012). Evidence-based practices in education. In K. R. Harris, S. Graham, & T. Urdan (Eds.), *APA educational psychology handbook: Vol. 1.* (pp. 495–528). Washington, DC: American Psychological Association.

Cook, B. G., Tankersley, M., & Landrum, T. J. (2009). Determining evidence-based practices in special education. *Exceptional Children, 75,* 365–383. doi:10.1177/001440290907500306

Cooper, J. O., Heron, T. E., & Heward, W. L. (2007). *Applied behavior analysis* (2nd ed.). Upper Saddle River, NJ: Pearson/Merrill–Prentice Hall.

Courtade, G. R., Spooner, F., & Browder, D. M. (2007). Review of studies with students with significant cognitive disabilities which link to science standards. *Research and Practice for Persons with Severe Disabilities, 32,* 43–49.

Courtade, G. R., Test, D. W., & Cook, B. C. (2015). Evidence-based practices for learners with severe intellectual disability. *Research and Practice for Persons with Severe Disabilities, 39,* 305–338. doi:10.1177/1540796914566711

Cronin, M. E., & Patton, J. R. (1993). *Life skills instruction for all students with special needs: A practical guide for integrating real-life content into the curriculum.* Austin, TX: Pro-Ed.

den Brok, W. L. J. E., & Sterkenburg, P. S. (2015). Self-controlled technologies to support skill attainment in persons with an autism spectrum disorder and/or intellectual disability: A systematic literature review. *Disability and Rehabilitation: Assistive Technology, 10*(1), 1–10. doi:10.3109/17483107.2014.921248

Doyle, P. M., Wolery, M., Ault, M. J., & Fast, D. L. (1988). System of least prompts: A literature review of procedural parameters. *Journal of the Association for Persons with Severe Handicaps, 13*(1), 28–40.

Drasgow, E., Wolery, M., Chezan, L. C., Halle, J., & Hajiaghamohseni, Z. (2017). Systematic instruction of students with significant cognitive disabilities. In J. M. Kauffman, D. P. Hallahan, & P. C. Pullen (Eds.), *Handbook of special education* (pp. 632–648). New York, NY: Routledge.

Edgar, E. (1987). Secondary programs in special education: Are many of them justifiable? *Exceptional Children, 63,* 555–561.

Flower, L., & Hayes, J. R. (1981). A cognitive process theory of writing. *College Composition and Communication, 32,* 365–387.

Fujiura, G. (2003). Continuum of intellectual disability: Demographic evidence for the "forgotten generation." *Mental Retardation, 41,* 420–429.

Gargiulo, R. M. (2015). *Special education in contemporary society* (5th ed.). Thousand Oaks, CA: Sage.

Giangreco, M. F., Cloninger, C. J., & Iverson, V. S. (1998). *Choosing outcomes and accommodations for children (COACH): A guide to educational planning for students with disabilities* (2nd ed.). Baltimore, MD: Paul H. Brookes Publishing.

Hudson, M. E., Browder, D. M., & Wood, L. A. (2013). Review of experimental research on academic learning by students with moderate and severe intellectual disability in general education. *Research & Practice for Persons with Severe Disabilities*, *38*(1), 17–29.

Hudson, M. E., & Test, D. W. (2011). Evaluating the evidence base of shared story reading to promote literacy for students with extensive support needs. *Research & Practice for Persons with Severe Disabilities*, *36*(1–2), 34–45.

Individuals with Disabilities Education Improvement Act of 2004. (2004). Pub. L. No. 108-446.

Iovannone, R., Dunlap, G., Huber, H., & Kincaid, D. (2003). Effective instructional practices for students with autism spectrum disorders. *Focus on Autism and Other Developmental Disabilities*, *3*, 150–165. doi:10.1177/1088 3576030180030301

Joseph, L. M., & Konrad, M. (2009). Teaching students with intellectual or developmental disabilities to write: A review of the literature. *Research in Developmental Disabilities*, *30*, 1–19.

Kolstoe, O. P. (1970). *Teaching educable mentally retarded children*. New York, NY: Holt, Rinehart, & Winston.

Konrad, M., & Trela, K. (2007). GO 4 IT … NOW! Extending writing strategies to support all students. *TEACHING Exceptional Children*, *39*(4), 38–47.

Konrad, M., Trela, K., & Test, D. W. (2006). Using IEP goals and objectives to teach paragraph writing to high school students with physical and cognitive disabilities. *Education and Training in Developmental Disabilities*, *41*, 111–124.

Koyama, T., & Wang, H. T. (2011). Use of activity schedule to promote independent performance of individuals with autism and other intellectual disabilities: A review. *Research in Developmental Disabilities*, *32*, 2235–2242.

Ley Davis, L., Spooner, F., & Saunders, A. (2017). Effects of peer-mediated instruction on mathematical problem solving for student with moderate/severe intellectual disability. Manuscript in preparation.

Mazzotti, V. L., Rowe, D. A., Cameto, R., Test, D. W., & Morningstar, M. E. (2013). Identifying and promoting transition evidence-based practices and predictors of success: A position paper of the Division on Career Development and Transition. *Career Development and Transition for Exceptional Individuals*, *36*, 140–151. doi:10.1177/2165143413503365

McDonnell, J., Johnson, J. W., Polychronis, S., Risen, T., Jameson, M., & Kercher, K. (2006). Comparison of one-to-one embedded instruction in general education classes with small group instruction in special education classes. *Education and Training in Developmental Disabilities*, *41*, 125–138.

Mechling, L. C. (2005). The effect of instructor-created video programs to teach students with disabilities: A literature review. *Journal of Special Education Technology*, *20*, 25–36.

Mechling, L. C., Gast, D. L., & Seid, N. H. (2010). Evaluation of a personal digital assistant as a self-prompting device for increasing multi-step task completion by students with moderate intellectual disabilities. *Education and Training in Autism and Developmental Disabilities*, *45*, 422–439.

National Reading Panel. (2000). *Teaching children to read: An evidence-based assessment of the scientific research literature on reading and its implications for reading instruction: Report of the subgroups.* Bethesda, MD: Author.

No Child Left Behind Act of 2001. (2002). Pub. L. No. 107-110, 115 Stat. 1425.

Patton, J. R., Cronin, M. E., & Jairrels, V. (1997). Curricular implications of transition: Life skills as an integral part of transition education. *Remedial and Special Education, 18,* 294–306.

Pennington, R., Courtade, G., Ault, M. J., & Delano, M. (2016). Five essential features of quality educational programs for students with moderate and severe intellectual disability: A guide for administrators. *Education and Training in Autism and Developmental Disabilities, 51,* 294–306.

Polloway, E. A. (2004). A eulogy for MMI. *DDD Express, 14,* 1, 8.

Polloway, E. A. (2005). Mild retardation: The status of a category of exceptionality. In J. J. Hoover & R. Hills (Eds.), *21st century issues in special education: Meeting diverse needs* (pp. 35–46). Boulder, CO: University of Colorado, BUENO Center.

Polloway, E. A. (2006). Mild mental retardation: A concept in search of clarity, a population in search of appropriate education and supports, a profession in search of advocacy. *Exceptionality, 14,* 183–190.

Polloway, E. A., Lubin, J., Smith, J. D., & Patton, J. R. (2010). Mild intellectual disabilities: Legacies and trends in concepts and educational practices. *Education and Training in Autism and Developmental Disabilities, 45,* 54–68.

Pugach, M. C., & Warger, C. L. (2001). Curriculum matters: Raising expectations for students with disabilities. *Remedial and Special Education, 22,* 194–196.

Ramdoss, S., Lang, R., Fragale, C., Britt, C., O'Reilly, M., Sigafoos, J., … Lacioni, G. E. (2012). Use of computer-based interventions to promote daily living skills in individuals with intellectual disabilities: A systematic review. *Journal of Developmental and Physical Disabilities, 24,* 197–215. doi:10.1007/s10882-011-9249-8

Root, J. R., Browder, D. M., Saunders, A. F., & Lo, Y.-y. (2017). Schema-based instruction with concrete and virtual manipulatives to teach problem solving to students with autism. *Remedial and Special Education, 38,* 42–52. doi:10.1177/0741932516643592

Sabornie, E. J., Evans, C., & Cullinan, D. (2006). Comparing characteristics of high-incidence disability groups: A descriptive review. *Remedial and Special Education, 27,* 95–104.

Saunders, A., Browder, D. M., Root, J., & Brosh, C. (2017). Teaching students with autism to solve word problems using modified schema-based instruction. Manuscript in preparation.

Savage, M. N., & Taber-Doughty, T. (2017). Self-operated auditory prompting systems for individuals with intellectual disability: A meta-analysis of single-subject research. *Journal of Intellectual & Developmental Disability, 42,* 249–258. doi:10.3109/1366825.2016.1229459

Schalock, R. L., Borthwick-Duffy, S. A., Bradley, V. J., Buntinx, W. H. E., Coulter, D. L., Braig, E. M., … Yeager, M. H. (2010). *Intellectual disability: Definition, classification, and systems of support* (11th ed.). Washington, DC: American Association on Intellectual and Developmental Disabilities.

Shurr, J., Jimenez, B., & Bouck, E. C. (in preparation). Acquisition. In J. Shurr, B. Jimenez., & E. C. Bouck (Eds.), *Evidence-based practices for teaching students with intellectual disability and autism.* Arlington, VA: Council for Exceptional Children.

Slavin, R. E. (2002). Evidence-based education policies: Transforming educational practice and research. *Educational Researcher, 31*(7), 15–21.

Smith, K. A., Shepley, S. B., Alexander, J. L., & Ayres, K. M. (2015). The independent use of self-instructions for the acquisition of untrained multi-step tasks for individuals with an intellectual disability: A review of the literature. *Research in Developmental Disabilities, 40*, 19–30. doi:10.1016/j.ridd.2015.01.010

Spooner, F., Knight, V., Browder, D., Jimenez, B., & DiBiase, W. (2011). Evaluating evidence-based practice in teaching science content to students with severe developmental disabilities. *Research and Practice for Persons with Severe Disabilities, 36*, 62–75.

Spooner, F., Knight, V. F., Browder, D. M., & Smith, B. R. (2012). Evidence-based practices for teaching academics to students with severe developmental disabilities. *Remedial and Special Education, 33*, 374–387. doi:10.1177/0741932511421634

Spooner, F., Saunders, A., Root, J., & Brosh, C. (2017). Promoting access to common core mathematics for students with severe disabilities through mathematical problem-solving. *Research and Practice for Persons with Severe Disabilities, 42*, 171–186. Advanced online publication. doi:10.1177/1540796917697119

Spriggs, A. D., Mims, P. J., van Dijk, W., & Knight, V. F. (2017). Examination of the evidence base for using visual activity schedules with students with intellectual disability. *The Journal of Special Education, 51*, 14–26. doi:10.1177/0022466916658483

Storey, K., & Miner, C. (2011). *Systematic instruction of functional skills for students and adults with disabilities.* Springfield, IL: Charles C. Thomas.

Test, D. W., Fowler, C. H., Richter, S., White, J. A., Mazzotti, V. L., Walker, A. R., … Kortering, L. (2009). Evidence-based practices in secondary transition. *Career Development for Exceptional Individuals, 32*, 115–128.

Test, D. W., Spooner, F., Holzberg, D., Roberston, C., & Davis, L. L. (2016). Planning for other educational needs and community-based instruction. In M. L. Wehmeyer & K. A. Shogren (Eds.), *Handbook of research-based practices for educating students with intellectual disability* (pp. 130–150). New York, NY: Routledge.

Wehmeyer, M. L., Lattin, D., & Agran, M. (2001). Achieving access to the general education curriculum for students with mental retardation: A curriculum decision-making model. *Education and Training in Mental Retardation and Developmental Disabilities, 36*, 327–342.

Wolery, M., Anthony, L., Synder, E. D., Werts, M. G., & Katzenmeyer, J. (1997). Training elementary teachers to embed instruction during classroom activities. *Education and Treatment of Children, 20*, 40–58.

Chapter 4

Interventions for Students Who Are Deaf/Hard of Hearing

*Christy M. Borders, Stacey Jones Bock, Karla Giese,
Stephanie Gardiner-Walsh and Kristi M. Probst*

Abstract

The world revolves around sound. Children who are deaf/hard of hearing (D/HH) lack access to sound, thus need careful monitoring and planning to ensure they have access to adequate language models and supports to develop a strong language foundation. It is this foundation that is needed to ensure D/HH children are able to achieve developmental and academic milestones. Research is emerging to suggest specific intervention strategies that can be used to support D/HH children from birth throughout their educational career. In this chapter, we highlight several strategies that can be used to support communication, language, academic, and social/emotional growth. We freely admit that this is in no way a comprehensive and exhaustive list, but rather only scratches the surface. The field of deaf education and related research and technology is constantly changing. To ensure adequate educational access, it is highly recommended that a professional specialized in hearing loss be a part of the educational team any time a child is identified as having any degree or type of hearing loss.

Keywords: Deaf/hard of hearing; intervention strategies; language and communication; academic; social/emotional

Viewpoints on Interventions for Learners with Disabilities
Advances in Special Education, Volume 33, 75–105
Copyright © 2018 by Emerald Publishing Limited
All rights of reproduction in any form reserved
ISSN: 0270-4013/doi:10.1108/S0270-401320180000033005

Deafness is a low-incidence disability, and many teachers will only experience having a student who is deaf or hard of hearing (D/HH) in their classroom a handful of times throughout their careers. The Individuals with Disabilities Education Act (1997, 2004) defines hearing loss as "an impairment in hearing, whether permanent or fluctuating, that adversely affects a child's educational performance" (). The prevalence of hearing loss remains a small percentage of the overall population, ranging from 1 to 6 per 1,000 babies born in the United States (Gifford, Holmes, & Bernstein, 2009; National Institute on Deafness and Other Comunication Disorders [NIDCD], 2017). Over 90% of children who are D/HH are born to parents who are hearing and have no prior exposure or experience with hearing loss (NIDCD, 2017). This results in a challenge for these families due to a knowledge deficit. As a response to this deficit, an emphasis was placed on early identification of hearing loss so early intervention could begin with families in their homes. Early intervention has proven critical for providing these parental supports and services (Harrington, DesJardin, & Shea, 2010; Joint Committee on Infant Hearing [JCIH], 2007; JCIH, American Academy of Pediatrics [AAP], & American Speech-Language-Hearing Association [ASHA], 2000; Moeller, Carr, Seaver, Stredler-Brown, & Holzinger, 2013) thus, impacting long-term communication outcomes (Yoshinago-Itano, 2003).

Hearing loss is complex and can be presented in a variety of ways. It can be caused by either genetic or syndromic conditions or be a result of medical intervention or illness and can occur in children with a family history of deafness or those without. Loss can be progressive over time, fluctuate, or it can be a static, one-time occurrence, either at birth or later in life. It can be present in one ear (unilateral) or both (bilateral), and it can occur in any part of the ear and range from a slight to complete absence of sound. Technology such as hearing aids and cochlear implants can sometimes alleviate this absence of sound and assist in both sound awareness and speech production; however, there are times when the use of technology is not beneficial for a variety of reasons. A hearing loss is typically classified as either deaf or hard of hearing, often based on the degree of loss or on personal preference. Anderson and Price (2015) created a chart summarizing the degrees of loss and the possible implications (see Table 1). It is important to remember that hearing loss affects each person differently based on a variety of factors. Additionally, the Supporting Success for Children with Hearing Loss website (http://successforkidswithhearingloss.com/) has a plethora of information for both

Table 1: Functional Interpretation of Hearing Thresholds on the Audiogram.

Degree of Hearing Loss	General Issues with this Degree of Hearing Loss	Audibility of Speech Sounds (Puzzle Pieces Available for Understanding) for Listening in QUIET. Will Be Significantly Poorer in Noise		
		"Soft Speech" 35 dB HL	"Conversational Speech" 45 dB HL	"Teacher Speech" 50 dB HL
20–25 dB	Impact of a 20–25 dB hearing loss can be compared to ability to hear when index fingers are placed in ears. A 20 dB or greater hearing loss in the better ear can result in absent, inconsistent, or distorted parts of speech, especially word endings (-s, -ed) and unemphasized sounds. Behavior may be confused for immaturity or inattention. May be unaware of subtle conversational cues that could cause child to be viewed as inappropriate or awkward.	Audibility 40% Missing sounds: f, s, th, p, k, v, z, g, sh, ch	Audibility 80% Missing sounds: f, s, th, p, k, v, z	Audibility 95% Missing sounds: all sounds detected but not as loud as normal

Table 1: *(Continued)*

Degree of Hearing Loss	General Issues with this Degree of Hearing Loss	Audibility of Speech Sounds (Puzzle Pieces Available for Understanding) for Listening in QUIET. Will Be Significantly Poorer in Noise		
		"Soft Speech" 35 dB HL	"Conversational Speech" 45 dB HL	"Teacher Speech" 50 dB HL
25–30 dB	Child can "hear" but misses fragments of speech leading to misunderstanding. Degree of difficulty experienced in school will depend upon noise level in the classroom, distance from teacher, and configuration of the hearing loss, even with hearing aids. Will miss unemphasized words and consonants, especially with a high-frequency hearing loss. Often experiences difficulty learning early reading skills, that is, letter/sound associations. Barriers begin to build with negative impact on self-esteem as child is accused of "hearing when he wants to," "daydreaming" or "not paying attention." May believe he/he is less capable due to difficulties understanding in class. Child begins to lose the ability for selective listening and has increasing difficulty	25% Missing sounds: f, s, th, p, k, v, z, g, sh, ch, l, a, j, m, d, b	65% Missing sounds: f, s, th, p, k, v, z, g, sh, ch	81% Missing sounds: f, s, th, p, k,
30–35 dB		15% Missing sounds: f, s, th, p, k, v, z, g, p, l, j, sh, ch, a, m, d, b, ng, o	45% Missing sounds: f, s, th, p, k, v, z, g, sh, ch, l, a, j, m, d, b	60% Missing sounds: f, s, th, p, k, v, z, g, sh, ch
35–40 dB		10% Perceived sounds: u, e, l, ng	30% Perceived sounds: j, m, d, b, ng, i, a	45% Perceived sounds: j, m, d, b, ng i, a, sh, ch, g

dB	Description			
40–45 dB	suppressing background noise causing the learning environment to be more stressful. Child is more fatigued due to effort needed to listen. FM needed to access verbal instruction. Repeat key student discussion.	0% Perceived sounds: none	15% Perceived sounds: u, e, l, ng	30% Perceived sounds: j, m, d, b, ng, i, a
45–50 dB	Even with hearing aids, child can "hear" but will miss much of speech if classroom is noisy or reverberant. Without early amplification, the child is likely to have delayed or disordered syntax, limited vocabulary, imperfect speech production, and flat voice quality. With personal hearing aids alone, high risk to effective learning in class; FM is necessary for access in class.	0%	0%	15%
55–60 dB+	Conversation is inaccessible without amplification.	0%	0%	0%

Source: K. Anderson (2015), revised from Making Sense of the Audiogram, November 2013 Teacher Tools. In Steps to Assessment.

parents and professionals, including materials and strategies that may be helpful in educational planning.

People who are D/HH choose from a variety of modes of communication, which include but are not limited to the use of signed languages, spoken language, or cued languages (e.g., Cued Speech). The National Association for the Deaf (NAD, 2017) defines American Sign Language (ASL) as a visual language, with its own grammar and phonology separate from any spoken language. Many countries have their own signed languages, with ASL primarily used in the United States. It is important to note that not every student in the United States who uses sign language uses ASL.

Spoken language is any verbal language used throughout the world, such as English, Spanish, or French. Cued Speech is a visual handshape system designed to represent the patterns of spoken language and is separate from signed language (National Cued Speech Association, 2017). Fig. 1 displays the hand shapes and positions used in Cued Speech. It is important to note that successful outcomes with each communication modality can vary widely among D/HH children and adults, and there is no strong evidence favoring one modality over the other (Ferrell, Bruce, & Luckner, 2014; Stredler-Brown, 2010).

The lack of access to sound substantially affects the overall development of the D/HH student. Numerous studies have shown that students who are D/HH often demonstrate significant delays in the areas of speech production, expressive and receptive vocabulary, school readiness/conceptual knowledge, vocabulary, grammar, English syntax and structure, language, reading, math, and comprehension skills (Gale & Schick, 2009; Harrington et al., 2010; Kritzer & Pagliaro, 2013; Lederberg, Miller, Easterbrooks, & Connor, 2014; Luft, 2017). Thus, it is critical that both parents and professionals become familiar with techniques that have shown promise in closing the gap in achieving typical developmental milestones (Ferrell et al., 2014; Harrington et al., 2010). In addition to coaching parents during the early intervention years, many researchers have uncovered the powerful effects of high expectations for the child's success from both parents and providers acknowledging that high expectations often lead to positive outcomes (Hayes, 2014; Metz, 2017; Wang, Engler, & Oetting, 2014).

There are many things to consider when planning for the educational needs of a student who is D/HH. Regardless of the age of onset, cause, type, degree (severity), or communication modality, a student who is D/HH works harder to access information from the world around them (Luft, 2017). Therefore, it is crucial that professionals who support

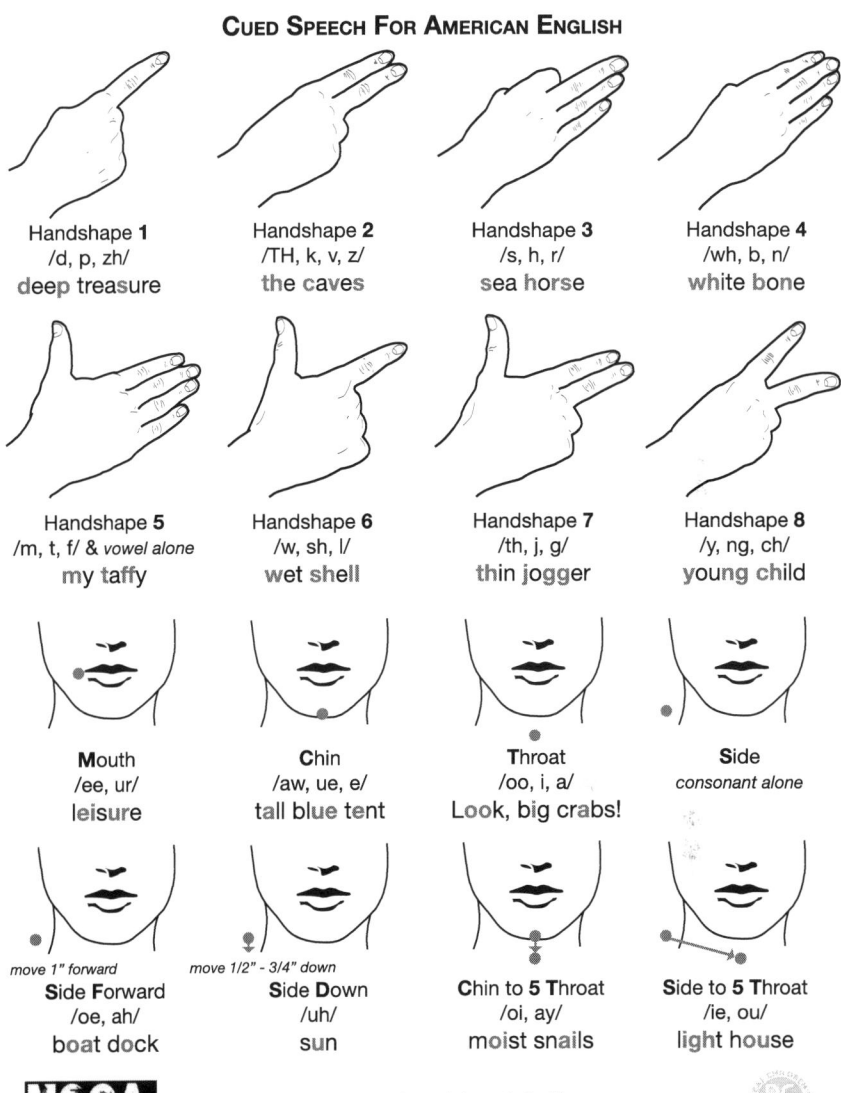

Fig. 1:

students that are D/HH are well-versed in the use of evidence-based practices (EBPs). Unfortunately, due to the low incidence nature of D/HH, there are often "misunderstandings, low expectations, and a lack of knowledge about EBPs simply because education personnel have lacked familiarity with how these students learn" (Ferrell et al., 2014, p. 8). This chapter will focus on recommended interventions to use with children who are D/HH, from birth through high school. We will look at interventions that support positive outcomes within the timeframes of early intervention, elementary, and secondary education. These interventions will be further separated to focus on the areas of communication and language, academics (literacy, math, science, and life skills) and social emotional development.

Practices in Deaf Education

Current Practices

Luckner, Sebald, Cooney, Young, and Muir (2005/2006) illuminated a lack of EBPs in the field of deaf education. They articulated that there are not only logistical and scientific difficulties associated with establishing EBPs in a low-incidence population, but very few professors and researchers in the field to establish such practices. Faculty is often overcommitted being the sole providers of coursework or program coordination at their respective universities. The field's constant struggle against emotional allegiances, often linked to modality and cultural identity, also make replication studies and establishment of practices impractical. Spencer and Marschark (2010) highlighted this issue by stating: "For too long, practice in education of deaf and hard-of-hearing students has been based more closely on beliefs and attitudes than on documented evidence from research or the outcomes of interventions" (p. 25).

Ferrell et al. (2014) worked with the Collaboration for Effective Educator, Development, Accountability, and Reform (CEEDAR) Center to launch an evaluation of practices in sensory disabilities. In their report, a shockingly low number of practices were shown to have more than a limited amount of evidence. For example, only early identification/early intervention and some areas of literacy were rated as having moderate evidence of effectiveness. Those areas with limited evidence included assessment, assistive technology, communication, life skills, some areas of literacy, mathematics, placement/inclusion, science, social-emotional/behavior, and transition.

Throughout the following sections, it is important to consider the limitations inherent in writing on this topic. Each of these topics has and could continue to fill its own volume. As authors, we have chosen to highlight some of these practices, fully acknowledging a lack of comprehensiveness. All educational practices are driven by solid assessment. However, assessment of educational skills in D/HH students can be complicated. The impact of communication, language, reading, and writing delays (Cawthon, 2009; Gilbertson & Ferre, 2008; Luckner & Bowen, 2006) can compromise the accuracy of assessments administered and conclusions drawn. The mode of delivery for assessments must be considered. If a D/HH student communicates through signed language, mismatch between the test administrator and student could clearly impact the process and validity warranting an interpreter who understands confidentiality and the assessment process (Ferrell et al., 2014; Gilbertson & Ferre, 2008; Maller & Braden, 2011; Wood & Dockrell, 2010).

As D/HH students move through their educational careers, quality of programming is a critical variable in success (Knoors & Hermans, 2010; Pianta et al., 2005). A quality program includes planning for transitions. Transition planning cannot and should not only occur at the legally mandated times. While planning for transitions between early childhood and school-aged services, elementary and middle, and high school and post-secondary are critical, there are also transitions to consider within each of those periods. For example, the multiple transitions in a school day (from the classroom to the gym, etc.), from teacher-to-teacher, and year-to-year must also be considered during intervention planning. It is important that plans for generalization and maintenance be considered for all skills to result in the greatest potential outcomes.

Recommended Practices

Interventions for Early Childhood

JCIH et al. (2000) proposed recommended guidelines for Early Hearing Detection and Intervention (EHDI) programs and providers throughout the United States. The guidelines recommended all babies with suspected hearing loss begin the diagnostic confirmation process by three months of age and begin receiving early intervention supports by six months of age from professionals with a background in hearing loss. JCIH et al. (2000) strongly recommended that early intervention services be family-centered and include the concept of informed choice by providing a variety of information and resources for parents including the opportunity to meet deaf and hard of hearing adults and children. In addition, the guidelines encouraged providers to ensure that families have "access to general information on child development and specific information on hearing loss and language development" (JCIH et al., 2000, p. 798). JCIH et al. (2000) emphasized the concept of "family centered" (p. 799) intervention and established eight principles to incorporate into programming. These guidelines were revised in 2007 to update and expand each of the eight principles due, in part, to the dramatic increase (38–95%) in the percentage of infants screened annually in the United States (JCIH, 2007). The revised JCIH (2007) recommendations continued to stress a team approach with family involvement. The idea of family-centered planning remained and continued to be addressed throughout the guidelines, benchmarks, and quality indicators.

In 2013, a supplement to the JCIH (2007) position statement was created and published by the American Academy of Pediatrics (AAP) and republished by Yoshinaga-Itano (2013). This supplement was created based on the work of an international panel of experts and listed 10 principles for family-centered early intervention (FCEI) programming for D/HH children and their families (see Table 2). Goals, rationales, and recommendations for achievement were listed along with guidelines detailing best practices for early intervention professionals working with D/HH children and their families. Implementation allowed for systematic EHDI programming and monitoring of service provision with increased fidelity (AAP, 2013; Yoshinaga-Itano, 2013).

Communication and language. Hearing loss directly impacts access to spoken language. Communication and language skill deficits are frequent among students who are D/HH. Several intervention strategies are recommended for addressing communication needs of D/HH infants and toddlers. Several researchers point out that fluent language input in the early years of life strongly impacts language and communication development (Ferrell et al., 2014; Spencer, 2004; Yoshinago-Itano, 2013) and could even positively impact overall brain development (Kritzer & Pagliaro, 2013). Regardless of the chosen mode of communication (Stredler-Brown, 2010), it is imperative that fluent language input happens prior to the age of two to increase the chances of reaching typical language milestones (Mayberry, 2010; Metz, 2017). Research specific to fluent visual language exposure in the early years has demonstrated a positive impact on reading (Allen, Letteri, Choi, & Dang, 2014; Mueller & Hurtig, 2010). One way to provide fluent language input is through use of daily routines within natural environments (Allen et al., 2014; Moeller et al., 2013).

Table 2: Best Practice Principles for FCEI.

Number	Best Practice Principle
1	Early, timely, and equitable access to services
2	Family/provider partnerships
3	Informed choice and decision making
4	Family social and emotional support
5	Family infant interaction
6	Use of assistive technologies and supporting means of communication
7	Qualified providers
8	Collaborative teamwork
9	Progress monitoring
10	Program monitoring

Source: Adapted from Moeller et al. (2013).

The use of daily routines allows for frequent repeated exposure to words; thus, allowing D/HH children repeated exposure so they can internalize words (Harrington et al., 2010; VanDam, Ambrose, & Moeller, 2012). Furthermore, increased conversations with parents (VanDam et al., 2012) based on the child's interest (Gale & Schick, 2009) positively impacts the development of vocabulary (Ferrell et al., 2014; Moeller et al., 2013) and language in young children. In addition, Rhoades (2013) suggests inserting intentional moments of silence or natural pauses while talking with D/HH children, to teach turn-taking and other important conversational skills.

Academics. Increased access to language facilitates academic learning of school readiness skills – a focus of quality early intervention services (Easterbrooks, Lederberg, Miller, Bergeron, & Connor, 2008; Harrington et al., 2010). Several reading and math intervention strategies show promising results in addressing preacademic skills for D/HH students at a young age.

Reading and math skills are important skills to learn in early childhood. Shared reading during the first five years of life reinforces preliteracy skills and provides D/HH students with a strong foundation to begin reading on their own (Andrews & Taylor, 1987; Delk & Weidekamp, 2001; Ferrell et al., 2014; Lutz, 2017). Strategies that may be beneficial include recasting (restatement of child's pronunciation into a question; DesJardin, Ambrose, & Eisenberg, 2009), use of open-ended questions, acting out stories, emphasizing facial expressions, altering speech inflections, focusing on pictures rather than the words, making the shared reading time an enjoyable bonding experience (Lutz, 2017), and capitalizing on joint attention through following the child's lead, and commenting on what they are interested in (Gale & Schick, 2009). Learning of mathematical concepts can occur during naturally occurring events and conversations (Kritzer, 2009). Conversations with young children can easily incorporate numbers, counting, quantity, time/sequence, and categorization concepts (Kritzer, 2009; Kritzer & Pagliaro, 2013). Parent confidence in presenting mathematical concepts in the home can be increased through specific parent training (Kritzer & Pagliaro, 2013).

Social/Emotional. Early intervention services and parental supports encourage healthy attachment between parents and D/HH babies (Ferrell et al., 2014; Moeller, 2007). Stika et al. (2015) discussed the connection between language delays and poor social–emotional relationships. They cautiously concluded that early identification and support can lessen the negative impact of hearing loss on social emotional development.

Interventions for Elementary D/HH Students

When a D/HH student exits early intervention, they enter P-12 education. They transition from a family-centered approach, where the home is a primary intervention location (Individualized Family Service Plan) to an academically focused approach primarily delivered in the school (Individualized Education Program, IEP). After the IEP team has articulated present levels of performance and goals for a student, selection of services and the most appropriate educational placement is determined. This consideration is made on a yearly basis. The Placement and Readiness Checklists for Students who are Deaf and Hard of Hearing (PARC; Johnson, 2011) are designed to aid IEP teams in planning the placement and support needs of D/HH students, based on language needs. Another evaluation that can be used to make similar considerations about language needs for the classroom setting is available for teacher use from the Boston Center for Deaf and Hard of Hearing Children, Children's Hospital of Boston (2003).

Communication/Language. Strong communication and language skills are critical to academic success. Instruction is built upon language skills. Deficits in language or communication can lead to widespread delays in content comprehension and increased impulsivity and behavioral outbursts in the classroom (Calderon & Greenberg, 2003). As discussed previously, language use in the home (Mayberry, 2010; Mitchell & Karchmer, 2004) and level of parental involvement (Calderon, 2000; DesJardin, 2006; Spencer, 2004) also impact communication skills in the school environment. Access to academic content is heavily reliant on language skills.

Academics. The core of academic learning is language. Eventual content learning relies heavily on literacy skills. Much of the literature in the field of deaf education focuses on literacy. Unfortunately, literacy outcomes for D/HH students have remained consistently delayed (Nunes, Burman, Evans, & Bell, 2010), with only 10% of students developing age-appropriate reading levels by graduation (Traxler, 2000). Some researchers posit lack of phonological memory of words and mismatch of phonemes in words and sign representation (Bochner & Bochner, 2009; Musselman, 2000), limited access to spoken language and word identification skills (Luckner & Handley, 2008; Marschark & Wauters, 2008), insufficient experience with literacy in early childhood (Luckner et al., 2005/2006), and delayed vocabulary acquisition (Luckner et al., 2005/2006; Marschark & Wauters, 2008) as primary causes for literacy delay. In an effort to address and remediate the delay, the National Reading Panel identified the five essential components of reading instruction as phonemic awareness, phonics, fluency, vocabulary, and comprehension (Eunice Kennedy Shriver National Institute of Child Health and Human Development, 2000). These components also apply when developing reading instruction for D/HH students.

Some researchers choose to discuss literacy interventions in a broad sense rather than skill-specific components. Easterbrooks and Stephenson (2006) identified the ten most frequently cited broad literacy interventions for D/HH students as independent reading, use of technology, phonemic awareness and phonics, metacognitive reading strategies, writing to promote reading, reading in content areas, shared reading and writing, semantic approaches to vocabulary, morphographemic approaches to vocabulary, and fluency interventions. Research indicates that while many researchers in the field of deaf education do not address phonemic awareness or phonics-based instruction for D/HH students, those who receive instruction with these components have positive outcomes (Luckner & Handley, 2008; Syverud, Guardino, & Selznick, 2009). Additionally, links to the phonemic or phonic system are sometimes addressed through a visual, or signed system for D/HH students. Although the use of fingerspelling to supplement instruction has not been rigorously tested, use of it to facilitate literacy shows promise (Haptonstall-Nykaza & Schick, 2007; Lederberg, Schick, & Spencer, 2013). The use of ASL has also been investigated to teach English literacy (Bailes, 2001).

Bailes conducted a qualitative study where connections between ASL and English where used to increase literacy in young D/HH students. Visual phonics is another signed system that combines hand cues with spoken language to enhance auditory information to illustrate English phonemes for D/HH students (Waddy-Smith & Wilson, 2003). The use of visual phonics has been shown to increase the phonological awareness and skills of D/HH students (Smith & Wang, 2010; Trezek & Malmgren, 2005). Researchers found that students were able to generalize the phonological awareness skills learned through visual phonics to reading (Smith & Wang, 2010; Trezek & Malmgren, 2005). Significant improvements in foundational reading skills of kindergarten students were also observed when strong curricula were paired with the use of visual phonics (Trezek, Wang, Woods, Gampp, & Paul, 2007). Cued speech has also been shown to be beneficial in addressing phonemic awareness and increasing reading skills (Bouton, Bertoncini, Serniclaes, & Colé, 2011; Wang, Trezek, Luckner, & Paul, 2008).

Repeated reading of passages has been identified as an effective intervention for improving word recognition, speed, accuracy, fluency, and comprehension among typical hearing readers (Luckner & Urbach, 2012; Mercer, Campbell, Miller, Mercer, & Lane, 2000; O'Connor, White, & Swanson, 2007; Therrien, 2004). Research results are variable for the effect of repeated readings for D/HH students. While some study results indicated that the repeated reading method was effective for improving reading fluency of these students (Ensor & Koller, 1987; Schirmer, Schaffer, Therrien, & Schirmer, 2012), Schirmer and McGough (2005) found no such indication for increased reading fluency in D/HH students.

D/HH students' vocabulary development and word acquisition are often delayed (Andrews & Mason, 1991; Geers & Moog, 1989; Lederberg & Spencer, 2001; Strassman, 1992). When Luckner and Cooke (2010) reviewed 41 studies on vocabulary interventions for D/HH students, they found that only two interventions (explicit teaching of vocabulary through a computerized program and aural/oral habilitation following cochlear implantation) demonstrated effects across more than one study. Visually based vocabulary strategies may help signing D/HH students develop a representational structure that can mediate word reading difficulties (Lederberg et al., 2013). Specific literature on reading comprehension strategies for D/HH students indicated five interventions to be promising including explicit comprehension strategy, teaching students story grammar, modified directed-reading thinking activity, activating background knowledge, and use of well-written, high interest text (Luckner & Handley, 2008).

The impact of language delays exhibited by many D/HH students is not limited to literacy or reading alone. Language delays also impact student outcomes in mathematics (Easterbrooks & Stephenson, 2006; Hyde, Zevenbergen, & Power, 2003; Kelly & Mousley, 2001; Kritzer, 2009; Pagliaro, 2010) and content areas, such as science (Barman & Stockton, 2002; Diebold & Waldron, 1988; Easterbrooks & Stephenson, 2006; Elefant, 1980; Jones, 2014; Lang & Pagliaro, 2007; Lang & Steely, 2003; Mertens, 1991; Vosganoff, Paatsch, & Toe, 2011). Easterbrooks and Stephenson (2006) identified the 10 most-used interventions for teaching science and mathematics to D/HH students as fluent teacher communication; instruction provided through the students' primary language; content specialization by the teacher; active learning; visual organizers; authentic, problem-based instruction; use of technology; instruction in specialized content vocabulary; focus on critical thinking skills; and mediation of textbook material.

Social/Emotional. Ferrell et al. (2014) note that a large number of D/HH students leave P-12 school lacking independence, demonstrating decreased employability, or having difficulty maintaining employment. Teachers should focus on providing programming that is not solely focused on academics but includes instruction on specific skills such as emotional self-awareness, emotional self-regulation, motivation, empathy, and social skills (Goleman, 2006). Instruction on independence skills can begin in early grades and helps to ensure adequate programming for knowledge and skills development across students' educational careers. Additionally, social skills training can be beneficial for D/HH students' social emotional outcomes (Antia, Kreimeyer, & Eldredge, 1994; Ducharme & Holborn, 1997; Kusche & Greenberg, 1993; Schloss & Smith, 1990; Schloss, Smith, & Schloss, 1984).

Interventions for Secondary D/HH Students

Much of the recommended practices discussed in literature focus on those delivered prior to secondary education. This may be due to the fact that while early interventions lay a groundwork, secondary educators are often utilizing the same interventions for students at this level if student levels of performance have not increased beyond an elementary level. The long-standing statistic of high school deaf students graduating with a 4th grade reading level (Watson, 1998) is perhaps an indication that interventions remain at the elementary level due to overall student outcomes.

Communication/Language. The Expanded Common Core for Students who are Deaf or Hard of Hearing addresses the comprehensive development of communication in children who are D/HH through the inclusion of receptive and expressive communication skills. Additionally, they offer developmental sequences of "optional" skills that may be developed further dependent on which communication modality is chosen. These skills include auditory, ASL, and speech. The common core also includes skills in self-advocacy or management of one's communication needs, including technology.

Little research focuses on strategies for increasing language development in D/HH students beyond early childhood. Several studies (Geers & Moog, 1989; Geers, Tobey, Moog, & Brenner, 2008; Yoshinaga-Itano, 2013) indicate outcomes for students in secondary settings that reinforce that those children who had early identification, early amplification, limited or no additional disabilities, and intense language rich environments (English or ASL) thrive in comparison to their D/HH peers who were late identified, amplified, or intervened.

Academics. Existing research related to the needs of middle and high school students focuses on the skills of literacy (phonological awareness, decoding/word recognition, vocabulary, fluency, comprehension, and composition) and not language development. Studies related to phonological awareness interventions at the middle and high school level are rare, as these skills are presumed to be developed in the preschool to third grade setting for children without hearing loss.

Full access to academic content and vocabulary for D/HH students who sign requires educationally trained interpreters who have complex knowledge of interpreting skills, language skills, and longitudinal academic development across age spans (Schick, Williams, & Kupermintz, 2006). This knowledge was present in about 40% of the 2,100 the interpreters (Schick et al., 2006) as measured by the Educational Interpreters Performance Assessment. In fact, the results from the study by Schick and colleagues indicates that the interpreting services received by many students who are D/HH severely hindered access to classroom curriculum. To build the vocabulary skills of high school students with severe to profound hearing loss, Hamilton (2012) compared the use of an online, bilingual, multimedia English-ASL dictionary (OBMEAD) to online monolingual English (OMED) dictionaries and paper English-ASL dictionaries (PBEAD). Results indicated that learners had stronger short-term recall of target vocabulary after using online OBMEAD as opposed to OMED and PBEAD. For longer-term recall, there was no difference between OBMEAD and PBEAD; however, recall from OMED was significantly weaker (Hamilton, 2012).

Low levels of reading comprehension will likely negatively impact many different aspects of a student's education. Since secondary educators primarily rely on informational texts when teaching, adolescents who do not have strong comprehension skills may quickly fall behind. Secondary-level students who rated themselves as good readers described their process of reading to include practicing and decoding. They employed comprehension strategies such as paying attention to detail, explaining, retelling, summarizing, visualizing, rereading, and identifying the meaning of unknown vocabulary (Donne & Rugg, 2015). These same students reported more frequent and longer interactions with text. Two studies explored types of comprehension strategies used by D/HH adolescents. Ewoldt, Israelite, and Dodds (1992) and Strassman (1992) reported that participants used the following strategies: rereading text, using prior knowledge, requesting help from someone else, and using picture cues. The strategy used most often was requesting an explanation from someone else. Additionally, the Reread-Adapt and Answer-Comprehend repeated reading strategy with added comprehension tracking positively impacted outcomes for secondary students (Schirmer et al., 2012). This strategy focuses on increasing reading fluency and overall reading achievement by first providing a prompting card with guiding questions (i.e., who, what, when, where, and how) followed by timed reading of an independent passage as quickly as possible. If an unknown word is encountered, the teacher states it while making notes about student errors and recording the reading time. After the first reading, the student is instructed to reread the story as many times as necessary to reach set criterion (no more than two errors or passage reading four times; Schirmer et al., 2012).

Writing involves the encoding of information. Encoding is more difficult for D/HH students than decoding because encoding requires experience and fluency with decoding. The grammatical structure of ASL differing from English creates a more prominent difficulty (Appanah & Hoffman, 2014). To add more complexity to this issue, some D/HH students may not have a strong foundation in either English or ASL. Several studies have identified interventions that could improve the writing skills of D/HH adolescents. The Strategic and Interactive Writing Instruction (SIWI) method increased English grammar skills and overall written language growth in middle school D/HH students (Wolbers, Dostal, & Bowers, 2012). SIWI explicitly teaches writing strategies through a collaborative or interactive writing session between the teacher and the student. During the interactive writing sessions, the teacher comments and expands on the student's use of grammar, vocabulary, and other linguistic characteristics in both ASL and English. Finally, when a student is having difficulty expressing ideas, a "language zone" is used to facilitate idea generation and communication through the use of other means (e.g., pictures, role play, drawings, and objects). Strassman and O'Dell (2012) paired writing with digital media for D/HH students in middle grades. Students who used closed captioned self-created materials had improved language form and use, increased use of unique and targeted vocabulary, and improved English conventions when compared to traditional writing methods (Strassman & O'Dell, 2012). Another study, conducted by Wolbers (2008), used Morning Message (MM), a balanced and interactive writing strategy which resulted in gains in editing and revising skills for middle-grade D/HH students. During a 15- to 30-minute MM session, the teacher and the students worked together to craft a writing passage. One student was designated the leader and would choose the topic. After the topic was chosen, the students would work together to construct the text. As the group constructed a phrase, the teacher would write the phrase word-for-word for the group to view, review, and edit. This process continued (planning, writing, revising, and editing), allowing the students to ask questions and the teacher to scaffold learning (i.e., structures such as compare/contrast and persuasion).

Social/Emotional. Life-skills instruction focuses on teaching students the skills needed for postsecondary independent living (e.g., cooking, budgeting, safety, and purchasing). Little research exists to provide guidance to teachers in life-skills instruction. Four principles have been associated with successful outcomes in education, employment, and independent living. These principles include purposeful inclusion in general education, paid employment or work experience, self-care/independent living skills, and support from family and friends (Ferrell et al., 2014; Test, Mazzotti, Mustian, Fowler, Kortering, & Kohler, 2009). Life-skills instruction grounded in these principles will likely result in positive outcomes.

Students with disabilities are more likely to engage in smoking and drinking alcohol (Hogan, McLellan, & Bauman, 2000), and they report increased struggles with psychosocial factors. D/HH students, specifically those who are hard of hearing, identified loneliness as an emotional experience more frequently than hearing peers (Kent, 2003). Kemmery and Compton (2014) identified interactions with others, settings and contexts of the exchanges, and life experiences as influences on the development of self-identification. Results of their study indicated that identity is a fluid concept that required a sense of management and resiliency.

Deafness with Additional Disabilities

While many students identify as D/HH, a large percentage of D/HH students also have an additional disability (Deaf with Disability, DWD). When a student is DWD, the effect of one disability upon another creates unique educational needs that are different than those displayed by any disability alone (Jones, Jones, & Ewing, 2006). For example, when a student has comorbid D/HH and autism spectrum disorder (ASD), the learning needs of this student will not be met by a standard curriculum or education program developed for students who are D/HH nor one developed for students who have ASD (Jones, 1984). To address the needs of DWD students, a compensatory curriculum that focuses on skill development through each child's unique strengths is most beneficial (Jones et al., 2006).

Impact on Communication Skill Development

DWD students demonstrate a slower rate of growth in perceptual skills and communication development than those who do not have additional disabilities (Waltzman, Scalchunes, & Cohen, 2000; Yoshinaga-Itano, Sedey, Coulter, & Mehl, 1998). To accommodate each student's unique learning, language, and communication needs, all experiences and curricula must be tailored to the individual student, often using modalities other than, or in conjunction with, vision, the primary teaching modality for children who are D/HH (Jones & Jones, 2003; Jones et al., 2006). For instance, to support students and increase comprehension as they process information, the addition of pictures, objects, or words can be helpful. When planning educational programs and interventions, it is important to identify the student's other disabilities (e.g., ASD, visual impairment, intellectual disability, and traumatic brain injury) and how those may interfere with learning. By combining modalities, the interferences that may emerge due to additional disabilities are reduced and DWD students may be more successful in attaining both receptive and expressive language skills (Jones et al., 2006).

Communicating with DWD students requires increased time from the teacher to both attract and maintain attention, and from the student to process the communicative information and craft responses (Jones et al., 2006). Some DWD students require augmentative communication (AAC) devices to aid in communication when additional disabilities restrict their ability to sign. Devices are used by D/HH students who have comorbid cerebral palsy, ASD, intellectual disability, and those learners with motor apraxia. Use of an AAC device to aid communication allows this population of students increased ability to express themselves (Jones et al., 2006).

Impact on Life-Skill Development

Only a small number of students with disabilities pursue postsecondary education at a university. In fact, in 2000–2001, the Twenty-Fourth Annual Report to Congress on Implementation of the Individuals with Disabilities Education Act (U.S. Department of Education, 2002) stated that only 26% of students with disabilities aged 17 or older achieved a high school academic diploma. Many students with disabilities were ineligible for college admission because they lacked a high school diploma (Bowe, 2003; Dew, 1999).

Curriculum used with DWD students must be tailored to each student's needs, functional for their life, and involve all people involved in the learner's life (Jones et al., 2006). These students participate in their educational program to develop life skills that will help them live as independently as they are able and be a part of their community. DWD students commonly need assistance in independent living skills (Wheeler-Scruggs, 2002). An important part of teaching life skills is self-advocacy training. This includes asserting one's rights (Bowe, 2003), communicating wants and needs, and requesting accommodations, when necessary. One functional way to start teaching these skills is to work with students to lead their IEP meetings. By leading such meetings, DWD students learn important self-advocacy skills such as making their needs known, requesting accommodations, communicating with others, and working with a team. These skills can be drawn upon and applied in future vocational experiences (e.g., requesting accommodations; Bowe, 2003).

Vocational education is ideally delivered in a systematic, developmental progression. This training could begin at a very young age where DWD students would be provided classroom or school jobs with a nondisabled peer (Jones et al., 2006). Beginning in middle school, vocational training experiences can be expanded into the community and, in high school, transition services could identify a community-based job specific to the skills, wants, and desires of the student. Once a student reaches 14 years of age, planning for transition after high school should begin in earnest. Another facet to vocational training for DWD students is learning how to effectively communicate with people who are hearing. This may include teaching students to use technology such as email, instant messaging, and the telephone relay center (Bowe, 2003). Students must also learn how to find a job (including searching for a job, providing all necessary documentation, completing application forms, and preparing for an interview), advocate for themselves and their needs, adhere to attendance and dress policies, communicate properly with others (Bowe, 2003), and transport themselves to and from their job (Wheeler-Scruggs, 2002).

One way to guide the transition process is through person-centered planning (PCP; Luft, 2015). PCP can begin earlier than high school in the education process to guide the educational team as they work to create a plan that sufficiently meets the needs of the student. During meetings where the PCP is discussed, education teams produce a long-term plan for the student that centers around their interests, strengths, and needs while linking the family with community support systems that will be required when the student eventually transitions to adulthood (Borders, Bock, Probst, & Kroesch, 2017, chapter 14). Two resources that provide a structured format and could be used when conducting PCP are Planning Alternative Tomorrows with Hope (Forest & O'Brien, 1993) and Making Action Plans (Vandercook, York, & Forest, 1989; Forest & Pearpoint, 1992).

The general education curriculum seldom incorporates the teaching of community living skills, therefore, it is imperative that educational teams integrate community living goals throughout the education plan of students who are DWD (Jones et al., 2006). Community living tasks include those that occur outside of the classroom (e.g., community safety, shopping, use of community services, travel, and eating out) (Jones et al., 2006). To effectively teach these skills and to allow for generalization, the DWD student must both learn and practice them in the community environment. Finally, fostering independence by teaching students who are DWD to safely use various forms of community transportation promotes self-esteem (Wheeler-Scruggs, 2002).

Conclusion

Hearing loss is complex and can be caused by either genetic or syndromic conditions or be a result of medical intervention or illness. Regardless of the cause, lack of access to sound substantially affects the overall development of D/HH students. Numerous studies have shown that students who are D/HH often demonstrate significant delays in the areas of speech production, expressive and receptive vocabulary, school readiness/conceptual knowledge, vocabulary, grammar, English syntax and structure, language, reading, math, and comprehension skills (Gale & Schick, 2009; Harrington et al., 2010; Kritzer & Pagliaro, 2013; Lederberg et al., 2014; Luft, 2017). Ferrell et al. (2014), in their work with the CEEDAR Center, reported a shockingly low number of EBPs with early intervention and some areas of literacy having moderate evidence of effectiveness and assessment, assistive technology, communication, life skills, some areas of literacy, mathematics, placement/inclusion, science, social-emotional/behavior, and transition having only limited evidence of effectiveness. Unfortunately, logistical and scientific difficulties impact the establishment of EBPs in this low-incidence population; however, intervention data does exist and programming should be based on these data. Thus, it is critical that both parents and professionals become familiar with interventions and techniques that have shown promise (Ferrell et al., 2014; Harrington et al., 2010). While many students identify as D/HH, a large percentage of D/HH students also present with an additional disability that creates unique educational challenges requiring functional curricula that is designed to meet each student's needs and include all people involved in the learner's life (Jones et al., 2006). Regardless of the strengths, deficits, or challenges, strong educational outcomes result from individualized, meaningful programming.

References

Allen, T. E., Letteri, A., Choi, S. H., & Dang, D. (2014). Early visual language exposure and emergent literacy in preschool deaf children: Findings from a national longitudinal study. *American Annals of the Deaf, 159*(4), 346–358. doi:10.1353/aad.2014.0030

Anderson, K. L., & Price, L. H. (2015). *Steps to assessment: A guide to identifying educational needs for students with hearing loss.* Minneapolis, MN: Supporting Success for Children with Hearing Loss.

Andrews, J. F., & Mason, J. M. (1991). Strategy usage among deaf and hearing readers. *Exceptional Children, 57*(6), 536–545. doi:10.1177/001440299105700607

Andrews, J. F., & Taylor, N. E. (1987). From sign to print: A case study of picture book "reading" between mother and child. *Sign Language Studies, 1056*(1), 261–274. doi:10.1353/sls.1987.0001

Antia, S. D., Kreimeyer, K. H., & Eldredege, N. (1994). Promoting social interaction between young children with hearing impairments and peers. *Exceptional Children, 60*(3), 262–275. doi:10.1177/001440299406000307

Appanah, T. M., & Hoffman, N. (2014). Using scaffolded self-editing to improve the writing of signing adolescent deaf students. *American Annals of the Deaf, 159*(3), 269–283. doi:10.1353/aad.2014.0024

Bailes, C. (2001). Integrative ASL-English language arts: Bridging paths to literacy. *Sign Language Studies, 1*(2), 147–174. doi:10.1353/sls.2001.0002

Barman, C. R., & Stockton, J. D. (2002). An evaluation of the SOAR-High Project: A web-based science program for deaf students. *American Annals of the Deaf, 147*(3), 5–10. doi:10.1353/aad.2012.0211

Bochner, J. H., & Bochner, A. M. (2009). A limitation on reading as a source of linguistic input: Evidence from deaf learners. *Reading in a Foreign Language, 21*(2), 143–158.

Bouton, S., Bertoncini, J., Serniclaes, W., & Colé, P. (2011) Reading and reading-related skills in children using cochlear implants: Prospects for the influence of cued speech. The Journal of Deaf Studies and Deaf Education, *16*, 458–473. https://doi-org.libproxy.lib.ilstu.edu/10.1093/deafed/enr014.

Bowe, F. G. (2003). Transition for deaf and hard-of-hearing students: A blueprint for change. *Journal of Deaf Studies and Deaf Education, 8*(4), 485–493. doi:10.1093/deafed/eng024

Borders, C. M., Bock, S. J., Probst, K. M., & Kroesch, A. M. (2017). Deaf/hard of hearing students with disabilities. In S. Lenihan (Ed.), *Preparing to teach, committing to learn: An introduction to educating children who are deaf/hard of hearing* (pp. 1–19). Retrieved from http://www.infanthearing.org/

Calderon, R. (2000). Parental involvement in deaf children's educational programs as predictor of child's language, early reading, and social-emotional development. *Journal of Deaf Studies and Deaf Education, 5*(2), 140–155. doi:10.1093/deafed/5.2.140

Calderon, R., & Greenberg, M. (2003). Social and emotional development of deaf children: Family, school, and program effects. In M. Marschark & P. E. Spencer (Eds.), *Oxford handbook of deaf studies, language, and education* (2nd ed., Vol. 1, pp. 188–199). New York, NY: Oxford University Press.

Cawthon, S. (2009). Making decisions about assessment practices for students who are deaf or hard of hearing. *Remedial and Special Education, 32*(4), 4–21. doi:10.1177/0741932509355950

Children's Hospital Boston. (2003). *Children with cochlear implants that sign: Guidelines for transitioning to oral education or a mainstream setting.* Retrieved from https://www.mbaea.org/documents/resources/Boston_Hospital_Checklist_F9DCBD401C81E.pdf

Delk, L., & Weidekamp, L. (2001). *Shared reading project: Evaluating implementation processes and family outcomes.* Washington, DC: Gallaudet University.

DesJardin, J. (2006). Family empowerment: Supporting language development in young children who are deaf or hard of hearing. *Volta Review, 106*, 275–298.

Dew, D. W. (Ed.). (1999). Serving individuals who are low functioning deaf. In *Twenty-fifth institute on rehabilitation issues.* Washington, DC: George Washington University, Regional Rehabilitation Continuing Education Program.

Diebold, T. J., & Waldron, M. B. (1988). Designing instructional formats: The effects of verbal and pictorial components of hearing impaired students' comprehension of science concepts. *American Annals of the Deaf, 133*(1), 30–35. doi:10.1353/aad.2012.0679

Donne, V., & Rugg, N. (2015). Comprehension practices of students who are deaf and hard of hearing. *Volta Review, 115*(2), 101–127.

Ducharme, D., & Holborn, S. (1997). Programming generalization of social skills in preschool children with hearing impairments. *Journal of Applied Behavior Analysis, 30*(4), 639–651. doi:10.1901/jaba.1997.30-639

Easterbrooks, S. R., Lederberg, A. R., Miller, E. M., Bergeron, J. P., & Connor, C. M. (2008). Emergent literacy skills during early childhood in children with hearing loss: Strengths and weaknesses. *Volta Review, 108*(2), 91–114.

Easterbrooks, S. R., & Stephenson, B. (2006). An examination of twenty literacy, science, and mathematics practices used to educate students who are deaf or hard of hearing. *American Annals of the Deaf, 151*(4), 385–399. doi:10.1353/aad.2006.0043

Elefant, E. F. (1980). Deaf children in an inquiry training program. *Volta Review, 82*, 271–279.

Ensor, A. D., & Koller, J. R. (1987). The effect of the method of repeated readings on the reading rate and word recognition accuracy of deaf adolescents. *Journal of Deaf Studies and Deaf Education, 2*(2), 61–70. doi:10.1093/oxfordjournals.deafed.a014313

Eunice Kennedy Shriver National Institute of Child Health and Human Development. (2000). *Report of the national reading panel: Teaching children to read: Reports of the subgroups (00-4754)*. Washington, DC: U.S. Government Printing Office.

Ewoldt, C., Israelite, N., & Dodds, R. (1992). The ability of deaf students to understand text: A comparison of the perceptions of teachers and students. *American Annals of the Deaf, 137*(4), 351–361. doi:10.1353/aad.2012.0493

Ferrell, K. A., Bruce, S., & Luckner, J. L. (2014). *Evidence-based practices for students with sensory impairments*. Document No. IC-4, University of Florida, Collaboration for Effective Educator, Development, Accountability, and Reform Center. Retrieved from: http://ceedar.education.ufl.edu/tools/innovation-configurations/

Forest, M., & O'Brien, J. (1993). *PATH: A workbook for planning positive possible futures: Planning alternative tomorrows with hope for schools, organizations, businesses, families*. Toronto, ON: Inclusion Press.

Forest, M., & Pearpoint, J. C. (1992). Putting all kids on the MAP. *Educational Leadership, 50*(2), 26–31. Retrieved from: http://www.ascd.org/publications/educational-leadership.aspx

Gale, E., & Schick, B. (2009). Symbol-infused joint attention and language use in mothers with deaf and hearing toddlers. *American Annals of the Deaf, 153*, 484–503. doi:10.1353/aad.0.0066

Geers, A., & Moog, J. (1989). Factors predictive of the development of literacy in profoundly hearing-impaired adolescents. *Volta Review, 91*(2), 69–86. doi:10.1044/jshd.5201.84

Geers, A., Tobey, E., Moog, J., & Brenner, C. (2008). Long-term outcomes of cochlear implantation in the preschool years: From elementary grades to high school. *International Journal of Audiology*, *47*(Suppl. 2), S21–S30. doi:10.1080/14992020802339167

Gifford, K. A., Holmes, M. G., & Bernstein, H. H. (2009). Hearing loss in children. *Pediatric Review*, *30*, 207–215. doi:10.1542/pir.30-6-207

Gilbertson, D., & Ferre, S. (2008). Considerations in the identification, assessment, and intervention process for deaf and hard of hearing students with reading difficulties. *Psychology in the Schools*, *45*(2), 104–120. doi:10.1002/pits.20286

Hamilton, H. (2012). The efficacy of dictionary use while reading for learning new words. *American Annals of the Deaf*, *157*(4), 358–372. doi:10.1353/aad.2012.1627

Haptonstall-Nykaza, T. S., & Schick, B. (2007). The transition from fingerspelling to English print: Facilitating English decoding. *Journal of Deaf Studies and Deaf Education*, *12*(2), 172–183. doi:10.1093/deafed/enm003

Harrington, M., DesJardin, J. L., & Shea, L. C. (2010). Relationships between early child factors and school readiness skills in young children with hearing loss. *Communication Disorders Quarterly*, *32*, 50–62. doi:10.1177/1525740109348790

Hayes, C. (2014). Teachers, parents, and – above all – students "Buy In" to raise expectations. *Odyssey: New Directions in Deaf Education*, *15*, 10–13.

Hogan, A., McLellan, L., & Bauman, A. (2000). Health promotion needs of young people with disabilities: A population study. *Disability and Rehabilitation*, *8*, 352–357. doi:10.1080/096382800296593

Hyde, M., Zevenbergen, R., & Power, D. (2003). Deaf and hard of hearing students' performance on arithmetic word problems. *American Annals of the Deaf*, *148*(1), 56–64. doi:10.1353/aad.2003.0003

Individuals with Disabilities Education Act. (2004). 20 U.S.C. § 1400.

Johnson, C. D. (2011). *PARC: Placement and readiness checklists*. Retrieved from http://www5.esc13.net/thescoop/deaf-ed/files/2011/12/PARC_2011.pdf

Joint Committee on Infant Hearing. (2007). Year 2007 position statement: Principles and guidelines for early hearing detection and intervention programs. *Pediatrics*, *120*, 898–921. doi:10.1542/peds.2007-2333

Joint Committee on Infant Hearing, American Academy of Pediatrics, & American Speech-Language-Hearing Association. (2000). Year 2000 position statement: Principles and guidelines for early hearing detection and intervention programs. *Pediatrics*, *106*, 798–817. Retrieved from http://jcih.org/jcih2000.pdf

Jones, L. (2014). Developing deaf children's conceptual understanding and scientific argumentation skills: A literature review. *Deafness and Education International*, *16*(3), 146–160. doi:10.1179/1557069x13y.0000000032

Jones, T. W. (1984). A framework for identification, classification and placement of multihandicapped hearing impaired students. *Volta Review*, *86*(2), 142–151.

Jones, T. W., & Jones, J. K. (2003). Educating young deaf children with multiple disabilities. In B. Bodner-Johnson & M. Sass-Lehrer (Eds.), *The young deaf or hard of hearing child: A family-centered approach to early education* (pp. 297–327). Baltimore, MD: Paul H. Brookes.

Jones, T. W., Jones, J. K., & Ewing, K. M. (2006). Students with multiple disabilities. In D. F. Moores & D. S. Martin (Eds.), *Deaf learners: Developments in curriculum and instruction* (pp. 127–143). Washington, DC: Gallaudet University Press.

Kelly, R. R., & Mousley, K. (2001). Solving word problems: More than reading issues for deaf students. *American Annals of the Deaf, 146*(3), 251–262. doi:10.1353/aad.2012.0088

Kemmery, M. A., & Compton, M. V. (2014). Are you deaf or hard of hearing? Which do you go by: Perceptions of identity in families of students with hearing loss. *Volta Review, 114*(2), 157–192.

Kent, B. A. (2003). Identity issues for hard-of-hearing adolescents aged 11, 13, and 15 in mainstream setting. *Journal of Deaf Studies and Deaf Education, 8*(3), 315–324. doi:10.1093/deafed/eng017

Knoors, H., & Hermans, D. (2010). Effective instruction for deaf and hard-of-hearing students: Teaching strategies, school settings, and student characteristics. In M. Marschark & P. E. Spencer (Eds.), *Oxford handbook of deaf studies, language, and education* (Vol. 2, pp. 57–71). New York, NY: Oxford University Press.

Kritzer, K. L. (2009). Families with young deaf children and the mediation of mathematically based concepts within a naturalistic environment. *American Annals of the Deaf, 153*, 474–483. doi:10.1353/aad.0.0067

Kritzer, K. L., & Pagliaro, C. M. (2013). An intervention for early mathematical success: Outcomes from the hybrid version of the building math readiness parents as partners (MRPP) project. *Journal of Deaf Studies and Deaf Education, 18*(1), 30–46. doi:10.1093/deafed/ens033

Kusche, C. A., & Greenberg, M. R. (1993). *The PATHS curriculum*. Seattle, WA: Developmental Research and Programs.

Lang, H., & Pagliaro, C. (2007). Factors predicting recall of mathematics terms by deaf students: Implications for teaching. *Journal of Deaf Studies and Deaf Education, 12*(4), 449–460. doi:10.1093/deafed/enm021

Lang, H. G., & Steely, D. (2003). Web-based science instruction for deaf students: What research says to the teacher. *Instructional Science, 31*(4), 277–298. doi:10.1023/a:1024681909409

Lederberg, A. R., Miller, E. M., Easterbrooks, S. R., & Connor, C. M. (2014). Foundations for literacy: An early literacy intervention for deaf and hard-of-hearing children. *Journal of Deaf Studies and Deaf Education, 19*(4), 438–455. doi:10.1093/deafed/enu022

Lederberg, A. R., Schick, B., & Spencer, P. E. (2013). Language and literacy development of deaf and hard-of-hearing children: Successes and challenges. *Developmental Psychology, 49*(1), 15–30. doi:10.1037/a0029558

Luckner, J. L., & Bowen, S. (2006). Assessment practices of professionals serving students who are deaf or hard of hearing: An initial investigation. *American Annals of the Deaf, 151*(4), 410–417. doi:10.1353/aad.2006.0046

Luckner, J. L., & Cooke, C. (2010). A summary of vocabulary research with students who are deaf or hard of hearing. *American Annals of the Deaf*, *155*(1), 38–67. doi:10.1353/aad.0.0129

Luckner, J. L., & Handley, C. M. (2008). A summary of reading comprehension research undertaken with students who are deaf or hard of hearing. *American Annals of the Deaf*, *153*(1), 6–36. doi:10.1353/aad.0.0006

Luckner, J. L., Sebald, A. M., Cooney, J., Young, J., & Muir, S. G. (2005/2006). An examination of the evidence-based literacy research in deaf education. *American Annals of the Deaf*, *150*(5), 443–456. doi:10.1353/aad.2006.0008

Luckner, J. L., & Urbach, J. E. (2012). Reading fluency and students who are deaf or hard of hearing: Synthesis of the research. *Communication Disorders Quarterly*, *33*(4), 230–241. doi:10.1177/1525740111412582

Luft, P. (2015). Transition services for DHH adolescents and young adults with disabilities: Challenges and theoretical frameworks. *American Annals of the Deaf*, *160*(4), 395–414. doi:10.1353/aad.2015.0028

Luft, P. (2017). What is different about deaf education? The effects of child and family factors on educational services. *The Journal of Special Education*, *51*(1), 27–37. doi:10.1177/0022466916660546

Lutz, L. (2017). The early years: Parents and young deaf children reading together. *Odyssey: New Directions in Deaf Education*, *18*, 4–10.

Maller, S., & Braden, J. (2011). Intellectual assessment of deaf people: A critical review of core concepts and issues. In M. Marschark & P. Spencer, (Eds.), *The Oxford handbook of deaf studies, language, and education* (Vol. 1, 2nd ed., pp. 473–485). New York, NY: Oxford University Press.

Marschark, M., & Wauters, L. (2008). Language comprehension and learning by deaf students. In M. Marschark & P. Hauser (Eds.), *Deaf cognition: Foundations and outcomes* (pp. 309–350). New York, NY: Oxford University Press.

Mayberry, R. I. (2010). Early language acquisition and adult language ability: What sign language reveals about the critical period for language. In M. Marschark & P. Spencer, (Eds.), *The Oxford handbook of deaf studies, language, and education* (Vol. 1, pp. 281–291). New York, NY: Oxford University Press.

Mercer, C. D., Campbell, K. U., Miller, M. D., Mercer, K. D., & Lane, H. B. (2000). Effects of a reading fluency intervention for middle schoolers with specific learning disabilities. *Learning Disabilities Research & Practice*, *15*(4), 179–189. doi:10.1207/sldrp1504_2

Mertens, D. M. (1991). Instructional factors related to hearing impaired adolescents' interest in science. *Science Education*, *75*(4), 429–442. doi:10.1002/sce.3730750405

Metz, K. K. (2017). Five factors leading to deaf and hard of hearing students' success: Perspectives of a veteran teacher. *Odyssey: New Directions in Deaf Education*, *18*, 58–61.

Mitchell, R. E., & Karchmer, M. A. (2004). When parents are deaf versus hard of hearing: Patterns of sign use and school placement of deaf and hard-of-hearing children. *Journal of Deaf Studies and Deaf Education*, *9*(2), 133–152. doi:10.1093/deafed/enh017

Moeller, M. P. (2007). Current state of knowledge: Psychosocial development in children with hearing impairment. *Ear and Hearing, 28*, 729–739. doi:10.1097/aud.0b013e318157f033

Moeller, M. P., Carr, G., Seaver, L., Stredler-Brown, A., & Holzinger, D. (2013). Best practices in family-centered early intervention for children who are deaf or hard of hearing: An international consensus statement. *The Journal of Deaf Studies and Deaf Education, 18*(4), 429–445. doi:10.1093/deafed/ent034

Mueller, V., & Hurtig, R. (2010). Technology-enhanced shared reading with deaf and hard-of-hearing children: The role of a fluent signing narrator. *Journal of Deaf Studies and Deaf Education, 15*(1), 72–101. doi:10.1093/deafed/enp023

Musselman, C. (2000). How do children who can't hear learn to read an alphabetic script? A review of literature on reading and deafness. *Journal of Deaf Studies and Deaf Education, 5*(1), 9–31. doi:10.1093/deafed/5.1.9

National Association of the Deaf. (2017). *What is American sign language?* Retrieved from https://www.nad.org/resources/american-sign-language/what-is-american-sign-language/

National Cued Speech Association. (2017). *About cued speech.* Retrieved from http://www.cuedspeech.org/cued-speech/about-cued-speech

National Institute on Deafness and Other Communication Disorders. (2017). *Quick statistics.* Retrieved from http://www.nidcd.nih.gov/health/statistics/Pages/quick.aspx

Nunes, T., Burman, D., Evans, D., & Bell, D. (2010). Writing a language that you can't hear. In N. Brunswick, S. McDougall, & P. de Mornay Davies (Eds.), *Reading and dyslexia in different orthographies* (pp. 109–126). New York, NY: Psychology Press.

O'Connor, R. E., White, A., & Swanson, H. L. (2007). Repeated reading versus continuous reading: Influences on reading fluency and comprehension. *Exceptional Children, 74*(1), 31–46. doi:10.1177/001440290707400102

Pagliaro, C. (2010). Mathematics instruction and learning of deaf and hard-of-hearing students: What do we know? Where do we go? In M. Marschark & P. Spencer (Eds.), *Oxford handbook of deaf studies, language, and education* (Vol. 2, pp. 156–171). New York, NY: Oxford University Press.

Pianta, R. C., Howes, C., Burchinal, M., Byrant, D., Clifford, R., Early, C., & Barbarin, O. (2005). Features of pre-kindergarten programs, classrooms, and teachers: Do they predict observed classroom quality and child–teacher interactions? *Applied Developmental Science, 9*(3), 144–159. doi:10.1207/s1532480xads0903_2

Rhoades, E. A. (2013). Interactive silences: Evidence for strategies to facilitate spoken language in children with hearing loss. *Volta Review, 113*, 57–73.

Schick, B., Williams, K., & Kupermintz, H. (2006). Look who's being left behind: Educational interpreters and access to education for deaf and hard-of-hearing students. *Journal of Deaf Studies and Deaf Education, 11*(1), 3–20.

Schirmer, B. R., & McGough, S. M. (2005). Teaching reading to children who are deaf: Do the conclusion of the National Reading Panel apply? *Review of Educational Research, 75*(1), 83–117. doi:10.3102/00346543075001083

Schirmer, B. R., Schaffer, L., Therrien, W. J., & Schirmer, T. N. (2012). Reread-adapt and answer-comprehend intervention with deaf and hard of hearing readers: Effect on fluency and reading achievement. *American Annals of the Deaf, 156*(5), 469–475. doi:10.1353/aad.2012.1602

Schloss, P. J., & Smith, M. A. (1990). *Teaching social-skills to hearing-impaired students.* Washington, DC: Alexander Graham Bell Association.

Schloss, P. J., Smith, M. A., & Schloss, C. N. (1984). Empirical analysis of a card game designed to promote consumer-related social competence among hearing-impaired youth. *American Annals of the Deaf, 129*(5), 417–423. doi:10.1353/aad.2012.0979

Smith, A., & Wang, Y. (2010). The impact of visual phonics on the phonologi-cal awareness and speech production of a student who is deaf: A case study. *American Annals of the Deaf, 155*(2), 124–130. doi:10.1353/aad.2010.0000

Spencer, P. E. (2004). Individual differences in language performance after cochlear implantation at one to three years of age: Child, family, and linguistic factors. *Jour-nal of Deaf Studies and Deaf Education, 9*(4), 395–412. doi:10.1093/deafed/enh033

Spencer, P. E., & Marschark, M. (2010). *Evidence-based practice in education deaf and hard-of-hearing students.* New York, NY: Oxford University Press.

Stika, C. J., Eisenberg, L. S., Johnson, K. C., Henning, S. C., Colson, B. G., Gan-guly, D. H., & DesJardin, J. L. (2015). Developmental outcomes of early-iden-tified children who are hard of hearing at 12 to 18 months of age. *Early Human Development, 91*(1), 47–55. doi:10.1016/j.earlhumdev.2014.11.005

Strassman, B. K. (1992). Deaf adolescents' metacognitive knowledge about school-related reading. *American Annals of the Deaf, 137*(4), 326–330. doi:10.1353/aad.2012.0456

Strassman, B. K., & O'Dell, K. (2012). Using open captions to revise writing in digital stories composed by d/Deaf and hard of hearing students. *American Annals of the Deaf, 157*(4), 340–357. doi:10.1353/aad.2012.1626

Stredler-Brown, A. (2010). Communication choices and outcomes during the early years: An assessment and evidence-based approach. In M. Marschark & P. Spencer (Eds.), *The Oxford handbook of deaf studies, language, and educa-tion* (Vol. 1, pp. 292–315). New York, NY: Oxford University Press.

Syverud, S. M., Guardino, C., & Selznick, D. N. (2009). Teaching phonological skills to a deaf first grader: A promising strategy. *American Annals of the Deaf, 154*(4), 382–388. doi:10.1353/aad.0.0113

Test, D. W., Mazzotti, V. L., Mustian, A. L., Fowler, C. H., Kortering, L., & Kohler, P. (2009). Evidence-based secondary transition predictors for improv-ing postschool outcomes for students with disabilities. *Career Development for Exceptional Individuals, 32*(3), 160–181. doi:10.1177/0885728809346960

Therrien, W. J. (2004). Fluency and comprehension gains as a result of repeated reading: A meta-analysis. *Remedial and Special Education, 25*(4), 252–261. doi: 10.1177/07419325040250040801

Traxler, C. B. (2000). The Stanford Achievement Test (9th ed.): National norming and performance standards for deaf and hard-of-hearing students. *Journal of Deaf Studies and Deaf Education, 5*(4), 337–348. doi:10.1093/deafed/5.4.337

Trezek, B. J., & Malmgren, K. W. (2005). The efficacy of utilizing a phonics treatment package with middle school deaf and hard-of-hearing students. *Journal of Deaf Studies and Deaf Education, 10*(3), 256–271. doi:10.1093/deafed/eni028

Trezek, B. J., Wang, Y., Woods, D. G., Gampp, T. L., & Paul, P. V. (2007). Using visual phonics to supplement beginning reading instruction for students who are deaf or hard of hearing. *Journal of Deaf Studies and Deaf Education, 12*(3), 373–384. doi:10.1093/deafed/enm014

U.S. Department of Education. (2002). *Twenty-fourth annual report to Congress on Implementation of the Individuals with Disabilities Education Act.* Washington, DC: Author.

VanDam, M., Ambrose, S. E., & Moeller, M. P. (2012). Quantity of parental language in the home environments of hard-of-hearing 2-year-olds. *Journal of Deaf Studies and Deaf Education, 17*(4), 402–420. doi:10.1093/deafed/ens025

Vandercook, T., York, J., & Forest, M. (1989). The McGill Action Planning System (MAPS): A strategy for building the vision. *Research and Practice for Persons with Severe Disabilities, 14*, 205–215. doi:10.1177/154079698901400306

Vosganoff, D., Paatsch, L. E., & Toe, D. M. (2011). The mathematical and science skills of students who are deaf or hard of hearing in inclusive settings. *Deafness & Education International, 13*(3), 70–88. doi:10.1179/1557069x11y.0000000004

Waddy-Smith, B., & Wilson, V. (2003). See that sound! Visual phonics helps deaf and hard of hearing students develop reading skills. *Odyssey, 5*, 14–17.

Waltzman, S. B., Scalchunes, V., & Cohen, N. L. (2000). Performance of multiply handicapped children using cochlear implants. *American Journal of Otology, 21*(3), 329–335. doi:10.1016/s0196-0709(00)80040-x

Wang, Y., Engler, K. S., & Oetting, T. L. (2014). Expectations lead to performance: The transformative power of high expectations in preschool. *Odyssey: New Directions In Deaf Education, 15*, 36–39.

Wang, Y., Trezek, B. J., Luckner, J. L., & Paul, P. V. (2008). The role of phonology and phonologically related skills in reading instruction for students who are deaf or hard of hearing. *American Annals of the Deaf, 153*(4), 396–407.

Watson, D. (1998). *The challenge of tomorrow for deafness: Rehabilitation of LFD persons in the United States: An executive summary.* Washington, DC: Office of Special Education and Rehabilitative Services.

Wheeler-Scruggs, K. (2002). Assessing the employment and independence of people who are deaf and low functioning. *American Annals of the Deaf, 147*(4), 11–17. doi:10.1353/aad.2012.0260

Wolbers, K. A. (2008). Using balanced and interactive writing instruction to improve the higher order and lower order writing skills of deaf students. *Journal of Deaf Studies and Deaf Education, 13*(2), 257–277. doi:10.1093/deafed/enm052

Wolbers, K. A., Dostal, H. M., & Bowers, L. M. (2012). "I was born full deaf." Written language outcomes after 1 year of strategic and interactive writing instruction. *Journal of Deaf Studies and Deaf Education, 17*(1), 19–38. doi:10.1093/deafed/enr018

Wood, N., & Dockrell, J. (2010). Psychological assessment procedures for assessing deaf or hard-of-hearing children. *Educational & Child Psychology, 27*(2), 11–22.

Yoshinaga-Itano, C. (2013). Principles and guidelines for early intervention after confirmation that a child is deaf or hard of hearing. *Journal of Deaf Studies and Deaf Education, 19*, 143–175. doi:10.1093/deafed/ent043

Yoshinaga-Itano, C., Sedey, A. L., Coulter, D. K., & Mehl, A. L. (1998). Language of early- and later-identified children with hearing loss. *Pediatrics, 102*(5), 1161–1171. doi:10.1542/peds.102.5.1161

Chapter 5

Interventions for Students with Visual Impairments

Stacy M. Kelly

Abstract

This chapter discusses the elements of interventions provided to students who are visually impaired within the context of past instructional advancements still in effect today and current instructional advancements preparing the field for tomorrow. Disability-specific interventions and the theoretical framework that encompasses the unique areas of instruction for students with visual impairments are described. Important additional considerations of interventions for students with visual impairments are presented. Needs of students who are visually impaired, alignment with state standards, management of limited instructional time, and shortage of qualified specialists who teach students with visual impairments are examples of significant matters to be considered for effective instructional practice in present-day classrooms.

Keywords: Assistive technology; blind; braille; career education; expanded core curriculum; independent living; low vision; orientation and mobility; recreation and leisure; self-determination

Viewpoints on Interventions for Learners with Disabilities
Advances in Special Education, Volume 33, 107–126
Copyright © 2018 by Emerald Publishing Limited
All rights of reproduction in any form reserved
ISSN: 0270-4013/doi:10.1108/S0270-401320180000033006

Incidental Learning

Much of what is learned by children is acquired using their vision in an automatic and instantaneous manner. Children learn to see and understand what is happening in the world around them just by looking around or watching others perform everyday tasks and activities (Turnbull, Turnbull, Wehmeyer, & Shogren, 2013). Instruction or guidance is not required, and the process is entirely incidental. For students with visual impairments (i.e., those who are blind or have low vision), these naturally occurring opportunities to gain visual information are not the same as they are for students who are sighted. Incidental learning opportunities must be explicitly taught to students with visual impairments through meaningful instruction that includes extra explanations, descriptions, real-world activities, and repeated experiences. Thus, the interventions for students with visual impairments often come in the form of a wide range of compensatory skills areas such as career education, independent living, orientation and mobility (O&M), recreation and leisure, self-determination, sensory efficiency, and social interaction. This targeted form of intervention enables students with visual impairments to learn what their sighted peers learn by watching and imitating others. Also, through interventions disability-specific skills are acquired by learners with visual impairments in such things as braille reading and writing, traveling with a long cane, and using screen reading software to search online.

This chapter examines the elements of these sorts of interventions for students who are visually impaired within the context of past instructional advancements that are still in effect and current instructional advancements that are preparing students who are visually impaired for tomorrow. Discussion is provided about how disability-specific instruction works for students with visual impairments. The framework that guides instructional interventions for students who are visually impaired is described. Important additional considerations of the implementation of the interventions for students with visual impairments in today's school climates are presented. Needs of students who are blind or visually impaired, alignment with state standards, management of limited instructional time, and shortage of qualified personnel are examples of significant issues to be addressed for effective practice in today's classrooms.

Historical Advancements in Interventions for Students with Visual Impairments Still in Effect Today

Principles of Learning from Long Ago

One of the early instructors of children with visual impairments was Lowenfeld and his instructional strategies continue to be significant principles with practical applications today (Lewis & Allman, 2014). Lowenfeld's instructional strategies specifically target three primary issues facing individuals who are visually impaired: lack of meaningful experiences, lack of independent travel, and lack of control over the environment (Lowenfeld, 1948). Since this was first documented by Lowenfeld nearly 70 years ago, interventions for students with visual impairments have addressed these basic limitations that visual impairment can have on incidental learning and development. Lowenfeld (1973) described three particular techniques useful when teaching students with visual impairments to facilitate their learning given the inherent challenges of visual impairment: (1) provide students with concrete experiences, (2) allow students to learn by doing, and (3) expose students to unifying experiences. Specific examples of Lowenfeld's principles of learning are provided.

Without concrete experiences, students who are visually impaired are not acquiring the experiences that their sighted peers learn incidentally. Students who are visually impaired need concrete experiences to facilitate their learning of abstract concepts such as "around," "energy," "sinking," and "outer space." Without the opportunity to participate in the activity, the learning experience is incomplete for students who are visually impaired. It is important to know that when teaching students with visual impairments just talking about information is not enough. Students with visual impairments need to be involved in activities to support their comprehension of information. For example, making a model volcano, baking a cake, raking the leaves, washing the car, or snowshoeing in the winter are activities that enable students who are visually impaired to learn by doing. Also, it is important to recognize that students who are blind or severely visually impaired are unable to gather the whole picture by quickly absorbing a lot of information using their vision. Those students with visual impairments who learn by touch first learn about the parts of something and then they put the parts together to form the whole concept. This type of learning is called part-to-whole learning and explains Lowenfeld's longstanding theory that students who are visually impaired require unifying experiences (1973). The "big picture" is not apparent to students with visual impairments who learn in a part-to-whole manner (Lewis & Allman, 2014). The overall scope needs to be provided to these students who are visually impaired along with every step, and all skills that are involved in activities or tasks (Lewis & Allman, 2014).

Goals of the National Agenda

The National Agenda for the Education of Children and Youth with Visual Impairments, Including Those with Multiple Disabilities (hereafter referred to as the National Agenda) was first published in 1995 (Corn, Hatlen, Huebner, Ryan, & Siller, 1995) and updated in 2004 (Huebner, Merk-Adam, Stryker, & Wolffe, 2004). The goal statements included in the National Agenda were identified as critical components of quality education for students with visual impairments. The goals of the National Agenda are designed to support the long-term success of students with visual impairments through the school years. The 10 goals of the National Agenda are shown in Table 1.

The goals of the National Agenda capture a variety of issues. Many of the goals have a clearly identifiable relationship to instructional interventions for students with visual impairments (e.g., Goal 8: importance of teaching the expanded core and common core curricula), while others have a more indirect relationship with the instructional interventions (e.g., Goal 5: assurance of array of school district service delivery options). Regardless of how each goal is situated, the National Agenda serves a broad summary of changes required in policy and practice for the effective instruction of all students who are visually impaired (Spungin & Huebner, 2017). The field is still striving to meet many of the National Agenda goals to this date and the National Agenda continues to facilitate changes in education policy and practice. One of the productive outcomes of the National Agenda was the development of the expanded core curriculum (ECC) that outlines the unique educational needs of students with visual impairments (Spungin & Huebner, 2017).

Introducing the ECC for Students with Visual Impairments

The disability-specific knowledge and skills required by students who are visually impaired have been known as the expanded core curriculum or ECC since the ECC was introduced by Hatlen in 1996. Students who are visually impaired need the ECC in addition to the common core

Table 1: Goals of the National Agenda.

Goal	Description of Goal
Goal 1: Referral	Students and their families will be referred to an appropriate education program within 30 days of identification of a suspect visual impairment. Teachers of students with visual impairments and O&M instructors will provide appropriate quality services.
Goal 2: Parent participation	Policies and procedures will be implemented to ensure the right of all parents to full participation and equal partnership in the education process.
Goal 3: Personnel preparation	Universities with a minimum of one full-time faculty member in the area of visual impairment will prepare a sufficient number of teachers and O&M specialists for students with visual impairments to meet personnel needs throughout the country.
Goal 4: Provision of services	Caseloads will be determined based on the assessed needs of students.
Goal 5: Array of services	Local education programs will ensure that all students have access to a full array of service delivery options.
Goal 6: Assessment	All assessments and evaluations of students will be conducted by or in partnership with personnel having expertise in the education of students with visual impairments and their parents.
Goal 7: Access to instructional materials	Access to developmental and educational services will include an assurance that textbooks and instructional materials are available to students in the appropriate media and at the same time as their sighted peers.
Goal 8: Core curriculum	All educational goals and instruction will address the academic and expanded core curricula based on the assessed needs of each student with visual impairments.
Goal 9: Transition services	Transition services will address developmental and educational needs (birth through high school) to assist students and their families in setting goals and implementing strategies through the life continuum, commensurate with the students' aptitudes, interests, and abilities.
Goal 10: Professional development	To improve students' learning, service providers will engage in ongoing local, state, and national professional development.

Source: Adapted from Huebner et al. (2004).

curriculum of general education. Disability-specific skills are taught to enable students who are visually impaired to function as independently as possible. For example, in O&M training, students who are visually impaired develop body, spatial, and environmental concepts (Fazzi & Klein, 2002; Skellenger & Sapp, 2010). Students with visual impairments may learn about such things as body awareness, systematic searching, directionality, route shapes, address systems, public transportation, and street crossings as part of their O&M training (Clark-Bischke & Kelly, 2011). Likewise, in the area of the ECC focused on the compensatory skill of communication modes, students with visual impairments learn to read and write in the particular media they will be using (i.e., braille, print, or a mixture of both braille and print materials) (McCarthy & Holbrook, 2017). In this way, ECC-specific instruction facilitates the participation of students who are visually impaired in school and society. There are nine unique areas that comprise the ECC. Each of the nine areas are overviewed in Table 2.

It is noted that the areas of the ECC are related to each other. The areas of the ECC are often interdependent and overlapping in many ways and, therefore, development in one area of the ECC promotes and supports development in other areas (Allman & Lewis, 2014).

Early Intervention for Students with Visual Impairments. Also, the importance of early intervention in the areas and components of the ECC outlined in Table 2 cannot be overstated. Instructional interventions for learners of all ages with visual impairments, including infants and toddlers, should be provided in an appropriate manner as Lowendfeld (1973) explained with concrete experiences, opportunities to learn by doing, and unifying experiences. Expanded experiences and targeted ECC-based interventions for infants and toddlers with visual impairments can include such things as exposure to multiple friends and family members, realistic praise for accomplishing tasks, exploration of familiar environments at home, in the yard, and around the neighborhood, encouragement of behaviors that initiate independence, fantasizing about the roles of adults, playing make-believe games, and assisting with teeth brushing and bath time (Allman & Lewis, 2014; Wolffe, 2017). Early childhood experiences for learners with visual impairments should include these sorts of tasks, skills, and behaviors that overlap and explicitly address several areas of the ECC (Allman & Lewis).

Ongoing School-age and Transition-age Interventions for Students with Visual Impairments. The importance of ongoing instructional interventions that include the areas and components of the ECC during the school-age and transition-age years cannot be overstated either.

Table 2: Overview of the ECC for Students with Visual Impairments.

Area of the ECC (Hatlen, 1996)	Description of the Areas of the ECC (Hatlen, 1996)	Components of the Areas of the ECC (Allman & Lewis, 2014)
Assistive technology	Includes no-tech, low-tech, and high-tech assistive and adaptive tools that are commercially or custom-made as well as optical devices.	Access to information, communication, and personal productivity.
Career education	Includes hands-on and meaningful explorations of careers as well as job-readiness skills that are often learned incidentally by sighted people and are often explicitly taught to students with visual impairments.	Career awareness, career exploration, career preparation, and career placement.
Compensatory skills to access the general curriculum or functional academic skills, including communication modes	Includes literary and mathematical braille codes, concept development, tactile graphics, and specialized communication skills.	Concept development, spatial understanding, communication modes, speaking and listening skills, study and organization skills, and use of adapted and specialized educational materials.
Independent living	Includes daily routines and tasks (e.g., personal care, food preparation, money management, and household tasks) that are often learned incidentally by sighted people and are often explicitly taught to students with visual impairments.	Organization, personal hygiene and grooming, dressing, clothing care, time management, eating, cooking, cleaning and general household tasks, telephone use, and money management.

Table 2: (*Continued*)

Area of the ECC (Hatlen, 1996)	Description of the Areas of the ECC (Hatlen, 1996)	Components of the Areas of the ECC (Allman & Lewis, 2014)
Orientation and mobility	Includes methods for safe and efficient travel as well as basic and advanced concept development in the areas of O&M in school, at home, and within communities.	Body concepts, environmental concepts, spatial concepts, perceptual/sensory skills, mobility skills, orientation skills, interpersonal skills, and decision-making skills.
Recreation and leisure	Includes development of skills for lifelong physical and leisure activities that are often learned incidentally by sighted people and are often explicitly taught to students with visual impairments.	Play, physical activity, health, fitness, and individual sports, team and spectator sports, leisure activities and hobbies.
Self-determination	Includes the skills such as decision-making and problem-solving that enhance self-advocacy and well-being in life.	Self-knowledge, awareness of individual rights and responsibilities, capacity to make informed choices, problem-solving and goal-setting skills.
Sensory efficiency	Includes efficient use of available senses (e.g., visual, tactual, and auditory skills) to maximize learning and participation in school, at home, and within communities.	Visual functioning, auditory function, tactile function, gustatory (taste) function, and olfactory (smell) function.
Social interaction	Includes the verbal and nonverbal social interaction skills that are often learned incidentally by sighted people and are often explicitly taught to students with visual impairments.	Appropriate body language, social communication, effective conversation patterns, cooperative skills, interactions with others, social etiquette, development of relationships and friendships, knowledge of self, and interpretation and monitoring of social behavior.

Source: Adapted from Hatlen (1996) and Allman and Lewis (2014).

Again, interventions should be rooted in concrete and unifying experiences that provide opportunities for students with visual impairments to learn by doing (Lowenfeld, 1973). ECC-related competencies for elementary and middle school learners with visual impairments may include such things as responsibility for household chores, following complex instructions, working individually and in groups, responding appropriately to peers and adults, organizing school and work materials (Wolffe, 2017). For high school and transition-age students with visual impairments, preparation in several areas of the ECC may involve tasks such as making plans for life after high school, volunteering to help others, participating in groups or school clubs, job shadowing others, performing work-related tasks at school and at home, and applying for, acquiring, and maintaining a paid job in the community (Wolffe). Each of these examples explicitly address many areas of the ECC that overlap and support each other as learners with visual impairments progress through the formative years and beyond.

Working Collaboratively with Other School Personnel to Support the ECC. Often, students who are visually impaired are included in general education or specialized classrooms with school professionals who may not have highly specialized training in teaching children with visual impairments. It is important that many of the interventions established by teachers and specialists in the field of visual impairments remain in place throughout the school day and not just during isolated periods when the vision professional (e.g., teacher of students with visual impairments [TVIs]) is teaching the learner with visual impairments. Hudson (1997) created a popular list of instructional practices for paraprofessionals and other school staff who provide students who are visually impaired with direct support on a regular basis. Table 3 lists an excerpt from "Ways to Step Back." Twenty years later, this list and the ideas within it are an example of a collaborative tool shared widely by TVIs with school staff members who directly work with students who are visually impaired but may not be as familiar with the disability-specific training for people with visual impairments.

Providing "Ways to Step Back" and a supporting discussion to go along with it may go a long way for those who otherwise may not have thought of interventions that are helping students with visual impairments complete a task being a sort of hindrance in the long run. For example, if every time a student who is visually impaired drops an object someone nearby picks the object up for them, it will be difficult for this student who is visually impaired to learn how to search for and locate a dropped object on their own. It will also be difficult for this student who is visually

Table 3: Ways to Step Back (Hudson, 1997).

It often feels right to give help to students with visual impairments, but this may not be in their best interest. Use this list to help yourself to step back.

1. You're stepping back so your students can step forward and become independent. Keep this in mind.
2. Clock how long it actually takes for students to start zippers, pick up dropped papers, or find page numbers. What's a few more seconds in the grander scheme?
3. Sit on your hands for a whole task while you practice giving verbal instead of touch cues. Hands off the hands!
4. If you need touch cues, try hand-under-hand instead of hand-over-hand. This gives students much more choice.
5. Let your students make mistakes and get into trouble. It's part of the human experience.
6. Acknowledge your own needs. There's a reason you chose the helping profession.
7. Sit further away. If you've been within arm's reach, sit just within earshot. If you've been sitting just within earshot, sit across the room.
8. Pat yourself on the back every time you help with seeing, not thinking. Your job is to give information.
9. Even though helping can feel right, be aware that too much assistance is short-sighted. Sometimes less is more, less is better.
10. Catch yourself before you correct your students' work. Don't cover for them. This is about their skills… not yours.

Source: Adapted from Hudson (1997).

impaired to learn that it is an expectation that they search for and locate something as simple as a dropped object on their own. The list "Ways to Step Back" and the information it conveys is a reminder of the ongoing effort to maximize the independence of learners with visual impairments across areas of the expanded and common core curricula. It is not the intention of the ECC that others impinge on students with visual impairments or that behaviors of learned helplessness are nurtured. In fact, it is the opposite. It is the intention of the ECC that students with visual impairments have opportunities for self-determined action throughout the school day and throughout their lives. It is important that the wide range of school professionals who may work directly with students who are visually impaired are working together and in sync with this approach to intervening with the appropriate supports.

Current Advancements in Interventions for Students with Visual Impairments

An ongoing challenge that has faced educators of students who are blind for over a century is figuring out appropriate systems for reading and writing for their students (Spungin & Huebner, 2017). Early efforts before braille was established as the method for tactile reading and writing included wax tablets, wood carvings, and wire letters (Illingworth, 1910; Lowenfeld, 1971). Today, students with visual impairments continue to need the same access to print and digital information as their sighted peers. Print and digital information continue to become more complex and difficult to manage for those who are visually impaired. Many interventions in the recent years have been targeted toward addressing this situation. Recent advancements in the compensatory skill areas of braille and technology (i.e., assistive technology [AT] for persons with visual impairments) are discussed next.

Global Braille Code Transition

Changes with Print. Ambiguity and complexity created the need for the worldwide English braille code change that recently occurred. There have been drastic changes in the appearance and production methods of print that have contributed to the need to update the braille code. This includes new characters, icons, layouts, and fonts. Print is increasingly read from screens. For example, schools are increasingly providing print textbooks digitally rather than on paper and an ever-growing and large percentage of the population goes to the Internet to get most of their news. Boundaries between "technical" materials and everyday materials have become increasingly blurred. For example, this includes website addresses and email addresses in the general literature.

Changes with Braille. Braille is also evolving. Braille is more widely available than ever before in history because of braille embossers, translation software, and refreshable braille. Digital text provides the capability for braille users to read the material in braille instantly with refreshable braille. Accurate translation of digital print text into braille remains far from perfect because of ambiguities in braille codes that existed prior to the recent braille code change. Backtranslation (i.e., the translation from braille to print) contained many errors when handled in a digital format prior to the recent braille code change.

Adoption of a New Braille Code to Address Well-Established Problems. The problems that have been identified were longstanding and in dire need of a solution. Back in 1980, for example, the Computer Braille Code was introduced and at that time, the complexity of it was a concern. Multiple braille symbols for the same print symbol resulted in the increased contextuality of braille. It was more than 25 years ago, that Drs. Abraham Nemeth and Tim Cranmer presented a paper stating the urgent need to unify various braille codes used in North America (Nemeth & Cranmer, 1991). They cited multiple examples of increasing difficulty in creating new code symbols to reflect changes in print (Nemeth & Cranmer).

Thus, for braille to remain viable it had to change as well. The Unified English Braille (UEB) Code started as a Braille Authority of North America (BANA) research project. This research project became international in the early 1990s. On November 2, 2012, BANA voted to adopt UEB as an official code in the United States after monitoring UEB adoption and implementation around the world. All International Council on English Braille members have now adopted UEB: Australia, New Zealand, South Africa, Nigeria, Canada, the United Kingdom, and now the United States. The date that implementation of the new UEB braille code began in the United States was January 4, 2016. January 4th is also the birthdate of Louis Braille.

Currently in the United States, students who are visually impaired and learning braille for the first time are to be taught UEB as part of their compensatory skill program in the ECC. Students who learned the braille code that was is existence prior to UEB in the United States are to be gradually been transitioned to the new code with targeted instruction that serves as a significant intervention to guide in this transition.

The changes involved in UEB and reasons for UEB adoption have been well documented in the literature prior to the decision (Bogart, Cranmer, & Sullivan, 2000; Bogart, D'Andrea, & Koenig, 2004; Bogart & Koenig, 2005; Knowlton & Wetzel, 2004; Steinman & Johnson, 2003). UEB is based on the braille codes that existed before its adoption such as English Braille American Edition. UEB is as clear and consistent as possible to allow for ease of braille reading, backtranslation, and braille transcribing. UEB eliminates some braille symbols to reduce ambiguity and adds new braille symbols to unify existing codes. UEB involves one set of rules that are the same everywhere in the world. For the first time, there is a braille code available that can be applied across various types of English-language material. This large-scale, global, and collaborative effort to unify the English braille codes is a major advancement in the disability-specific skill of braille literacy.

Assistive Technology (AT) Certification to Support Twenty-First Century Learners with Visual Impairments

Technology is driving an unprecedented wave of innovation in education. The most successful learning environments, for example, are those that use multimodal presentations (Moreno & Meyer, 2007). This premise paired with the increased availability of emerging technology has caused unprecedented growth in the range of types and formats of instructional materials, from complex graphics and video to interactive games, and shifts in how educational content is produced and by whom. For students with a visual impairment that impacts their ability to access learning materials, these new types and formats and their related creation methods present new and multifaceted accessibility challenges that AT training can help resolve through instant access to digital media. Unfortunately, the conclusion based on data generated in recent studies is clear that the majority of students with visual impairments who can benefit from training interventions in the use of AT are not receiving that training (Abner & Lahm, 2002; Candela, 2003; Kapperman, Sticken, & Heinze, 2002; Kelly, 2008, 2009, 2011). One of the major reasons for this unfortunate situation is that many teachers of students with visual impairments have little or no exposure to the specialized technology, and do not understand it or know how to use it; therefore, it is a difficult if not impossible proposition to provide this training for their students who are visually impaired (Abner & Lahm, 2002; Edwards & Lewis, 1998; Kapperman et al., 2002; Zhou, Parker, Smith, & Griffin-Shirley, 2011; Zhou, Smith, Parker, & Griffin-Shirley, 2011; Zhou et al., 2012).

New Specialization in AT for Instructing Learners with Visual Impairments

Kelly's (2008) research summarized the need for a national effort to develop a new specialization in AT for people with visual impairments:

> Further study that takes into account the need for this innovative aspect of education can best be geared toward

gradually expanding a specialty in assistive technology training for the blind that reflects existing, emerging, and ever-changing technologies relevant to the field of visual impairment...this new aspect of education that embraces the existing, emerging, and ever-changing aspects of assistive technology is ready for immediate attention. If the necessary research was generated and policies were adopted, the education of visually impaired students could reorient itself immediately with this emphasis. (p. 96)

As of May 1, 2016, the Academy for Certification of Vision Rehabilitation and Education Professionals (ACVREP) launched the Certified Assistive Technology Instructional Specialist for People with Visual Impairments (CATIS) credential (Kelly, 2016). After more than three decades of working toward such an outcome (ACVREP, 2016), there is finally an opportunity to train, qualify, and certify personnel in the area of AT for people with visual impairments.

The first university training program in AT for learners with visual impairments was started at Northern Illinois University on the same date as the CATIS certification was launched (Kelly, 2016). In the first year of the Northern Illinois University CATIS program (from May of 2016 to May of 2017), more than 100 individuals have been trained by the program. The newly trained personnel have met new standards and acquired new qualifications to provide instructional interventions in the area of AT for students with visual impairments.

Additional Considerations of Implementing Disability-Specific Interventions for Students with Visual Impairments

Variation in Needs of Students with Visual Impairments

There are several additional matters that must be considered when teaching students who are visually impaired the disability-specific skills presented in this chapter. Perhaps one of the most compelling factors is the heterogeneity of the population of students with visual impairments. Every individual who is visually impaired with remaining or residual vision uses their remaining sight differently (Corn & Lusk, 2010). Also, estimates that pertain to the population of students with visual impairments consistently demonstrate that well over half of students with visual impairments have multiple disabilities (Bishop, 1991; Ferrell, Shaw, & Deitz, 1998; Hatton, Ivy, & Boyer, 2013; Sacks, 1998). Thus, students who are visually impaired often have other disabilities such as autism, intellectual disability, specific learning disability, or traumatic brain injury. The interventions provided to learners with visual impairments with and without additional disabilities consider, assess, and accommodate for these wide variations in functioning that present differently from one student who is visually impaired to the next.

Aligning the ECC and Common Core State Standards

A pressing challenge experienced by teachers of students with visual impairments is alignment of their instruction in areas of the ECC with Common Core Curriculum and Common Core State Standards (CCSS). The environmental shift of standards-based education includes students with visual impairments who must also meet these mandates that are required of all students (Kendall, 2011). However, the CCSS do not easily lend themselves to O&M, independent living, social interaction, or sensory efficiency skills, for example. As outlined in this chapter, the ECC includes distinct knowledge and skill sets for students who are visually impaired. Whereas, the CCSS establish clear expectations for what students should be learning in language arts and mathematics at every grade level from pre-kindergarten through twelfth grade. The CCSS apply to the academic standards and expectations for all children, including those who have disabilities (Kendall). The ECC on the other hand applies very specifically to children who have visual disabilities.

Nevertheless, the state standards and the ECC must be aligned and integrated with each other. In fact, they must be integrated together to facilitate the provision of instruction to students with visual impairments given the emphasis on the common core. Some principles within the CCSS that lend themselves to ECC-specific instruction for students with visual impairments are as follows: emphasis on critical thinking and concept mastery, using evidence to back claims, expanding academic vocabulary, applying and demonstrating knowledge in real-world settings. During O&M lessons, for example, each of these CCSS principles can be directly applied on a regular basis to facilitate the design of standards-based instruction for students who are visually impaired. Thus, it is possible to find a CCSS to apply to vision-related goals, activities, and interventions with this approach.

Management of Limited Resources

Limited Instructional Opportunities. The common core curriculum and state standards that are a driving force can easily encompass every available minute in the contemporary school day. A major challenge in the implementation of the ECC is finding the additional instructional time in the school day for these disability-specific skills. When Hatlen (1996) conceptualized the ECC, it was also identified by Hatlen that this would be a problem:

> The additional learning experiences contained in the expanded core curriculum are not easy to implement. They would be difficult to complete in 12 years of education, especially for students who are high academic learners. They require time to teach, and the need for them does not diminish with age or competency. At this time, no single, simple method assures visually impaired students of accessing both traditional and expanded core curricula within the same length of time as their sighted peers. This remains a significant, but attainable challenge. (p. 27)

Sizeable time periods are required to master competencies that are required in the ECC (Hatlen, 1996). More than two decades later, the lack of available instructional time for instruction in the ECC continues to be a pressing issue. As Hatlen explained, the ECC does not go away as children grow or progress. It is important to recognize this and value the instructional time that is in high demand for students with visual impairments who are learning both expanded and common core curricula during their busy school days year after year.

Shortage of Specialized Vision Teachers. As outlined by both the original and revised editions of the National Agenda, not only is there a shortage of required instructional time available to teach learners with visual impairments, but there is also a severe shortage of qualified specialists who teach students with visual impairments (Corn et al., 1995; Huebner et al., 2004). According to Kirchner and Diament (1999), there were only 7,000 teachers of the visually impaired available to serve students with visual impairments in 1999, and there was an immediate need for an additional 4,700 teachers of the visually impaired if the recommended teacher–student ratio was applied (Mason & Davidson, 2000). There is no evidence to indicate that the situation has improved in the last 18 years. The need is even greater today due to the increased numbers of students with visual impairments who would benefit from specialized services, and the inadequate number of new professionals to provide the disability-specific interventions outlined in this chapter.

Conclusion

This chapter presented a wide range of information related to the disability-specific interventions for students with visual impairments. Advancements in instruction for students with visual impairments that were developed years ago are still useful today. Recent changes pertaining to instructional approaches for learners with visual impairments are also discussed as specific examples of the ongoing progress of the profession. It is emphasized that qualified specialists who teach students with visual impairments do not work in isolation on targeted interventions for their students. Teachers of the visually impaired and O&M specialists work collaboratively on teams to achieve many of the disability-specific interventions described in this chapter. Also, by working together this helps alleviate some of the other extraordinary real-world challenges of disability-specific instruction for learners with visual impairments in twenty-first century classrooms.

References

Abner, G., & Lahm, E. (2002). Implementation of assistive technology with students who are visually impaired: Teachers' readiness. *Journal of Visual Impairment & Blindness, 96*, 98–105.

Academy for Certification of Vision Rehabilitation and Education Professionals. (2016). *Certified assistive technology instructional specialist handbook.* Retrieved from www.acvrep.org/certifications/catis

Allman, C. B., & Lewis, S. (2014). The importance of the expanded core curriculum. In C. B. Allman & S. Lewis (Eds.), *ECC essentials: Teaching the expanded core curriculum to students with visual impairments* (p. 1530). New York, NY: AFB Press.

Bishop, V. E. (1991). Preschool visually impaired children: A demographic study. *Journal of Visual Impairment & Blindness, 85*, 69–74.

Bogart, D. E., Cranmer, T. V., & Sullivan, J. E. (2000). Unifying the braille codes. In J. Dixon (Ed.), *Braille: Into the next millennium* (pp. 160–181). Washington, DC: National Library Service for the Blind and Physically Handicapped.

Bogart, D., D'Andrea, F. M., & Koenig, A. (2004) *A comparison of the frequency of number/punctuation and number/letter combinations in literary and technical materials.* Retrieved from http://www.brailleauthority.org/research-ueb/content analysisfinal11-15-04.pdf

Bogart, D., & Koenig, A. (2005). Selected findings from the first international evaluation of the proposed Unified English Braille Code. *Journal of Visual Impairment & Blindness, 99,* 233–238.

Candela, A. R. (2003). A pilot course in teaching skills for assistive technology specialists. *Journal of Visual Impairment & Blindness, 97,* 661–666.

Clark-Bischke, C., & Kelly, S. M. (2011). Orientation and mobility. In C. Simpson & J. P. Bakken (Eds.). *A full circle approach to multidisciplinary instruction: A teacher's guide to collaboration for successful inclusion of students with disabilities* (pp. 269–280). Waco, TX: Prufrock Press.

Corn, A. L., Hatlen, P., Huebner, K. M., Ryan, F., & Siller, M. A. (1995). *The national agenda for the education of children and youths with visual impairments, including those with multiple disabilities.* New York, NY: AFB Press.

Corn, A. L., & Lusk, K. E. (2010). Perspectives on low vision. In A. L. Corn & J. N. Erin (Eds.), *Foundations of low vision: Clinical and functional perspectives* (2nd ed., pp. 3–34). New York, NY: AFB Press.

Edwards, B. J., & Lewis, S. (1998). The use of technology in programs for students with visual impairments in Florida. *Journal of Visual Impairment & Blindness, 92,* 302–312.

Fazzi, D. L., & Klein, M. D. (2002). Cognitive focus: Developing cognition, concepts, and language. In R. L. Pogrund & D. L. Fazzi (Eds.), *Early focus: Working with young children who are blind or visually impaired and their families* (2nd ed., pp. 107–155). New York, NY: AFB Press.

Ferrell, K. A., Shaw, A. R., & Deitz, S. J. (1998). *Project PRISM: A longitudinal study of developmental patterns of children who are visually impaired.* Final Report, CFDA 84.023C, Grant H023C10188. University of Northern Colorado, Division of Special Education.

Hatlen, P. (1996). The core curriculum for blind and visually impaired students, including those with additional disabilities. *RE:view, 28,* 25–32.

Hatton, D. D., Ivy, S. E., & Boyer, C. (2013). Severe visual impairments in infants and toddlers in the United States. *Journal of Visual Impairment & Blindness, 107,* 325–336.

Hudson, L. J. (1997). *Classroom collaboration.* Watertown, MA: Perkins School for the Blind.

Huebner, K. M., Merk-Adam, B., Stryker, D., & Wolffe, K. (2004). *The national agenda for the education of children and youths with visual impairments, including those with multiple disabilities* (Rev. ed.). New York, NY: AFB Press.

Illingworth, W. H. (1910). *History of the education of the blind.* London: Sampson, Low, Marston.

Kapperman, G., Sticken, J., & Heinze, A. (2002). Survey of the use of assistive technology by Illinois students who are visually impaired. *Journal of Visual Impairment & Blindness, 96,* 106–108.

Kelly, S. M. (2008). *Correlates of assistive technology use by students who are visually impaired in the U.S.: Multilevel modeling of the Special Education*

Elementary Longitudinal Study. Unpublished Ed.D., Northern Illinois University, Illinois.

Kelly, S. M. (2009). Use of assistive technology by students with visual impairments: Findings from a national survey. *Journal of Visual Impairment & Blindness, 103,* 470–480.

Kelly, S. M. (2011). Assistive technology use by high school students with visual impairments: A second look at the current problem. *Journal of Visual Impairment & Blindness, 105,* 235–239.

Kelly, S. M. (2016). Introducing the new assistive technology training credential and Project VITALL university training program. *Division on Visual Impairments Quarterly, 61*(4), 25–29.

Kendall, J. (2011). *Understanding common core state standards.* Alexandria, VA: ASCD.

Kirchner, C., & Diament, S. (1999). Estimates of the number of visually impaired students, their teachers, and orientation and mobility specialists: Part 1. *Journal of Visual Impairment & Blindness, 93,* 600–606.

Knowlton, M., & Wetzel, R. (2004). *Research investigating implications of adopting the Unified English Braille code.* Retrieved from http://www.brailleauthority.org/research-ueb/reportfromknowlton2004.pdf

Lewis, S., & Allman, C. B. (2014). Learning, development, and children with visual impairments: The evolution of skills. In C. B. Allman & S. Lewis (Eds.), *ECC essentials: Teaching the expanded core curriculum to students with visual impairments* (pp. 3–14). New York, NY: AFB Press.

Lowenfeld, B. (1948). Effects of blindness on the cognitive functions of children. *Nervous Child, 7,* 45–54.

Lowenfeld, B. (1971). *Our blind children* (3rd ed.). Springfield, IL: Charles C Thomas.

Lowenfeld, B. (1973). *The visually handicapped child in school.* New York, NY: John Day.

Mason, C., & Davidson, R. (2000). *National plan for training personnel to serve children with blindness and low vision.* Reston, VA: The Council for Exceptional Children.

McCarthy, T., & Holbrook, M. C. (2017). Compensatory skills. In M. C. Holbrook, C. Kamei-Hannan, & T. McCarthy (Eds.), *Foundations of education: Volume II instructional strategies for teaching children and youths with visual impairments* (3rd ed., pp. 350–373). New York, NY: AFB Press.

Moreno, R., & Mayer, R. E. (2007). Interactive multimodal learning environments. *Educational Psychology Review, 19,* 309–326.

Nemeth, A., & Cranmer, T. (1991). *A uniform braille code.* Retrieved from http://www.iceb.org/cranem.html

Sacks, S. Z. (1998). Educating students who have visual impairments with other disabilities: An overview. In S. Z. Sacks & R. K. Silberman (Eds.), *Educating students who have visual impairments with other disabilities* (pp. 3–38). Baltimore, MD: Paul H. Brookes Publishing.

Skellenger, A. C., & Sapp, W. K. (2010). Teaching orientation and mobility for the early childhood years. In W. R. Wiener, R. L. Welshe, & B. B. Blasch (Eds.),

Foundations of orientation and mobility: Vol. 2. Instructional strategies and practical applications (3rd ed., pp. 163–207). New York, NY: AFB Press.

Spungin, S. J., & Huebner, K. M. (2017). Historical perspectives. In M. C. Holbrook, C. Kamei-Hannan, & T. McCarthy (Eds.), *Foundations of education: Volume II instructional strategies for teaching children and youths with visual impairments* (3rd ed., pp. 3–49). New York, NY: AFB Press.

Steinman, B., & Johnson, F. (2003). *Literary Unified English Braille Code versus standard Braille: A pilot study comparing experienced Braille readers' reading rates, miscues, and regressions.* Retrieved from http://www.brailleauthority.org/research-ueb/rrtc-ueb-pilotstudy2003.pdf

Turnbull, A. P., Turnbull, H. R., Wehmeyer, M. L., & Shogren, K. A. (2013). *Exceptional lives: Special education in today's schools* (7th ed.). Upper Saddle River, NJ: Pearson Education.

Wolffe, K. E. (2017). Career education. In W. R. Wiener, R. L. Welshe, & B. B. Blasch (Eds.), *Foundations of orientation and mobility: Vol. 2. Instructional strategies and practical applications* (3rd ed., pp. 831–874). New York, NY: AFB Press.

Zhou, L., Smith, D. W., Parker, A. T., & Griffin-Shirley, N. (2011). Assistive technology competencies of teachers of students with visual impairments: A comparison of perceptions. *Journal of Visual Impairments & Blindness, 105,* 533–547.

Zhou, L., Parker, A. T., Smith, D. W., & Griffin-Shirley, N. (2011). Assistive technology for students with visual impairments: Challenges and needs in teachers' preparation programs and practice. *Journal of Visual Impairment & Blindness, 105,* 197–210.

Zhou, L., Griffin-Shirley, N., Kelley, P., Banda, D. R., Lan, W. Y., Parker, A. T., & Smith, D.W. (2012). The relationship between computer and internet use and performance on standardized tests by secondary students with visual impairments. *Journal of Visual Impairment & Blindness, 106,* 609–621.

Chapter 6

Interventions for Students with Autism

Shannon Stuart

Abstract

This chapter provides evidence-based supports for communication, social skills, and for using restricted patterns of interests and activities educationally for students with autism. Supports for receptive language, expressive language, Picture Exchange Communication System (PECS), visual supports, social narratives, and augmentative and alternative communication are included. Discussion on evidence-based social supports include using peer-mediated instruction and intervention, video modeling, and support for inclusive education. Supports for restricted patterns of behavior, interests, and activities cover how to include special interests, rituals, and routines in educational planning and how to recognize when restricted patterns of behavior are detrimental to education. Repetitive behaviors associated with anxiety and self-injury are also discussed. All supports can be combined and address more than one characteristic or need.

Keywords: Augmentative and alternative communication; autism spectrum disorders; functional based assessment; language and communication supports; picture exchange communication system; restricted patterns of interest; social narratives; social supports; video modeling; visual supports

Viewpoints on Interventions for Learners with Disabilities
Advances in Special Education, Volume 33, 127–142
Copyright © 2018 by Emerald Publishing Limited
All rights of reproduction in any form reserved
ISSN: 0270-4013/doi:10.1108/S0270-401320180000033012

The American Psychiatric Association (APA, 2013) characterizes autism spectrum disorder (ASD) as:

> Persistent deficits in social communication and social inter-action across multiple contexts, including deficits in social reciprocity, nonverbal communicative behaviors used for social interaction, and skills for developing, maintaining, and understanding relationships. In addition to the social communication deficits, the diagnosis of autism spectrum disorder requires the presence of restrictive, repetitive pat-terns of behavior, interests, or activities.

The APA revised its presentation about ASD with the publication of the fifth edition of the Diagnostic and Statistic Manual of Mental Disor-ders (DSM) in 2013. The current terminology, ASD, is characterized as a neurodevelopmental disorder (along with, e.g., learning disabilities and attention-deficit hyperactivity disorder) rather than a pervasive develop-mental disorder. The 2013 edition of the DSM consolidates autistic dis-order, Asperger disorder, and pervasive developmental disorder under the heading ASD. The rationale for this change is that "these disorders repre-sent a single continuum of mild to severe impairments in the two domains of social communication and restrictive/repetitive interests rather than being distinct disorders" (APA, 2013, p. xliii).

Although all students with ASDs show characteristic deficits in social communication and restrictive behaviors and patterns and interests, each person is unique. The degree that these features are demonstrated, in com-bination with intellectual ability, helps to define each student's academic strengths and challenges.

Students with ASD benefit from educational interventions, social opportunities, and inclusion in school and community activities. Because students with ASD represent a heterogeneous population, they require diverse educational interventions and teaching strategies. It is well docu-mented that effective instructional approaches are structured, predictable, and geared to the student's level of functioning (Heflin & Alaimo, 2007). Most students with ASD display appropriate behavior in structured rather than unstructured situations, and special education programs with more structure are generally associated with better outcomes.

This chapter provides evidence-based supports for communication, social skills, and for using restricted patterns of interests and activities educationally. The most successful supports for students with ASD are those that begin early and are intensive, continuous, and multidisciplinary

(Hyman & Levy, 2013; Levy, White, & Pinto-Martin, 2008). Supports should incorporate evidence-based best practice, and most use principles of applied behavior analysis or rely on structured teaching methodologies (Hall, 2013, National Autism Center, 2015; Ryan, Hughes, Katsiyannis, McDaniel, & Sprinkle, 2011). The National Professional Development Center (NPDC) used rigorous criteria to classify 27 focused interventions as evidence-based best practices in 2014. To translate this scientific review into practice, NPDC investigators and staff developed online training modules, which can be accessed from the NPDC website http://afirm. fpg.unc.edu/afirm-modules (Wong et al., 2015). Educators can register for a free account to assess training modules for each of these practices. See Table 1 for a description of some of the programs discussed in this chapter.

Educators can combine all supports presented in this chapter, because each support addresses more than one characteristic or need. For example, video-based instruction can be used as part of a peer-mediated intervention to address social skills and it can also enhance language and communication skills.

Language and Communication Supports

Communication encompasses a broad range of challenges for individuals with autism, from intake and processing of information, verbal or representational output, to reading and writing skills. Noticing nonverbal cues, body language and subtle intent, intonation, and interpretation are also difficult for students with ASD. For students without verbal language, the speech pathologist should assist in formulating plans and supports for alternate modes of communication, such as sign language, PECS, or augmentative devices. For students with emerging verbal language, building on receptive and expressive language skills will be ongoing, and for those with high verbal skills, working on the more subtle aspects of pragmatics and conversational reciprocity should be the focus. Speech pathologists can be instrumental in helping to drive the social, as well as the language components of interaction, because these are commonly intertwined. However, the development of communication skills in a student with ASD cannot be the sole responsibility of the speech pathologist. Communication regarding wants and needs, as well as social interactions, occurs throughout the day and across settings, and the entire school team should be involved. While some students are predominantly auditory learners,

Table 1: Selected Evidence-Based Interventions for Students with ASD.

Intervention	Program Description	Module Website
Picture Exchange Communication System (PECS)	The PECS is used to teach learners with limited functional communication skills to initiate communicative exchanges and interactions within a social context.	http://afirm.fpg.unc.edu/picture-exchange-communication-system
Visual supports (VS)	By using VS, the learner with ASD might be able to process information easier and more quickly than without support.	http://afirm.fpg.unc.edu/visual-supports
Video modeling	Video modeling is an assistive technology method that has become increasingly popular as a way to teach a wide range of skills to persons with ASD, other disabilities, and typical peers. Video modeling can be used as a stand-alone method or be integrated within other methods such as an activity schedule or a social narrative.	http://www.autisminternetmodules.org/mod_intro.php?mod_id=30
Peer-mediated instruction and intervention (PMII)	With a foundation in behaviorism and social learning theory, PMII involves systematically teaching peers without disabilities ways of engaging learners with ASD in positive and meaningful social interactions.	http://afirm.fpg.unc.edu/peer-mediated-instruction-and-intervention
Social narratives (SN)	SN describe social situations for learners by providing relevant cues, explanation of the feelings and thoughts of others, and descriptions of appropriate behavior expectations.	http://afirm.fpg.unc.edu/social-narratives
Functional behavior assessment (FBA)	An FBA can be used when the intensity, duration, or type of interfering behavior creates safety concerns or impacts a child's development.	http://afirm.fpg.unc.edu/functional-behavior-assessment

many tend to be visual learners, meaning they understand or retain what they see more effectively than what they hear. Visual Supports (VS) are often helpful since they provide extra processing time. This section is divided into receptive language supports, expressive language supports, and augmentative and alternative communication (AAC) supports.

Supporting Receptive Language

Receptive language is the ability to understand what is said or written. Suggestions to support students' receptive language skills include the following:

- Make sure you have the student's attention before you deliver an instruction or ask a question.
- Consider the student's processing challenges and timing (e.g., begin an instruction with the student's name – this increases the likelihood that he/she may be attending by the time you deliver the direction).
- Avoid complex verbal directions, information, and discussion. Keep instructions short or give information in chunks.
- Give positive directions to allow for incomplete language processing.
- Minimize the use of "don't" and "stop." For example, "Please stay on the sidewalk" can be much more effective than "Don't walk on the grass" for a student who might not hear the "don't" – or for one who isn't sure where the acceptable place to walk might be. This lets the student know exactly what you want them to do.
- Allow "wait time" (be prepared to wait for a response, whether it is an action or answer). Avoid immediately repeating an instruction or inquiry. Sometimes it is helpful to think of a student with auditory processing challenges like a computer – when it is processing, hitting the command again does not make it go any faster, but rather sends it back to the beginning to start the process all over again. Model and shape correct responses to build understanding (e.g., for a younger student, to teach the meaning of "stop": run on the playground holding hands with the student, say "stop"; stop yourself and the student; repeat until you can fade the handholding and then fade the modeling).
- Supplement verbal information with pictures, visual schedules, gestures, visual examples, and written directions.
- Do not reprimand a student for "not listening or responding" as it only serves to highlight their challenges.

Supporting Expressive Language

Expressive language is spoken language as well as any communicative output such as picture exchange, written language, etc.

Take responsibility for finding a way to access the student's need for communication. Many people with autism have word retrieval issues – even if they know an answer, they may not be able to come up with the words. For example, a student with ASD who knows state capitals may offer the same verbal answer, "Lansing," when prompted for any capital. However, if that student is provided with a visual United States map with the names of all state capitals printed on stickers, they might be able to place every capital in the correct state, especially if handed the names of the capitals, in small groups (e.g., three at a time). Another example is the situation of a student who requests the same daily snack, but when it is given, gets upset and throws it. The teacher verbally presents choices of pretzels, apples, or graham crackers to the student in the same order each day. The student verbally repeats the last snack they hear, "graham crackers," when they want pretzels. If the teacher would print pictures of pretzels, graham crackers, and apples then put them in front of the student, while asking what they want for snack, the student would be able to choose the picture of pretzels, repeat it verbally, and eat what was given without throwing the snack as a means to communicate dissatisfaction.

Supports for expressive language include the following:

- Use of VS to prompt language or give choices. For example, if you are teaching a student to ask for help, have a cue card available at all times, and prompt its use whenever it is time for him to request help. This can be used by the student instead of spoken language, or as a support for developing language and teaching when it might be appropriate to use this phrase.
- Teach and use scripts – words, pictures, etc., for communication needs or exchanges (e.g., "I like... What do you like?" "I like..."). Use cue cards and fade over time as the student develops an understanding of how to use the phrase or the pattern of the exchange.
- Teach the student to communicate or say "I don't know" to reduce the anxiety associated with not being able to answer a question. Later teach the student how to ask for additional information (Who? What? Where? When? etc.).
- Add VS to the environment as needed (e.g., label "IN" and "OUT" boxes).

- Teach students to look for and use VS that already exist in the environment: calendars, signs, door numbers, name placards, drawer labels, the display on a cash register, and body language.
- Use a communication board, PECS, pictures or sign language to support or provide communication options for students with low verbal output.
- If your student has been provided with an augmentative or alternative communication device, learn how to use it too. These devices can range considerably in terms of sophistication, with some offering either written or speech output. Ask the student's special education staff or tech support for programming specific to his needs and help guide them to communication options that will be helpful.
- Sing! Musical processing occurs separately from language processing, and singing can be used to promote both receptive and expressive skills (e.g., for younger children, "The fork goes on the left, the fork goes on the left, hi ho the dairy- o, the fork goes on the left!") as well as motivation.
- Provide verbal prompts or models with care, knowing that these can sometimes cause pronoun confusion and challenges due to perspective taking (e.g., from the student's perspective, when a teacher says "I want a cookie" does that mean that the teacher wants a cookie or is prompting him to say, "I want a cookie?")
- Be aware of echolalia, in which a student repeats phrases they have heard before. Sometimes this is seemingly self-stimulatory behavior, but many individuals with ASD also use functional echolalia to comment, inform, or request.
- Always look for a student's communicative intent (e.g., if a student often reverses pronouns or employs functional echolalia, then "Does your head hurt?" might be his way of telling you that their head hurts).
- For a student who is inclined to use echolalia, try to model language (and VS and SN) using language forms that would be appropriate when the student uses it so that pronoun reversals do not occur (e.g., when creating a visual for a child with frequent headaches, one might use a picture of a person holding his head and the words "My head hurts.")

Augmentative and Alternative Communication

AAC describes any means of communication, aside from traditional speech, that allows someone to use language. This can include using pictures, gestures, sign language, visual aids, or speech-output devices like computers. These can be aided (e.g., speech-generating devices) or unaided (e.g., PECS, sign language). The use of AAC does not prevent verbal language and, in fact, may increase verbal language (Iacono, Trembath, & Erickson, 2016). In addition, students can learn the needed skills for AAC (e.g., being able to push a button), while they are already using it to communicate.

Low-tech communication involves using devices made out of paper, pictures, or other classroom items that are easily created. There are also many different devices on the market that will allow for a simple layout where the student can touch a picture of what they want and the device speaks the word out loud. These range from a single button that says only one message to a board with several buttons, each with a different message. Educators can also print pictures of common objects and actions in the student's educational environment. These add a visual component to support verbal speech development. Educators can also create a sturdy board of laminated poster material about the size of a lunch tray. Pictures that represent the things the student may want to communicate are imaged on the board. The student can then point to the picture of what they want. Educators can also use signs from the American Sign Language along with spoken speech because it adds a visual component to language. Because students with ASD are often visual learners, this may make language easier to comprehend.

The more sophisticated communication devices are similar to tablet computers with touch-screens. The student can navigate through pages of icons that represent different things and will communicate different messages when pushed. These range from very easy to use for the student (one button on the screen) up through very complex. Computer-based instruction involves the use of computer technology (e.g., iPADs) and/ or computerized programs for teaching language skills, including vocabulary, social skills, social understanding, and social problem-solving. Examples include the TouchChat application and the Language Acquisition through Motor Planning application (Vance, Voreis, & Scott, 2013).

Social Supports

Peer Supports

Researchers have investigated the role that typically developing peers may be able to play in the social learning of students with ASD (DiSalvo & Oswald, 2002). PMII is an evidence-based best practice identified by the NPCD. As a result, there are currently many evidence-based social skills training paradigms that involve training peers to work as "buddies" or "tutors" with their classmates on the autism spectrum. Some of the approaches involve training a group of students, the entire class, or assigning an individual student to work with a target classmate with ASD. Types of Peer-mediated instruction and intervention (PMII) include integrated playgroups, peer buddies and peer tutors, group-oriented contingency, peer networks, and pivotal response training (PRT).

In integrated playgroups, an experienced adult guides typical peers and students with ASD in a structured and supportive environment through activities purposefully chosen to encourage interaction. The role of the adult is to establish a consistent schedule, coach the peers through play sessions, and encourage the students with ASD to stay engaged using cues that the child is familiar with. The involvement of the adult can vary and some groups choose to spend time educating typically developing peers about ASD before the playgroup begins.

Peer buddies and peer tutors assign typically developing peers to be a "tutor" or "buddy" to a specific student with ASD. The typically developing peer is trained to keep a close eye on their buddy, talking to them, playing with them, and staying by their side. This strategy hopes to create opportunities for natural interactions between children with ASD and their typical peer that encourage incidental learning about social behaviors. Unlike a buddy or tutor system, the group-oriented contingency strategy involves training an entire classroom of students on some social skill behaviors and techniques in hopes of promoting supportive behaviors among all of the students in a classroom with one or more students with ASD. This option can be useful when educators have limited additional personnel, but would like to provide encouragement for the social growth of a student with ASD.

A peer network intervention trains a group of peers to form a social "network" to provide support for students with ASD. Peer networks may learn the communication system used by the child with ASD, how to initiate and maintain conversations, and how to help provide instructions. In PRT, adults can intervene by using role-play to train peers to engage in specific behaviors with students with ASD by: taking turns, providing narration for play activities, encouraging conversation, and modeling appropriate social behaviors.

Video Modeling

Video modeling is a mode of teaching that uses video recording and display equipment to provide a visual model of the targeted behavior or skill (Franzone & Collet-Klingenberg, 2008). Types of video modeling include basic video modeling, video self-modeling, point-of-view video modeling, and video prompting. Basic video modeling involves recording someone besides the learner engaging in the target behavior or skill (i.e., models). The student with ASD views the video at a later time. Video self-modeling is used to record the learner displaying the target skill or behavior and is reviewed later. Point of-view video modeling is when the target behavior or skill is recorded from the perspective of the learner. Video prompting involves breaking the behavior skill into steps and recording each step with incorporated pauses during which the learner may attempt the step before viewing subsequent steps. Video prompting may be done with either the learner or someone else acting as a model.

Strategies for Inclusive Classrooms

Most students with ASD are included in the general education environment for some or all of the school day. Working with the student's family is essential to academic and social success. Parent teacher conferences and individual education plan meetings should be held with all members of the student's education team, and educators should be familiar with community resources outside of school as families may be overwhelmed and not know where to look for outside support. Specific strategies for inclusive classrooms include the following:

- Bring examples of AAC and accommodations to planning sessions among educators. It is more effective to show a team a support strategy than discussing it generally.
- Provide evidence-based best practice briefs from the NPDC for educators who are interested in learning more about a strategy or ASD in general. http://autismpdc.fpg.unc.edu/npdc-resources
- Make sure fidgets and other small sensory items meet the student's needs without disrupting the rest of the class. Sensory strategies should be discussed between general and special educators before they are implemented. Sensory supports (e.g., fidget items) can provide a benefit to a student with ASD and should not be taken away because a student with ASD is using it to "fidget." It may be beneficial to explain the importance of a sensory item to the other students in the classroom to eliminate possible "I want what they have" sensory item/toy battles.
- Provide seating options (e.g., beanbag chairs, rocking chairs, lawn chairs, seat cushions, couches, stuffed footstools, therapy balls, and armchairs).

- Reduce direct light when possible (e.g., use only some banks of light and turn off others, use upward projecting light, provide a visor or baseball cap to a student who is especially sensitive).
- Minimize distracting noises (e.g., provide earplugs or headphones during certain activities, install carpeting when possible, ban whistles from physical education class).

Supports for Restricted Patterns of Behavior, Interests, and Activities

According to the DSM-5 (American Psychological Association, 2013) restricted, repetitive patterns of behavior, interests, or activities are defined by the presence of at least two of the following:

- Stereotyped or repetitive motor movements, use of objects, or speech (e.g., simple motor stereotypes, lining up toys or flipping objects, echolalia, and idiosyncratic phrases).
- Insistence on sameness, inflexible adherence to routines, or ritualized patterns of verbal or nonverbal behavior (e.g., extreme distress at small changes, difficulties with transitions, rigid thinking patterns, greeting rituals, need to take same route or eat same food every day).
- Highly restricted, fixated interests that are abnormal in intensity or focus (e.g., strong attachment to or preoccupation with unusual objects, excessively circumscribed or perseverative interests).
- Hyper- or hyporeactivity to sensory input or unusual interest in sensory aspects of the environment (e.g., apparent indifference to pain/ temperature, adverse response to specific sounds or textures, excessive smelling or touching of objects, visual fascination with lights or movement).

These restricted patterns of behavior, interests, and activities serve a functional purpose for students with ASD; therefore, this section provides supports for educators to use these patterns productively.

Special Interests

Some students with ASD develop a special talent or skill that becomes a special interest. They may excel at playing or singing songs by ear, or perhaps they know the make, model, and car of every teacher in their school.

Some individuals can tell you which day of the week any date, past or future, occurs on. Educators can incorporate areas of interest into lesson planning and allow students with ASDs who have specialized interests to use these in project based learning to demonstrate academic competencies. If a student likes car racing an educator might use car stickers on their papers or reward systems, or use phrases like, "Rev up your engines, it's time for reading," and find a way to use car racing for math problems or history. Educators can also define a time, place, and duration for the student's specialized interest. For example, a student with ASD may be allowed to use the computer for 20 minutes to look up information about nuclear submarines after they finish a math assignment.

Henry and Myles (2007) suggest using special interests for social practice. The student with ASD or someone in his or her life can find an environment where the interest is valued and explored. Educators might encourage families to look for a club, group, or organization that will help the student increase their knowledge and provide a comfortable social environment for discussing these special interests.

Adreon and Myles (2001) emphasize using special interests to lead to a vocation. In particular, they discuss using an interest that the person can transition in and out of easily and one the individual will not lose interest in. Making the connection from the interest to a future job may take input and support from all those involved in the person's life. For instance, if a student enjoys putting items in order by the alphabet or by numbers, an education team might teach that student to learn filing so they will be able to work in an office or learn how to shelve books to work in a library.

However, students with ASD may have a special interest that interferes with academic or social expectations. Educators can do the following:

- Provide scheduled opportunities to discuss this topic. If appropriate, use a visual schedule to establish these boundaries.
- Set a timer to establish duration for the specialized interest.
- Support strategies for expanding to other topics.
- Reinforce the student for talking about other subjects or the absence of the specialized interest.

Routines and Rituals

Rituals are a pattern of behavior regularly performed in a specific sequence with no obvious function. Students with ASD can be very rigid and may want to do things the same way at the same time. Use consistent classroom routines to lower all students' anxiety and increase students' with ASD abilities to function independently in the classroom. Give visual instructions, provide visual rules, and use visual classroom schedules. Picture icons help to increase student understanding. Use a picture or words system for independent work listing the procedures and tasks to be completed. Educators can also develop social narratives (SN) (Sam & Afirm Team, 2015) to describe social situations for students with ASD by providing relevant cues, explanation of the feelings and thoughts of others, and descriptions of appropriate behavior expectations.

Repetitive Motor Behaviors

Repetitive behaviors may include motor movements, also referred to as self-stimulation, or verbal repetitions, such as words, phrases, or lines from songs. These behaviors can happen in any situation at any time. The purposes they may serve are unique to the individual. Repetitive movement may include the use of objects. Turning on water to play in, spinning the wheels on a toy car, or tearing paper or magazines are some of the movements educators might observe. A student with ASD might be allowed to spin tops for 15 minutes in their bedroom when they return back from school as a way to transition from school to home.

Some motor movements involve verbal repetitions. Students with ASD may repeat a sound, a word, or a phrase, perhaps from a song or television commercial. They may also ask the same question over and over or repeat information, such as telephone numbers, important dates, or the weather forecast (Honey, Rodgers, & McConachie, 2012). In many cases, this is an attempt to communicate, learn language, or practice language. Educators should be mindful that echolalia serves a function; therefore, educators should determine what function the echolalia serves rather than extinguish it.

Repetitive Behaviors Associated with Anxiety

It is also possible that students with ASD are trying to relieve anxiety and stress by using behaviors and interests as a coping mechanism (White, Oswald, Ollendick, & Scahill, 2009). Educators can help students with ASD put labels on emotions by using cartoons and VS to build emotional fluency (Sam & Afirm Team, 2015). Exercise is considered an evidence-based practice for students with ASD, according to the NPDC (Cox, 2013). Maybe the student with ASD can be supported to learn how to calm their body through relaxation practices, like deep breathing or yoga, or perhaps some physical exercise built into the day will help relieve the stress.

Another possibility is that students with ASD get tired of working and resort to behaviors and interests that provide an escape from demands, allowing them to relax and find pleasure in their selection. Restricted patterns of behavior and interests may also be indicative that the individual with autism does not find people or the environment interesting (Leekam, Prior, & Uljarevic, 2011). In this case, the behaviors or interests allow them to occupy themselves with something they enjoy. It is important for those educators to understand the possible reasons for their interests and behaviors. Being able to examine a situation and decide whether a student is anxious, bored, overworked, or understimulated can assist in problem-solving.

Self-Injury

Another area of motor movements involves self-injury. Sometimes, students with ASD engage in motor movements such as biting the wrist, head banging, or hitting themselves repeatedly (Leekam et al., 2011). If a student with ASD engages in self-injurious behaviors, enlist the help of professionals to individualize a behavior intervention plan after an Functional Behavior Assessment (FBA) is conducted. An FBA is used when the intensity, duration, or type of interfering behavior creates safety concerns or impacts a student's development (Sam & AFIRM Team, 2015). Examples of commonly used behavioral interventions include removing the antecedent that had been prompting the behavior, reinforcing a more appropriate behavior via positive attention, or extinguishing the self-injury by deliberately ignoring it.

Remember, restrictive patterns of behavior, interests, and activities are one of the triad characteristics of autism, along with communication and social interaction problems. When displaying such behaviors or activities, students with ASD are not purposefully misbehaving, but are probably anxious, or trying to communicate. Taking this perspective helps see the student with ASD in a different light and allows educators to develop supports. If educators wish to change a particular behavior, they must replace it with one that is more acceptable and useful.

Conclusion

This chapter provided examples of evidence-based supports for students with ASD. All supports can be used in inclusive education settings and educators should combine them as needed to address more than one need. Educators should recognize the communicative intent of problematic behavior and consider supports for receptive language, expressive language, and AAC. This chapter also included discussion on how to use PMII, video modeling, VS, and SN.

Educators should also recognize when restricted patterns of behavior are detrimental to education and when they serve functional purposes for students with ASD. The chapter included a section with examples of supports for educators to use these patterns productively. Supports should incorporate the type of evidence-based best practices included in the chapter. Most of these supports use principles of applied behavior analysis or rely on structured teaching methodologies (Hall, 2013, National Autism Center, 2015; Ryan et al., 2011).

Supports should begin early when possible and are most effective when provided in school, home, and community (Hyman & Levy, 2013; Levy et al., 2008). A multidisciplinary approach is virtually always beneficial because each team member brings a unique perspective, set of observational information, and skills. In addition, it is important to employ the knowledge and perspective of the family, since they offer another valuable and longitudinal view. Parents can contribute information and a history of successful (and unsuccessful) strategies, and they may benefit from information on strategies and successes at school that can help to extend learning into the home setting.

References

Adreon, D., & Myles, B. S. (2001). *Asperger syndrome and adolescence: Practical solutions for school success.* Shawnee Mission, KS: Autism Asperger Publishing Company.

Cox, A. W. (2013). *Exercise (ECE) fact sheet.* Chapel Hill, NC: The University of North Carolina, Frank Porter Graham Child Development Institute, The National Professional Development Center on Autism Spectrum Disorders.

Franzone, E., & Collet-Klingenberg, L. (2008). *Overview of video modeling.* Madison, WI: The National Professional Development Center on Autism Spectrum Disorders, Waisman Center, University of Wisconsin.

Hall, L. (2013). *Autism spectrum disorders* (2nd ed.). Upper Saddle River, NJ: Pearson Education.

Heflin, L., & Alaimo, D. (2007). *Students with autism spectrum disorders.* Upper Saddle River, NJ: Pearson Education.

Honey, E., Rodgers, J., & McConachie, H. (2012). Measurement of restricted and repetitive behaviour in children with autism spectrum disorder: Selecting a questionnaire or interview. *Research in Autism Spectrum Disorders, 6*(2), 757–776.

Hyman, S., & Levy, S. (2013). Autism spectrum disorders. In M. Batshwa, N. Rozen, & G. Loctrecchiano (Eds.), *Children with disabilities* (7th ed., pp. 345–367). Baltimore, MD: Paul H. Brookes.

Iacono, T., Trembath, D., & Erickson, S. (2016). The role of augmentative and alternative communication for children with autism: Current status and future trends. *Neuropsychiatric Disease and Treatment*, *12*, 2349–2361. http://doi.org/10.2147/NDT.S95967

Levy, S., Hyman, S., & Pinto-Martin, J. (2008). Autism spectrum disorders: Overview and diagnosis. In P. Accardo (Ed.), *Capute & Accordo's neurodevelopmental disabilities in infancy and childhood* (3rd ed., Vol. 2, pp. 495–511). Baltimore, MD: Paul H. Brookes.

National Autism Center. (2015). *Findings and conclusions: National standards project, Phase 2*. Randolph, MA: Author.

Ryan, J., Hughes, E., Katsiyannis, A., McDaniel, M., & Sprinkle, C. (2011). Research-based educational practices for students with autism spectrum disorders, *Teaching Exceptional Children*, *43*(3), 56–64.

Sam, A., & AFIRM Team. (2015a). *Functional behavior assessment*. Chapel Hill, NC: National Professional Development Center on Autism Spectrum Disorder, FPG Child Development Center, University of North Carolina. Retrieved from http://afirm.fpg.unc.edu/functional-behavior-assessment.

Sam, A., & AFIRM Team. (2015b). *Peer-mediated interventions and instruction*. Chapel Hill, NC: National Professional Development Center on Autism Spectrum Disorder, FPG Child Development Center, University of North Carolina. Retrieved from http://afirm.fpg.unc.edu/peer-mediated-instruction-and-intervention

Sam, A., & AFIRM Team. (2015b). *Picture exchange communication system*. Chapel Hill, NC: National Professional Development Center on Autism Spectrum Disorder, FPG Child Development Center, University of North Carolina. Retrieved from http://afirm.fpg.unc.edu/picture-exchange-communication-system

Sam, A., & AFIRM Team. (2015d). *Social narratives*. Chapel Hill, NC: National Professional Development Center on Autism Spectrum Disorder, FPG Child Development Center, University of North Carolina. Retrieved from http://afirm.fpg.unc.edu/social-narratives

Sam, A., & AFIRM Team. (2015e). *Visual supports*. Chapel Hill, NC: National Professional Development Center on Autism Spectrum Disorder, FPG Child Development Center, University of North Carolina. Retrieved from http://afirm.fpg.unc.edu/visual-supports

Vance, M., Voreis, G., & Scott, V. (2013). iPad® use in children and young adults with Autism Spectrum Disorder: An observational study. *Child Language Teaching and Therapy*, *30*(2), 159–173.

White, S. W., Oswald, D., Ollendick, T., & Scahill, L. (2009). Anxiety in children and adolescents with autism spectrum disorders. *Clinical Psychology Review*, *29*(3), 216–229.

Wong, C, Odom, S. L., Hume, K. A., Cox, A. W., Fettig, A., Kucharczyk, … Schultz, T. R. (2015). Evidence-based practices for children, youth, and young adults with autism spectrum disorder: A comprehensive review. *Journal of Autism Developmental Disorders*, *45*(7), 1951–1966.

Chapter 7

Viewpoints on Interventions for Students with Extensive and Pervasive Support Needs

Jennifer Kurth, Alison Zagona, Amanda Miller and Michael Wehmeyer

Abstract

This chapter provides "viewpoints" on the education of learners with extensive and pervasive support needs. That is, students who require the most support to learn, often categorized as having intellectual disability, multiple disabilities, autism spectrum disorder, or related disabilities. The lenses through which we provide these viewpoints are historical and future-oriented; we begin with historic perspectives on the education of students with extensive and pervasive support needs, and then provide 21st century viewpoints for these learners. We interpret the notion of viewpoints in two ways: first, consistent with a viewpoint as indicating an examination of objects (in this case, practices and interventions) from a distance so as to be able to compare and judge; and, second, viewpoint as indicating our perspective on said interventions and practice.

Keywords: Extensive support needs; inclusive education; severe disability; assessment; individualized education program; access; strengths-based

Viewpoints on Interventions for Learners with Disabilities
Advances in Special Education, Volume 33, 143–167
Copyright © 2018 by Emerald Publishing Limited
All rights of reproduction in any form reserved
ISSN: 0270-4013/doi:10.1108/S0270-401320180000033007

Historic Viewpoints on the Education of Students with Extensive and Pervasive Support Needs

Educating students with extensive and pervasive support needs was not even on the public agenda, in reality, until the passage of Public Law 94-142 in 1975. By then, how disability was understood as it pertained to this population was well established and, so implementers of the then-titled *Education for All Handicapped Children Act* immediately established a "continuum" of "special education" settings in which such children were to be educated (Jackson, Ryndak, & Wehmeyer, 2008–2009). By "well established," we mean that from the earliest efforts to habilitate (and eventually just to segregate) people who were determined (by whatever means was in use at the time) to have intellectual impairments onward, their "disability" was understood to be a personal pathology; something was wrong with them, they were broken, diseased, defective, atypical, and different (Wehmeyer, 2013a). We phrase this in ways (intentionally) that sound harsher than what was perceived; indeed, the notion that disability is a problem within the person is the dominant way our society thinks about disability today and, we believe, that is primarily why learners with extensive and pervasive support needs remain largely segregated in schools (Wehmeyer et al., 2016).

When disability is attributed to disease and deficit and seen as a characteristic of the person, it is inevitable that people with disability will be viewed as different from "the rest of us." And that is exactly what has happened over time. People with disability, and particularly people with intellectual, developmental, and multiple disabilities, have, throughout history, been viewed as menaces to society and to the social good (Smith & Wehmeyer, 2012). With the advent of intelligence testing as the dominant means to determine "differentness," people with intellectual disability were stigmatized (1) by the notion that so-called "intelligence" was a fixed trait, inherited and genetically determined; and (2) by the questionable notion of a calculated mental age, promulgating the notions of eternal children.

Fast forward to 1975: there is a century's worth of practice segregating people, stigmatizing them by their purported level of intelligence and mental age, and generally having low expectations for them. When public schools are forced to finally "educate" students with extensive and pervasive support needs, the systems set in place replicated practice to that point: segregated classrooms (the better to provide the myriad of services the children needed, parents were told), so-called "functional curriculum" (since "these" students couldn't learn actual school content), and a focus on "behavior" emanating from operant, behavioral psychology.

It should be noted, perhaps, that we don't believe the framers of what we now call Individuals with Disabilities Education Improvement Act (IDEA, 2004) intended that the system would evolve as it has. In 1975, a separate classroom in a public school for children with what we now refer to as intellectual disability seemed like a quantum leap ahead; parents' groups had begun setting up such classes in church basements and nonprofit agencies in the 1950s. And, as hard as it might be to see today, even the well-known abuses inherent with institutions toward the mid-20th century were not widely exposed or understood until the 1970s. The fact is, however, that the nation had a century's worth of experiences in institutionalization to know that segregated settings are not equal and lead to discrimination, low expectations, and inequity.

Lest we be accused of being too cynical, let us be clear. Public Law 94-142 was a watershed moment for students who require the most extensive educational supports to learn and progress. It was necessary because most children and youth with extensive and pervasive support needs were excluded entirely from the education system in America. In landmark civil rights cases on behalf of children with intellectual disability and their families, the courts interpreted the Due Process Clause of the 14th Amendment as requiring equal protection under the law with regard to the right to education for all. It is not coincidental or trivial that the 14th Amendment was adopted in the wake of the Civil War and the passage of the Civil Rights Act of 1866, and has been used to ensure citizenship rights and equal protection in situations ranging from the rights of former slaves, to women's voting rights, to the inherent inequality of racially-segregated public schools, and, in 1975, to IDEA's assurance of access to a free, appropriate public education for all students. For children and youth with extensive and pervasive support needs and their families, IDEA is first and foremost a civil rights Act.

Further, P.L. 94-142 did more than simply open the school door; from the beginning, the law prioritized educating students with disabilities alongside their nondisabled peers in general education settings. The least restrictive environment (LRE) language as it was originally written in 1975 in P.L. 94-142, and as it exists today in IDEA (2004) varies slightly, but the intent has not changed; that children with disabilities be educated in regular classes with their nondisabled peers with the supplementary aids and services they need to succeed. The fundamentals of inclusive practices are based upon these foundational IDEA presumptions and that they have not come to fruition yet is an aberration of historical viewpoints of how disability is understood and how we respond to disability.

Twenty-First Century Viewpoints on the Education of Students with Extensive and Pervasive Support Needs

So, to move us forward into a 21st century viewpoint of disability, we begin by describing how understandings of disability have changed in ways that will allow us to move beyond historic perspectives. In 1980, the World Health Organization (WHO) introduced a new classification system, the International Classification of Impairments, Disabilities, and Handicaps (ICIDH) as a means to describe the impact of a health condition on human functioning. Prior to this, any disability-related issue was classified as a disease or disorder under the WHO's International Classification of Diseases. The ICIDH was the first classification system to "externalize" the notion of disability; that is, rather than simply disability being understood as identical to the impairment, disease, or pathology and, thus, internal to the person, the ICIDH proposed a taxonomy of the consequences of disease, injuries, and other disorders and their implications for the person experiencing such conditions (Wehmeyer, 2013b).

In 2001, the WHO issued a revision of the ICIDH, titled the International Classification of Functioning, Disability, and Health (ICF) in response to criticisms of the ICIDH. The ICF was, according to its originators, a "radical shift" in that it moved from "emphasizing people's disabilities...to focus on their level of health" (WHO, 2002, p. 3). In essence, the ICF proposed a universal classification of disability in which disability was understood only as the gap between a person's capacities and the demands of the environment (Thompson, Wehmeyer, & Hughes, 2010). According to the WHO (2002):

> ICF is named as it is because of its stress is on health and functioning, rather than on disability. Previously, disability began where health ended; once you were disabled, you were in a separate category. We want to get away from this kind of thinking. We want to make ICF a tool for measuring functioning in society, no matter what the reason for one's impairments. So it becomes a much more versatile tool with a much broader area of use than a traditional classification of health and disability. (p. 2)

In essence, the ICF model, referred to as a social–ecological model or a person–environment fit model, conceptualizes disability not as identical to the impairment that resulted in disability, but in the lack of fit between what a person can do and what the person wants to do (in typical settings).

Students with extensive support needs who may not read cannot participate meaningfully in classwide discussions about a text-based young adult novel in a sixth grade language arts class. Students with extensive support needs who have access to a digital talking book version of the young adult novel, however, can participate meaningfully. In this case, what changed was a modification of the delivery of the curricular content (e.g., young adult novel) from print to e-text. The gap between what the student could do and the demands of the context were, essentially, narrowed. There are many examples of how enhancing personal capacity, modifying the environment or context, and providing additional supports and accommodations can enable someone with a disability to function successfully in typical environments, be they work, school, community, or other. In the ICF perspective, then, if the person is functioning successfully in typical settings and contexts, while the person's impairment does not change, the "disability" becomes irrelevant. It is not the person who is broken, it is the lack of supports to promote greater capacity, environmental or contextual modifications, and other supports that results in the "disability."

Such models reframe education from deficits-based models of disability to strengths-based models of disability and allow educators to consider how supports in the way of education, opportunities and experiences, modifications, technology, and other supports can interplay to enable the person to function successfully. Traditional models viewed people with extensive and pervasive support needs as apart from typical function; the ICF and social–ecological models view people with extensive and pervasive support needs as part of typical functioning.

General Education is Where Students with Extensive and Pervasive Support Needs Should Receive Special Education Supports

Students with extensive and pervasive support needs have long been excluded from schools and communities (Kurth, Morningstar, & Kozleski, 2014). This exclusion has persisted despite the IDEA mandate for students with disabilities to be educated in the LRE. In addition to mandating the education of students with disabilities in the LRE, IDEA also specifies that students with disabilities must have access to the general education curriculum. In addition to the legal mandate for students with extensive and pervasive support needs to be educated in the general education classroom, the ICF and social–ecological models of disability set the context for school teams to plan individualized *supports* for students with extensive and pervasive support needs that can be implemented in the general education classroom, rather than identifying the reasons why they should be educated in separate settings. (Shogren, Wehmeyer, Schalock, & Thompson, 2017).

Outcomes of Inclusive Education

Inclusive education, or the provision of necessary special education supports and services in general education settings, is the preference of Congress, as described in IDEA. Research substantiates this stance, noting students with extensive and pervasive support needs experience more positive outcomes and have the opportunity to participate in meaningful, grade-level activities with their peers more frequently than if they are placed in separate, self-contained classrooms (Matzen, Ryndak, & Nakao, 2010). Early research documented that students with extensive and pervasive support needs are more engaged in activities in general education classrooms, compared to separate settings (Hunt, Farron-Davis, Beckstead, Curtis, & Goetz, 1994), and more recent research has documented similar findings. For example, Kurth and Mastergeorge (2012) found that students with autism who were learning in inclusive classrooms spent more time engaged in activities linked to the grade-level curriculum, compared to students who were learning in self-contained classrooms. Others have found students with extensive and pervasive support needs are able to successfully access the general education curriculum within general education classrooms (Hudson, Browder, & Wood, 2013), and are able to learn skills linked with grade-level concepts more frequently than students taught in separate settings (Soukup, Wehmeyer, Bashinski, & Bovaird, 2003; Wehmeyer, Lattin, Lapp-Rincker, & Agran 2003). Further, students with extensive and pervasive support needs have access to more instructional opportunities in inclusive classrooms, as compared to separate classrooms (Matzen et al., 2010).

Assessment is Ecological, Person-Centered, and Strengths-Based

The most meaningful assessments for students with extensive and pervasive support needs are person-centered and strengths-based. However, school systems continue to use norm-referenced assessments for special education eligibility determination (Trent, Artiles, & Englert, 1998). Normative principles ascribe an individual's attributes and skills as a position along the curve in relation to other persons' measured attributes.

Students' scores are defined by the extent which they vary from the average population (Skrtic, 1995). This model is typical for special education evaluation and placement. However, it is a "deficit-based diagnostic model" used to differentiate learning differences as deficits (Trent et al., 1998, p. 282). Such "deficits-focused" processes are not appropriate for examining a student's strengths and growth across standard-based academic goals and quality of life outcomes (Hunt, McDonnell, & Crockett, 2012; Yell, Ryan, Rozalski, & Katsiyannis, 2009). There are other methods to assess students authentically in ways that capitalize on students' strengths, learning priorities, and broader connections to varied learning communities (Ruppar, 2015). The assessment framework discussed in this chapter considers the environment and the instructional strategies used across settings in combination with how the ecologies and techniques interact with the student's strengths, goals, and supports.

Person-Centered and Strengths-Based

Meaningful, authentic assessment is person-centered and strengths-based (Buntinx & Schalock, 2010; Field, 2014). Person-centered assessment embraces students and families as team members in the evaluation process. Through this multidimensional and interdisciplinary path, assessment is both subjective and objective (Buntinx, 2014). Objective measures, such as curriculum-based assessments, are integrated into the assessment process with subjective quality of life markers, including life experiences, desires, and ambitions (Buntinx & Schalock, 2010). Person-centered assessments collect student-based data, including information on student needed supports (Schalock et al., 2010) and support needs (Thompson et al., 2002, 2009). *Supports* describe the resources and strategies necessary to promote education, development, personal interests, and well-being (Schalock et al., 2010; Thompson et al., 2009). In conjunction, *support needs* outline the pattern and intensity of person-centered supports necessary for participation in activities associated with everyday life (Thompson et al., 2002, 2009). Ecological assessment is one person-centered approach used to determine individualized supports and environmental arrangements for students with extensive support needs (Hunt et al., 2012).

Strengths-based assessment also includes instructionally relevant student factors (McCart, Sailor, Bezdek, & Satter, 2014). Such strengths-based assessment provides information that can be incorporated into instruction, enabling educators to focus on skills that promote personal, social, and academic development; this is contrasted with more traditional deficit-oriented assessments used to identify weaknesses and eligibility for special education (Cosden, Koegel, Koegel, Greenwell, & Klein, 2006). Further, most traditional assessments are completed in contextually irrelevant settings such as the offices of school psychologists. Thus, taking data as formative assessment measures and using established rules to make data-based decisions is a preferred manner for understanding student ability in the context of routine instruction, using typical instructional materials (Jimenez, Mims, & Browder, 2012). Finally, strengths-based assessment incorporates information gathered with families, educators, and reflects student interests and priorities (Turnbull, Turnbull, Erwin, Soodak, & Shogren, 2015).

Data-Driven Decision-Making

An assessment framework that seeks to understand students' strengths and supports is ongoing and formative. Teachers, related service providers, families, and students all play an active role in ongoing assessment. Progress monitoring data are used to adjust or develop approaches that are distinctive to learning contexts and settings. For example, a team assesses the effectiveness of instructional strategies in supporting a student's progress and then makes decisions about the efficacy of the approach based on the student's responses (Kleinhammer-Tramill, Burrello, & Sailor, 2012). School personnel might use work samples, task analyses, portfolios, observations, and commercially or locally produced performance samples for progress monitoring (Field, 2014; Test, Spooner, Holzberg, Robertson, & Davis, 2017). Families may provide data through interviews, narratives, and observations. Examples of data collection for progress monitoring used by students with extensive and pervasive support needs include, but are not limited to, checklists, task analyses, and self-graphing tools (Test et al., 2017). Ongoing, formative data collection should be used to make timely instructional decisions, monitor progress, and understand students' strengths.

Inclusive Individualized Education Programs

Once assessments are completed with input from all stakeholders, teams use this knowledge to develop a student's Individualized Education Program (IEP). For students with extensive and pervasive support needs receiving special education services in schools, this includes developing

IEPs that can be implemented inclusively. Teams must develop IEPs in which goals can be addressed within the ongoing routines and contexts of general education settings, and in such a manner that students do not need to leave those settings to obtain needed instruction or services. Determining which IEP goals to prioritize must be a team decision, reflecting the preferences and priorities of the student, family, and all teachers. To facilitate inclusive education, all goals must be linked to grade-appropriate content standards (Browder, Spooner, & Jimenez, 2010). Such linkage aligns general education instruction with special education services. Importantly, this alignment prevents situations in which the IEP content is so different as to be incompatible with instruction in general education settings. To date, many state departments of education, along with alternate assessment organizations, facilitate the development of grade-referenced, standards-based IEP goals by crosswalking standards (as written) with essential elements, or access points, to each standard.

Collaborative IEP Development

As specified in IDEA, general and special education teachers, parents, administrators, psychologists, and the child (when appropriate) are required IEP team members. As discussed later, however, we advocate for inclusion of students with disabilities of any age in all IEP meetings. Often, IEP teams are much larger than described in IDEA, as related services providers, advocates, and allies may all be present as well. Perhaps as a consequence of these large school teams, equity is often not achieved among members. For example, school personnel are reported to speak far more frequently in IEP meetings than parents (Ruppar & Gaffney, 2011), with special education teachers speaking the most (Martin, Marshall, & Sale, 2004). Further, parents report disenfranchisement in meetings due to pre-IEP meetings held without them (Bray & Russell, 2016). Additionally, many general education teachers feel ill-prepared to both participate in IEP meetings and implement IEP team decisions (Berry, 2011). While general education teacher attendance at IEP meetings benefited IEP team members, they report being unsure of what to do in meetings, knowing the reason for meetings, and understanding what was said in meetings (Martin et al., 2004). Finally, students are often unaware of the purpose of the meeting or their role in it (Martin et al., 2004), and are simply often not invited to attend their own IEP meetings (Martin et al., 2006; Van Dycke, Martin, & Lovett, 2006).

Researchers and practitioners have identified a variety of strategies to improve collaboration among IEP team members. As content curriculum experts, general education teacher involvement in development and implementation of the IEP is critical for inclusive education. Providing clear information about the purpose of the meeting is one way to facilitate general education teacher involvement (Diliberto & Brewer, 2012). Other practical solutions offered include scheduling IEP team meetings when general education teachers are available, and providing release time as needed for teachers to prepare for and attend the meeting (Menlove, Hudson, & Suter, 2001). Finally, because many general education teachers perceive IEP goals to be disconnected from the curriculum they are teaching (Menlove et al., 2001), developing IEP goals clearly aligned to grade-level content standards is essential (Browder, Spooner, Wakeman, Trela, & Baker, 2006). General education teachers are well-positioned to work with other IEP team members to review grade-level standards and identify the essential elements of those standards to be taught to students with extensive support needs (Ballard & Dymond, 2017).

Including students themselves in the IEP team meeting is another strategy for improving collaboration and developing inclusive IEPs. Researchers have investigated how students in elementary (Danneker & Bottge, 2009) through secondary (Mason, McGahee-Kovac, Johnson, & Stillerman, 2002) school have been involved in leading meetings and developing their own IEPs. Participation of students in their own IEP development is a natural method of promoting self-determination, particularly related to goal setting and attainment (Lee, Palmer, & Wehmeyer, 2009). Yet other positive outcomes are associated with student participation and leadership in their IEP meetings. For example, student participation in meetings is associated with improved academic outcomes (Barnard-Brak & Lechtenberger, 2010), greater participation in the IEP meeting (Danneker & Bottge, 2009; Martin et al., 2006), greater motivation to achieve transition goals (Benz, Lindstrom, & Yovanoff, 2000), improved self-determination related skills (Williams-Diehm, Wehmeyer, Palmer, Soukup, & Garner, 2008), and student knowledge of their rights (Mason et al., 2002). Teachers have further reported improvements in choice-making, self-advocacy, self-awareness, and self-reflection when students lead their own IEPs (Hapner & Imel, 2002). Benefits extend to other team members, as well. Team members, including teachers and parents, report that student-led IEPs result in parent pride, improved climate of meetings, and streamlining the meeting (Eisenman, Chamberlin, & McGahee-Kovac, 2005).

Strategies for Accessing General Education Curriculum

Access to the general education curriculum is an ongoing process that school teams discuss during the IEP meeting and throughout the school year as curricula standards change in different instructional content areas. As IEP teams plan for students with extensive and pervasive support needs to access the general education curriculum, they do so by identifying and implementing accommodations and modifications. Accommodations and modifications support students to complete class activities and assignments. Accommodations are changes to how the student may experience a class activity or test, such as extended time and frequent breaks. An important distinction between accommodations and modifications is that accommodations do not change the learning objective of the assignment (Janney & Snell, 2013). Rather, accommodations support the student to complete the same assignment or test as his peers with greater flexibility than the original assignment (Janney & Snell, 2013). In addition to accommodations, students with extensive and pervasive support needs often benefit from modifications to access the general education curriculum. Modifications change the learning objective for an activity and support the student to actively participate with an adjusted and individualized objective appropriate for the student's strengths and support needs (Janney & Snell, 2013). Decisions about the design and implementation of a student's modifications should be made by the IEP team, in alignment with the student's annual IEP goals.

In addition to accommodations and modifications, teachers who implement differentiated instruction support all students to access the curriculum by adjusting activities and assignments for the range of student support needs in the class (Tomlinson, 2001). Differentiated instruction refers to the adjustment of the complexity of materials and activities in a classroom, rather than adding or reducing work for certain students (Tomlinson, 2001). Additionally, when teachers implement differentiated instruction, they provide all students with various ways to receive the information and various ways for the students to demonstrate their learning. Conceptually, differentiated instruction is closely linked with Universal Design for Learning (UDL).

UDL is an instructional approach guided by a framework of three principles designed to decrease barriers to learning by creating different ways for students to access class content and demonstrate learning. There are three main principles of UDL: "multiple means of representation," "multiple means of action and expression," and "multiple means of engagement" (Meyer, Rose, & Gordon, 2014, p. 7). Each of these principles includes a set of guidelines suggesting the importance of designing instruction to meet the needs of a wide variety of learners by providing visual supports for a lecture, or providing a verbal narration for visual content posted on the class website, for example. Additionally, UDL suggests the importance of providing students with a variety of ways to demonstrate their learning; for example, students may prefer to handwrite their responses, or they may prefer to dictate their answers in an audio file (Meyer et al., 2014). Researchers have documented the use of these strategies in general education classrooms that include students with extensive and pervasive support needs (Kurth, Lyon, & Shogren, 2015; Morningstar, Shogren, Lee, & Born, 2015).

Another strategy that can be used to support student's access to the general education curriculum is through the implementation of assistive technology (AT). AT may be implemented as part of a curriculum modification, or it may be used to support a student to access the physical environment of the school and classroom. As mandated by IDEA, IEP teams must consider providing students who are receiving special education and related services with AT as a support to "increase, maintain, or improve" a specific skill (IDEA, 2004, Sec. 602(1)(A))). AT devices may include items or systems that range from being "low-tech" (e.g., pencil grips and highlighters) to "high-tech" (e.g., laptops and mobile devices; Bryant & Bryant, 2012). AT devices may support students with extensive and pervasive support needs with a range of skills and activities in the general education classroom.

Designing and Implementing Inclusive Instruction

Student learning outcomes are priority within inclusive instructional design as part of the person-centered and strengths-based approach discussed in the *Assessment* section. As with ongoing assessment, the student and their family play an active role in determining learning outcomes. The outcomes ought to be academic, nonacademic, and extracurricular and dependent on the student's strengths, supports, interests, and futures planning. Prioritizing learning outcomes reflects students with extensive support needs have access to "the full range of learning experiences, environments, and social networks offered to students without disabilities" (Kurth, Marks, & Bartz, 2017, p. 280).

Context and Content

Supported by federal mandates and research-based strategies, effective inclusive instructional design requires a focus on context and content.

IDEA (2004) and Every Student Succeeds Act (2015) both emphasize student access, participation, and progress in the general education curriculum within general education contexts (Ryndak, Moore, Orlando, & Delano, 2008–2009). Said differently, effective inclusive instruction requires learning to occur in meaningful contexts with general education curricula. Instruction provided in context happens within natural, inclusive school settings such as general education classrooms and common areas like playgrounds, gymnasiums, and cafeterias where peers are engaged in context-specific activities (Jackson, Ryndak, & Billingsley, 2000). Embedded systematic instruction is one method that capitalizes on general education context and content for students with extensive support needs.

Embedded Systematic Instruction Across Academic Domains

Embedded systematic instruction focuses on the general education curriculum through repeated direct-trial instruction and takes place within the flow of instruction in inclusive settings (Johnson, McDonnell, Holzwarth, & Hunter, 2004). This method may incorporate systematic strategies such as task analysis, time delay, feedback schemes, and prompting and fading systems (Jackson et al., 2000). Embedded systematic instruction has been found to be successful in teaching vocabulary (McDonnell, Johnson, Polychronis, & Risen, 2002; McDonnell et al., 2006) and sight words (Johnson & McDonnell, 2004). Further, research has identified peers (Jameson, McDonnell, Polychronis, & Riesen, 2008) and paraprofessionals (Johnson & McDonnell, 2004) can support this method in inclusive settings. Embedded instruction is an evidenced-based practice (Hudson et al., 2013) used to design inclusive instruction across academic domains (Jameson, McDonnell, Johnson, Riesen, & Polychronis, 2007; Jimenez, Browder, Spooner, & DiBiase, 2012).

Embedded Systematic Instruction for Nonacademic Skills

Embedded systematic instruction is also used to teach and practice nonacademic skills within general education activities and settings, including communication, social-emotional, and behavior skills and supports. Systematic strategies, such as the ones mentioned above (e.g., task analysis, prompting, and fading systems) should be integrated in nonacademic skill instruction. Nonacademic activities embedded in inclusive spaces results in an increase in instructional time (Jackson et al., 2008–2009). In addition, combining embedded instruction with collaboration and co-teaching models (Solis, Vaughn, Swanson, & Mcculley, 2012) further facilitates effective inclusive design. Research indicates systematic embedded instruction is an effective practice for teaching nonacademic skills inclusively (Ryndak, Jackson, & White, 2013).

Self-Determination

Closely related to the shift toward strengths-based approaches to disability has been the instructional focus on promoting the self-determination of children, youth, and adults with disabilities. Self-determination refers to a:

> dispositional characteristic manifested as acting as the causal agent in one's life. Self-determined people (i.e., causal agents) act in service to freely chosen goals. Self-determined actions function to enable a person to be the causal agent in his or her life." (Shogren et al., 2015, p. 258)

Being a causal agent refers to making or causing things to happen in one's life. A dispositional characteristic is "an enduring tendency used to characterize and describe differences between people; it refers to a tendency to act or think in a particular way, but presumes contextual variance" (Shogren et al., 2015, p. 258). Thus, people who are self-determined have a tendency to act in ways that are self-caused, rather than other-caused. Choice-making, decision-making, problem-solving, goal-setting and attainment, self-management, self-advocacy, self-awareness, and self-knowledge are all skills and processes associated with self-determination (Shogren, 2013). By teaching students these skills and creating opportunities for them to apply them throughout their life, causal agency and self-determination develop.

Students with disabilities, including students with extensive and pervasive support needs, have far fewer opportunities to learn and engage in actions leading to self-determination and, as such, are less self-determined than their peers (Wehmeyer, Shogren, Little, & Lopez, 2017). Research has also established that students with disabilities can acquire skills leading to later self-determination if provided opportunities; that if they do so, they become more self-determined; and, if they are more self-determined, they achieve more positive school and postschool outcomes (Shogren, Wehmeyer, Palmer, Rifenbark, & Little, 2015). This has been shown to be the case for students with more extensive support needs, keeping in mind that being self-determined means making things happen in one's life, and not doing everything oneself. Research has established that if provided opportunities to be engaged in learning (and practicing) skills such as choice-making, problem-solving, goal-setting, and so forth, students with more extensive support needs can acquire skills in these areas and that they benefit when they do (Wehmeyer, 2014), including improved educational goal attainment, improved transition outcomes, and enhanced access to the general education curriculum (Wehmeyer et al., 2017).

Inclusive Extracurricular Instruction

Participation in extracurricular activities is critical for students with extensive and pervasive support needs (Kleinert, Miracle, & Sheppard-Jones, 2007). Students pursue personal interests, build academic and nonacademic skills, and explore career pathways through extracurricular activities throughout the year, including clubs, camps, and service learning opportunities (Carter, Swedeen, Moss, & Pesko, 2010). A person-centered and strengths-based approach to designing effective inclusive instruction can be transferred to school- and community-based extracurricular settings (Pence & Dymond, 2015). Further, ecological (Hunt et al., 2012) and supports inventories (Thompson et al., 2009) blended with co-teaching and collaboration provide information for modifications and communication and assistive technologies necessary to guide students contingent on their interests and future goals. Students with extensive and pervasive support needs have a wide range of interests and assets that can be explored and strengthened in inclusive extracurricular settings.

Teaming to Implement Inclusive Instruction

A team approach is essential for ensuring the full and meaningful inclusion. As students with extensive and pervasive support needs often have many members on their educational team, identifying roles and responsibilities for each team member to support the student inclusively is essential. Co-planning and co-teaching are effective strategies to support students in general education classrooms. Typically, general and special education teachers co-teach; however, utilizing the strengths of other team members (e.g., speech-language pathologists) as co-teachers is both possible and advantageous. Co-teaching depends upon advance planning, enabling all team members opportunities to develop lessons that fully include students with extensive support needs. Ideally, this is accomplished during consistent, duty-free co-planning periods (e.g., Murawski, 2012).

While few studies have directly investigated the impact of co-teaching on student achievement, preliminary research suggests its effectiveness. For example, Hang and Rabren (2009) found significant positive impact of co-teaching on student academic and behavioral performance. The presence of co-teachers has also been found to increase rates of positive feedback, opportunities for students to respond, use of small group instruction, and more one-to-one instruction (Sweigart & Landrum, 2015). Teachers further report using differentiated instruction and assessment, such as more hands-on activities and visual supports such as graphic organizer in co-taught classrooms (Cramer, Liston, Nevin, & Thousand, 2010). Finally, teachers report being able to better meet the needs of all learners in a co-taught classroom (Downing & Peckham-Hardin, 2008).

While related services providers can act as co-teachers, researchers have identified other mechanisms for these team members to provide inclusive instruction and therapy. Notably, both direct- and indirect-services, such as speech or occupational therapy, can be delivered in general education classrooms to students with extensive and pervasive support needs (Giangreco, Prelock, Reid, Dennis, & Edleman, 2000). Although limited research has investigated effectiveness of inclusive related services, existing research has demonstrated benefits to students (e.g., Kellegrew & Allen, 1996) and teachers (e.g., Downing & Peckham-Hardin, 2008). Often, the benefits are to both groups. For example, inclusive related services reduces disruptions for students and teachers, increasing instructional time for both (Rainforth & York-Barr, 1997). Further, inclusive related services allows teams to address IEP goals throughout the day, rather than only in therapy sessions (Downing & Peckham-Hardin, 2008).

Co-planning and co-teaching are also effective strategies for expanding students' social relationships. At times, students with extensive and pervasive support needs and their peers may require adult facilitation and faded supports for creating and maintaining friendships and social connections (Rossetti, 2012). Team members explicitly facilitate social interactions by embedding direct social skill instruction into general education curricula, providing feedback, teaching restorative problem-solving, and reinforcing interactions. Collaborative teaching partners can also implicitly expand social relationships by modeling positive interactions, demonstrating respectful communication exchanges, and redirecting interactions (Biggs & Carter, 2017). As collaborative teams, teachers, related services providers, and paraprofessionals encourage social relationship development across grade levels, with varying supports and levels of independence (Rosetti & Goessling, 2010).

In addition to implementing supports through co-planning and co-teaching, educators in general education classrooms plan and facilitate peer supports for students with extensive and pervasive support needs. Peer support strategies are intended to "facilitate the development of a normalized range of positive and age-appropriate social relationships" (Janney & Snell, 2006, p. 45). Peers can also support students with extensive and pervasive support needs to access the general education curriculum (Carter & Kennedy, 2006). During the adolescent and high school years, peer supports are particularly important as they may be a way to support a student that is less stigmatizing than if the student were to receive support from an adult, for example. Formalized peer supports and interventions are supervised by the adults at the school, and they are specifically designed to provide individualized support for students. The adults at the school may invite specific peers to participate and then teach or train them on how to provide support for that student effectively and appropriately (Carter & Kennedy, 2006; Carter et al., 2016).

Conclusion

In this chapter, we grounded current educational practices of separating and segregating students with extensive and pervasive support needs in an historical understanding of disability, and then contrasted that with a 21st century viewpoint on both the construct of disability and provision of education services. This included discussions of the critical role of inclusive education for students with extensive and pervasive support needs, along with emerging research-based strategies for delivering inclusive, strengths-based education supports and services. The supports and services included assessment, planning, accessing general education curriculum, and strategies for designing curriculum and teaming to support inclusive instruction.

As discussed in this chapter, our viewpoint is firmly rooted in a commitment to strengths-based, inclusive education for learners with extensive and pervasive support needs. While this viewpoint reflects a substantial shift from the status quo of schools today (i.e., separating and segregating students with extensive and pervasive support needs), we believe the strategies and supports articulated here, when enacted, will result in positive lifelong outcomes for students, teachers, and families. There is today a substantial body of research demonstrating the feasibility and appropriateness of this viewpoint, and we anticipate a future in which all learners are valued and welcomed in their schools and communities, with strengths recognized and capitalized.

References

Ballard, S. L., & Dymond, S. (2017). Addressing the general education curriculum in general education settings with students with severe disabilities. *Research and Practice for Persons with Severe Disabilities, 42*, 155–170. doi:10.1177/1540796917698832

Barnard-Brak, L., & Lechtenberger, D. (2010). Student IEP participation and academic achievement across time. *Remedial and Special Education, 31*, 343–349. doi:10.1177/0741932509338382

Benz, M., Lindstrom, L., & Yovanoff, P. (2000). Improving graduation and employment outcomes of students with disabilities: Predictive factors and student perspectives. *Exceptional Children, 66*, 509–529. doi:10.1177/001440290006600405

Berry, R. A. (2011). Voices of experience: General education teachers on teaching students with disabilities. *International Journal of Inclusive Education, 15*, 627–648. doi:10.1080/13603110903278035

Biggs, E. E., & Carter, E. W. (2017). Supporting the social lives of students with intellectual disability. In M. L. Wehmeyer & K. A. Shogren (Eds.), *Handbook of research-based practices for educating students with intellectual disability* (pp. 235–254). New York, NY: Routledge.

Bray, L. E., & Russell, J. L. (2016). Going off script: Structure and agency in individualized education program meetings. *American Journal of Education, 122*, 367–398. doi:10.1086/685845

Browder, D., Spooner, F., & Jimenez, B. A. (2010). Standards-based individualized education plans and progress monitoring. In D. Browder & F. Spooner (Eds.), *Teaching students with moderate and severe disabilities* (pp. 42–91). New York, NY: Guilford Press.

Browder, D., Spooner, F., Wakeman, S., Trela, K., & Baker, J. N. (2006). Aligning instruction with academic content standards: Finding the link. *Research and Practice for Persons with Severe Disabilities, 31*, 309–321. doi:10.1177/154079690603100404

Bryant, D. P., & Bryant, B. R. (2012). *Assistive technology for people with disabilities.* Upper Saddle River, NJ: Pearson.

Buntinx, W. H. E. (2014). Understanding disability: A strengths-based approach. In M. L. Wehmeyer, (Ed.), *The Oxford handbook of positive psychology and disability* (pp. 7–18). New York, NY: Oxford University Press.

Buntinx, W. H. E., & Schalock, R. L. (2010). Models of disability, quality of life, and individualized supports: Implications for professional practice in intellectual disability. *Journal of Policy and Practice in Intellectual Disabilities, 7*, 283–294. doi:10.1111/j.1741-1130.2010.00278.x

Carter, E. W., Asmus, J., Moss, C. K., Biggs, Elizabeth E., Bolt, ... Weir, K. (2016). Randomized evaluation of peer support arrangements to support the inclusion of high school students with severe disabilities. *Exceptional Children, 82*, 209–233. doi:10.1177/0014402915598780

Carter, E. W., & Kennedy, C. H. (2006). Promoting access to the general curriculum using peer support strategies. *Research and Practice for Persons with Severe Disabilities, 31*(4), 284–292.

Carter, E. W., Swedeen, B., Moss, C. K., & Pesko, M. J. (2010). "What are you doing after school?" Promoting extracurricular involvement for transition-age youth with disabilities. *Intervention in School and Clinic, 45*, 275–283. doi:10.1177/1053451209359077

Cosden, M., Koegel, L. K., Koegel, R. L., Greenwell, A., & Klein, E. (2006). Strength-based assessment for children with autism spectrum disorders. *Research and Practice for Persons with Severe Disabilities, 31*, 134–143. doi:10.1177/154079690603100206

Cramer, E., Liston, A., Nevin, A., & Thousand, J. (2010). Co-teaching in urban secondary school districts to meet the needs of all teachers and learners: Implications for teacher education reform. *International Journal of Whole Schooling, 6*, 59–76.

Danneker, J. E., & Bottge, B. A. (2009). Benefits of and barriers to elementary student-led individualized education programs. *Remedial and Special Education, 30*, 225–233. doi:10.1177/0741932508315650

Diliberto, J. A., & Brewer, D. M. (2012). Six tips for successful IEP meetings. *Teaching Exceptional Children, 44*, 30–37. doi:10.1177/0040059914553205

Downing, J. E., & Peckham-Hardin, D. (2008). Inclusive education: What makes it a good education for students with moderate to severe disabilties? *Research and Practice for Persons with Severe Disabilities, 32*, 16–30. doi:10.2511/rpsd.32.1.16

Eisenman, L. T., Chamberlin, M., & McGahee-Kovac, M. (2005). A teacher inquiry group on student-led IEPs: Starting small to make a difference. *Teacher Education and Special Education, 28*, 195–206. doi:10.1177/088840640502800406

Every Student Succeeds Act. (2015). § P.L. 114-95.

Field, S. L. (2014). Education. In M. L. Wehmeyer (Ed.), *The Oxford handbook of positive psychology and disability* (pp. 393–408). Oxford: Oxford University Press.

Giangreco, M., Prelock, P., Reid, R., Dennis, R., & Edleman, S. (Eds.). (2000). *Roles of related services personnel in inclusive schools* (2nd ed.). Baltimore, MD: Paul H. Brookes.

Hang, Q., & Rabren, K. (2009). An examination of co-teaching: Perspectives and efficacy indicators. *Remedial and Special Education, 30*, 259–268. doi:10.1177/0741932508321018

Hapner, A., & Imel, B. (2002). The students' voices: Teachers started to listen and show respect. *Remedial and Special Education, 23*, 122–126. doi:10.1177/074193250202300209

Hudson, M. E., Browder, D. M., & Wood, L. A. (2013). Review of experimental research on academic learning by students with moderate and severe intellectual disability in general education. *Research and Practice for Persons with Severe Disabilities, 38*, 17–29. doi:10.2511/027494813807046926

Hunt, P., Farron-Davis, F., & Beckstead, S., Curtis, D., & Goetz, L. (1994). Evaluating the effects of placement of students with severe disabilities in general education versus special classes. *Journal of the Association for Persons with Severe Handicaps, 19*, 200–214. doi:10.1177/154079699401900308

Hunt, P., McDonnell, J., & Crockett, M. A. (2012). Reconciling an ecological curricular framework focusing on quality of life outcomes with the development and instruction of standards-based academic goals. *Research and Practice for Persons with Severe Disabilities, 37*, 139–152. doi:10.2511/027494812804153471

Individuals with Disabilities Education Improvement Act. (2004). H.R. 1350, Pub. L. No. P.L. 108-446.

Jackson, L., Ryndak, D. L., & Billingsley, F. (2000). Useful practices in inclusive education: A preliminary view of what experts in moderate to severe disabilities are saying. *Journal of the Association for Persons with Severe Handicaps, 25*, 129–141.

Jackson, L. B., Ryndak, D. L., & Wehmeyer, M. L. (2008–2009). The dynamic relationship between context, curriculum, and student learning: A case for inclusive education as a research-based practice. *Research & Practice for Persons with Severe Disabilities, 33–34*, 175–195. doi:10.2511/rpsd.33.4.175

Jameson, J. M., McDonnell, J., Johnson, J. W., Riesen, T. J., & Polychronis, S. (2007). A comparison of one-to-one embedded instruction in the general education classroom and one-to-one massed practice instruction in the special education classroom. *Education and Treatment of Children, 30*, 23–44. doi:10.1353/etc.2007.0001

Jameson, J. M., McDonnell, J., Polychronis, S., & Riesen, T. J. (2008). Embedded, constant time delay instruction by peers without disabilities in general education classrooms. *Intellectual and Developmental Disabilities, 46*, 346–363. doi:10.1352/2008.46:346-363

Janney, R., & Snell, M. E. (2006). *Social relationships and peer support.* Baltimore, MD: Brookes.

Janney, R., & Snell, M. E. (2013). *Modifying schoolwork.* Baltimore, MD: Brookes.

Jimenez, B., Browder, D. M., Spooner, F., & Dibiase, W. (2012). Inclusive inquiry science using peer-mediated embedded instruction for students with moderate intellectual disability. *Exceptional Children, 78*, 301–317. doi:10.1177/001440291207800303

Jimenez, B. A., Mims, P. J., & Browder, D. (2012). Data-based decisions guidelines for teachers of students with severe intellectual and developmental disabilities. *Education and Training in Autism and Developmental Disabilities, 47*(4), 407–413.

Johnson, J. W., & McDonnell, J. (2004). An exploratory study of the implementation of embedded instruction by general educators with students with developmental disabilities. *Education and Treatment of Children, 27*(1), 46–63.

Johnson, J. W., McDonnell, J., Holzwarth, V. N., & Hunter, K. (2004). The efficacy of embedded instruction for students with developmental disabilities enrolled in general education classes. *Journal of Positive Behavior Interventions, 6*, 214–227. doi:10.1177/10983007040060040301

Kellegrew, D. H., & Allen, D. (1996). Occupational therapy in full-inclusion classrooms: A case study from the Moorpark model. *The American Journal of Occupational Therapy, 50*, 718–724.

Kleinert, H. L., Miracle, S. A., & Sheppard-Jones, K. (2007). Including students with moderate and severe intellectual disabilities in extracurricular and community recreation activities. *Intellectual & Developmental Disabilities, 45*, 46–55. doi:10.1352/1934-9556(2007)45[46:ISWMAS]2.0.CO;2

Kleinhammer-Tramill, J., Burrello, L. C., & Sailor, W. (2012). A critical perspective on reframing public policy for students with disabilities. In L. C. Burrello, W. Sailor, & J. Kleinhammer-Tramill (Eds.), *Unifying educational systems: Leadership and policy perspectives* (pp. 3–20). New York, NY: Routledge.

Kurth, J., & Mastergeorge, A. M. (2012). Impact of setting and instructional context for adolescents with autism. *The Journal of Special Education, 46*, 36–48. doi:10.1177/0022466910366480

Kurth, J. A., Lyon, K. J., & Shogren, K. A. (2015). Supporting students with severe disabilities in inclusive schools. *Research and Practice for Persons with Severe Disabilities, 40*, 261–274. doi:10.1177/1540796915594160

Kurth, J. A., Marks, S. U., & Bartz, J. (2017). Educating students in inclusive classrooms. In M. L. Wehmeyer & K. A. Shogren (Eds.), *Handbook of research-based practices for educating students with intellectual disability* (pp. 274–295). New York, NY: Routledge.

Kurth, J. A., Morningstar, M. E., & Kozleski, E. (2014). The persistence of highly restrictive special education placements for students with low-incidence disabilities. *Research and Practice for Persons with Severe Disabilities, 39*, 227–239. doi:10.1177/1540796914555580

Lee, S. H., Palmer, S., & Wehmeyer, M. L. (2009). Goal setting and self-monitoring for students with disabilities: Practical tips and ideas for teachers. *Intervention in School and Clinic, 44*, 139–145. doi:10.1177/1053451208326053

Martin, J., Van Dycke, J., Greene, B., Gardner, J., Christensen, W., Woods, L., & Lovett, D. (2006). Direct observation of teacher-directed IEP meetings: Establishing the need for student IEP meeting instruction. *Exceptional Children, 72*, 187–200. doi:10.1177/001440290607200204

Martin, J. E., Marshall, L. H., & Sale, P. (2004). A 3-year study of middle, junior high, and high school IEP meetings. *Exceptional Children, 70*, 285–297. doi:10.1177/001440290407000302

Martin, J. E., Van Dycke, J. L., Christensen, W. R., Greene, B. A., Gardner, J. E., & Lovett, D. L. (2006). Increasing student participation in IEP meetings:

Establishing the self-directed IEP as an evidence-based practice. *Exceptional Children, 72*, 299–316. doi:10.1177/001440290607200303

Mason, C. Y., McGahee-Kovac, M., Johnson, E., & Stillerman, S. (2002). Implementing student-led IEPs: Student participation and student and teacher reactions. *Career Development for Exceptional Individuals, 25*, 171–192. doi:10.1177/088572880202500206

Matzen, K., Ryndak, D., & Nakao, T. (2010). Middle school teams increasing access to general education for students with significant disabilities: Issues encountered and activities observed across contexts. *Remedial and Special Education, 31*, 287–304. doi:10.1177/0741932508327457

McCart, A., Sailor, W., Bezdek, J., & Satter, A. (2014). A framework for inclusive educational delivery systems. *Inclusion, 2*, 252–264. doi:10.1352/2326-6988-2.4.252

McDonnell, J., Johnson, J. W., Polychronis, S., & Risen, T. (2002). Effects of embedded instruction on students with moderate disabilities enrolled in general education classes. *Education and Training in Developmental Disabilities, 37*(4), 363–377.

McDonnell, J., Johnson, J. W., Polychronis, S., Riesen, T., Jameson, M., & Kercher, K. (2006). Comparison of one-to-one embedded instruction in general education classes with small group instruction in special education classes. *Education and Training in Developmental Disabilities, 41*(2), 125–138.

Menlove, R. R., Hudson, P. J., & Suter, D. (2001). A field of IEP dreams: Increasing general education teacher participation in the IEP development process. *Teaching Exceptional Children, 33*, 28–33. doi:10.1177/004005990103300504

Meyer, A., Rose, D. H., Gordon, D. (2014). *Universal design for learning: Theory and Practice.* Wakefield, MA: CAST.

Morningstar, M. E., Shogren, K. A., Lee, H., & Born, K. (2015). Preliminary lessons about supporting participation and learning in inclusive classrooms. *Research and Practice for Persons with Severe Disabilities, 40*, 192–210. doi:10.1177/1540796915594158

Murawski, W. W. (2012). 10 tips for using co-planning time more efficiently. *Teaching Exceptional Children, 44*, 8–15. doi:10.1177/004005991204400401

Pence, A. R., & Dymond, S. K. (2015). Extracurricular school clubs: A time for fun and learning. *Teaching Exceptional Children, 47*, 281–288. doi:10.1177/0040059915580029

Rainforth, B., & York-Barr, J. (1997). *Collaborative teams for students with severe disabilities: Integrating therapy and educational services* (2nd ed.). Baltimore, MD: Paul H. Brookes Publishing Co.

Rossetti, Z. S. (2012). Helping or hindering: The role of secondary educators in facilitating friendship opportunities among students with and without autism or developmental disability. *International Journal of Inclusive Education, 16*, 1259–1272. doi:10.1080/13603116.2011.557448

Rossetti, Z. S., & Goessling, D. P. (2010). Paraeducators' roles in facilitating friendships between secondary students with and without autism spectrum disorders or developmental disabilities. *Teaching Exceptional Children, 42,* 64–70. doi:10.1177/004005991004200608

Ruppar, A. L. (2015). A preliminary study of the literacy experiences of adolescents with severe disabilities. *Remedial and Special Education, 36,* 235–245. doi:10.1177/0741932514558095

Ruppar, A. L., & Gaffney, J. S. (2011). Individualized education program team decisions: A preliminary study of conversations, negotiations, and power. *Research and Practice for Persons with Severe Disabilities, 36,* 11–22. doi:10.2511/rpsd.36.1-2.11

Ryndak, D., Jackson, L. B., & White, J. M. (2013). Involvement and progress in the general education curriculum for students with extensive support needs: K-12 inclusive-education research and implications for the future. *Inclusion, 1,* 28–49. doi:10.1352/2326-6988-1.1.028

Ryndak, D. L., Moore, M. A., Orlando, A. M., & Delano, M. (2009). Access to the general curriculum: The mandate and role of context in research-based practice for students with extensive support needs. *Research and Practice for Persons with Severe Disabilities, 33,* 199–213. doi:10.2511/rpsd.33.4.199

Schalock, R. L., Borthwick-Duffy, S., Bradley, V. J., Buntix, W. H. E., Coulter, D. L., Craig, E. M. P., ... Yeager, M. H. (2010). *Intellectual disability: Definition, classification, and systems of support* (11th ed.). Washington, DC: American Association on Intellectual and Developmental Disabilities.

Shogren, K. A. (2013). A social–ecological analysis of the self-determination literature. *Intellectual and Developmental Disabilities, 51,* 496–511. doi:10.1352/1934-9556-51.6.496

Shogren, K. A., Wehmeyer, M. L., Palmer, S. B., Forber-Pratt, A., Little, T., & Lopez, S. (2015). Causal agency theory: Reconceptualizing a functional model of self-determination. *Education and Training in Autism and Developmental Disabilities, 50*(3), 251–263.

Shogren, K. A., Wehmeyer, M. L., Palmer, S. B., Rifenbark, G., & Little, T. (2015). Relationships between self-determination and postschool outcomes for youth with disabilities. *Journal of Special Education, 48,* 256–267. doi:10.1177/0022466913489733

Shogren, K. A., Wehmeyer, M. L., Schalock, R. L., & Thompson, J. R. (2017). Reframing educational supports for students with intellectual disability through strengths-based approaches. In M. L. Wehmeyer & K. A. Shogren (Eds.), *Handbook of research-based practices for educating students with intellectual disability* (pp. 17–30). New York, NY: Routledge.

Skrtic, T. M. (Ed.). (1995). *Disability and democracy: Reconstructing (special) education for postmodernity.* New York, NY: Teachers College Press.

Smith, J. D., & Wehmeyer, M. L. (2012). *Good blood, bad blood: Science and nature and the myth of the Kalikaks.* Washington, D.C.: American Association on Intellectual and Developmental Disabilities.

Solis, M., Vaughn, S., Swanson, E., & Mcculley, L. (2012). Collaborative models of instruction: The empirical foundations of inclusion and co-teaching. *Psychology in the Schools, 49,* 498–510. doi:10.1002/pits.21606

Soukup, J. H., Wehmeyer, M. L., Bashinski, S. M., & Bovaird, J. A. (2007). Classroom variables and access to the general curriculum for students with disabilities. *Exceptional Children, 74*, 101–120. doi:10.1177/001440290707400106

Sweigart, C. A., & Landrum, T. J. (2015). The impact of number of adults on instruction: Implications for co-teaching. *Preventing School Failure, 59*, 22–29. doi:10.1080/1045988X.2014.919139

Test, D. W., Spooner, F., Holzberg, D., Robertson, C., & Davis, L. L. (2017). Planning for other educational needs and community-based instruction. In M. L. Wehmeyer & K. A. Shogren (Eds.), *Handbook of research-based practices for educating students with intellectual disability* (pp. 130–150). New York, NY: Routledge.

Thompson, J. R., Bradley, V. J., Buntinx, W. H. E., Schalock, R. L., Shogren, K. A., Snell, M. E., ... Yeager, M. H. (2009). Conceptualizing supports and the support needs of people with intellectual disability. *Intellectual and Developmental Disabilities, 47*, 135. doi:10.1352/1934-9556-47.2.135

Thompson, J. R., Hughes, C., Schalock, R. L., Silverman, W., Tasse, M. J., Bryant, B., ... Campbell, E. M. (2002). Integrating supports in assessment and planning. *Mental Retardation, 40*, 390–405. doi:10.1352/0047-6765(2002)0402.0.CO2

Thompson, J. R., Wehmeyer, M. L., & Hughes, C. (2010). Mind the gap! Implications of person–environment fit models of intellectual disability for students, educators, and schools. *Exceptionality, 18*, 168–181. doi:10.1080/09362835.2010.513919

Tomlinson, C. A. (2001). *How to differentiate instruction in mixed-ability classrooms.* Upper Saddle River, NJ: Pearson Education, Inc.

Trent, S. C., Artiles, A. J., & Englert, C. S. (1998). From deficit thinking to social constructivism: A review of theory, research, and practice in special education. *Review of Research in Education, 23*, 277–307. doi:10.3102/0091732X023001277

Turnbull, A., Turnbull, R., Erwin, E. J., Soodak, L. C., & Shogren, K. A. (2015). *Families, professionals, and exceptionality: Positive outcomes through partnerships and trust* (7th ed., pp. 217–246). Boston, MA: Pearson.

Van Dycke, J., Martin, J., & Lovett, D. (2006). Why is this cake on fire? Inviting students into the IEP process. *Teaching Exceptional Children, 38*, 42–47. doi:10.1177/004005990603800306

Wehmeyer, M. L. (Ed.). (2013a). *The story of intellectual disability: An evolution of meaning, understanding, and public perception.* Baltimore, MD: Paul H. Brookes.

Wehmeyer, M. L. (2013b). Disability, disorder, and identity. *Intellectual and Developmental Disabilities, 51*, 122–126. doi:10.1352/1934-9556-51.2.122

Wehmeyer, M. L. (2014). Disability in the 21st century: Seeking a future of equity and full participation. In M. Agran, F. Brown, C. Hughes, C. Quirk, & D. Ryndak (Eds.), *Equity and full participation for individuals with severe disabilities: A vision for the future* (pp. 3–23). Baltimore, MD: Paul H. Brookes.

Wehmeyer, M. L., Lattin, D. L., Lapp-Rincker, G., & Agran, M. (2003). Access to the general curriculum of middle school students with mental retardation. *Remedial and Special Education, 24*, 262–272. doi:10.1177/07419325030240050201

Wehmeyer, M. L., Shogren, K. A., Kurth, J. A., Morningstar, M. E., Kozleski, E. B., Agran, M., ... Ryndak, D. L. (2016). Including students with extensive and pervasive support needs. In J. P. Bakken & F. E. Obiakor (Eds.), *Advances in special education. Volume 31: General and special education inclusion in an age of change: Impact on students with disabilities* (pp. 129–155). London: Emerald Group Publishing.

Wehmeyer, M. L., Shogren, K. A., Little, T. D., & Lopez, S. J. (2017). *Development of self-determination across the life course.* New York, NY: Springer.

Williams-Diehm, K., Wehmeyer, M. L., Palmer, S., Soukup, J. H., & Garner, N. (2008). Self-determination and student involvement in transition planning: A multivariate analysis. *Journal of Developmental Disabilities, 14*(1), 25–36.

World Health Organization. (2002). *Towards a common language for functioning, disability, and health (ICF)*. Geneva, Switzerland: Author.

Yell, M. L., Ryan, J. B., Rozalski, M. E., & Katsiyannis, A. (2009). The U.S. Supreme Court and special education: 2005 to 2007. *Teaching Exceptional Children, 41*, 68–75. doi:10.1100/004005990904100308

Chapter 8

Interventions for Learners with Traumatic Brain Injuries

Angela I. Canto and Danielle M. Eftaxas

Abstract

Hospital emergency rooms document approximately 500,000 traumatic brain injuries (TBIs) in children and adolescents aged 0–14 annually; these prevalence rates do not include those learners evaluated in primary care facilities nor those never evaluated by medical professionals. In this chapter, information on TBI and its effect on learners is provided with emphasis on the idiosyncratic nature of the injury and, thus, the need for individualized reintegration and educational plans. The role of educators in the identification, assessment, reintegration, disability classification, intervention delivery, and progress monitoring is described. Lastly, specific intervention options are presented with cautions that interventions should not be simply picked from a menu, but rather targeting key observations and reported deficits in the physical, cognitive, emotional, social, and behavioral domains.

Keywords: Traumatic brain injuries, TBIs; interventions; accommodations; modifications; educators

Traumatic brain injury (TBI) affects 1.7 million people annually and can range in severity from mild to severe. TBI-related emergency department visits are most frequent in ages 0–4 years (2,193.8 per 100,000), followed

Viewpoints on Interventions for Learners with Disabilities
Advances in Special Education, Volume 33, 169–182
Copyright © 2018 by Emerald Publishing Limited
All rights of reproduction in any form reserved
ISSN: 0270-4013/doi:10.1108/S0270-401320180000033008

by ages 15–24 years (981.9 per 100,000) and ages 5–14 years (888.7 per 100,000). The number of school-aged children who visit an emergency department due to sustaining a TBI is not completely accurate, as mild injuries often go unreported (Chesire, Canto, & Buckley, 2011; Davies, Trunk & Kramer, 2014) or unevaluated by emergency room medical personnel from which prevalence statistics are often derived. Deaths due to TBI are much more prevalent in older adults aged 65 years and up, accounting for 45.2 per 100,000 people (Centers for Disease Control and Prevention [CDC], 2010). Deaths due to TBI in school-aged children (0–24 years old) combined account for 21.8 per 100,000 people.

A common misperception is that most TBI in school-aged children are caused by sports-related injuries. Being struck by or against an object does account for a large portion of emergency department visits; however, falls are the most common cause of TBI in children ages 0–15 years old. The most common mechanism of injury in children ages 15–24 years is assault, followed by falls (CDC, 2010). Incidentally, falls are also the leading cause of TBI in older adults (aged 65 years old and up).

In contrast, TBI in schools is considered a "low incidence disability classification" – a designation that, perhaps, perpetuates the common belief that this injury is rare. Thus, TBIs among learners may be infrequently identified and targeted for services. It is important to note that these injuries are commonly occurring on our school campus and among our learners and students with the deficits resulting from TBI may be eligible for services.

In this chapter, information on TBI and its effect on learners is provided with emphasis on the idiosyncratic nature of the injury and, thus, the need for individualized reintegration and educational plans. The role of educators in the identification, assessment, reintegration, disability classification, intervention delivery, and progress monitoring is described. Lastly, intervention options are presented with cautions that interventions should not be simply picked from a menu, but rather targeting key observations and reported deficits in the physical, cognitive, emotional, social, and behavioral domains of the student.

Traumatic Brain Injuries

The CDC (2010) defines TBI as a "bump, blow, or jolt to the head that disrupts the normal function of the brain." Severity classifications of TBI are commonly determined by a score on the Glasgow Coma scale (Laurer, Meaney, Marguiles, & Mcintosh, 2002). The scale is divided into three categories, indicating if the presenting symptoms relate to a mild, moderate, or severe injury. The most common type of TBI, accounting for 75% of all cases, are classified as mild (mTBI), also known as concussions (CDC, 2010).

Symptoms

Symptoms of postinjury will depend on the level of severity and can affect individuals cognitively, physically, and emotionally. It is common for school-aged children to experience difficulties when returning to school after sustaining a TBI. After sustaining a concussion, common symptoms and complaints at school may include headaches, nausea or vomiting, fatigue, feeling disoriented or confused, and loss of consciousness (Lewandowski & Rieger, 2009). Learners may also experience sensory disturbances, such as blurry vision and ringing in the ears. It is also important to recognize the psychological effects that injured individuals may experience, such as feeling anxious or depressed, and mood instability (CDC, 2010; Mayo Foundation for Medical Education and Research, 2014).

Moderate-to-severe TBIs have more exaggerated symptoms, like confusion and loss of consciousness. Symptoms can also include convulsions or seizures, dilated pupils, and numbness in fingers and toes. These symptoms may appear within the first hour after injury, or days later (Mayo Foundation for Medical Education and Research, 2014). Young children who sustain a TBI may react differently, as they may be unable to express their symptoms. These symptoms may manifest as unusual irritability, changes in sleeping habits, loss of interest, and persistent crying (Mayo Foundation for Medical Education and Research, 2014).

Role of Educators

Given the definition and high prevalence rates of TBI among children and adolescents, it is likely that many educators will have the opportunity to experience the challenges and rewards of working with learners with TBI. This experience is not limited to the classroom teacher, however. Many school personnel, including teachers, will encounter learners with TBI including regular education teachers, special education teachers, administration/staff, school psychologists, school social workers, school nurses, speech/language pathologists, occupational therapists, physical therapists, and athletics personnel. The roles and duties of educators in working with these students are as multifaceted as is the range of educators who may be involved in this process. Educators are key players in the identification, assessment, classification/organization of service delivery, reintegration, intervention implementation, and progress monitoring of learners with TBI.

Identification

For a variety of reasons, educators are unlikely to be aware that a student has sustained a TBI, especially if a mTBI (i.e., concussion). First and foremost, many injuries go unevaluated and untreated by medical personnel. Prevalence statistics cited previously include only those individuals who were evaluated within a medical facility and reported accordingly. Many caregivers of students with concussion may seek the advice of online resources, call the family physician, or simply monitor the student themselves to gauge how severe the injury may be. Thus, prevalence statistics are likely a significant under-representation of the actual number of students with TBI at any given time (Chesire et al., 2011).

However, even for those students who were evaluated and diagnosed with TBI, the identification rate in schools remains alarmingly low (Chesire et al., 2011). Due to Health Insurance Portability and Accountability Act of 1996 (HIPPA) regulations and logistical impediments, communication transfer between medical and school personnel is abysmally low (Bradley-Klug, Fundman, Nadeau, Cunningham, Ogg, 2010; Bradley-Klug, Garafano, Lynn, DeLoatch, Lam, 2015; Chesire et al., 2011). Physicians cite lack of central school-based point of contact and lack of time (Bradley-Klug et al., 2010) as primary barriers to continuity of care across settings, relying instead on providing the medical information to the caregivers. Unfortunately, caregivers also often underestimate the impact the injury may have on the student's academic trajectory as well as the availability of school-based resources to assess, monitor, and intervene and/or accommodate if needed (Canto, Chesire, Buckley, Andrews, & Roehrig, 2014). Thus, if the student attends school subsequent to injury, the educators may, in fact, have to rely on their own observations and comparisons to baseline functioning in identifying students who may have sustained a TBI.

As discussed previously, the range of deficits for even the mild forms of TBI can vary across physical, cognitive, emotional, social, and behavioral domains (see Fig. 1) in varying degrees of severity. These observed deficits can mimic a variety of other commonly occurring disorders affecting learners in classrooms (e.g., Attention deficit hyperactivity disorder (ADHD).

Neurological/Physical Symptoms	Cognitive Impairments	Emotional Symptoms	Social Effects	Behavioral Symptoms
Headaches	Attention	Irritability	Over/under reactive	Increased aggression
Sleep disturbances	Concentration	Anger/labile mood	Social awkwardness	Substance use or abuse
Seizures	Auditory processing	Apathy	Withdrawal or isolation	Impulsive behavior
Sensory/motor impairments	Executive functioning	Emotional regression	Difficulty perspective taking	Conflict with authority
Light/sound sensitivities	Word retrieval	Egocentrism	Disrupted peer relations	Noncompliance
Dizziness	Working memory	Anxiety		Sexual acting out
Blurred vision		Decreased motivation		
		Depression		
		Posttraumatic Stress disorder		

Fig. 1: Effects of TBI and mTBI across Domains.

Note: Adapted from Jantz, Comerchero, Canto, and Pierson (2015); reprinted with permission from Emerald.

If teachers do not carefully screen and assess students' knowledge, skills, and achievement, the presentation of new symptoms across the aforementioned domains may lead educators to consider erroneous explanations. Observed cognitive deficits can mimic learning disorders, disorders in executive functioning, processing disorders, and even ADHD (Jantz, Davies, & Bigler, 2014). Emotional, social, and behavioral changes could easily be attributed to any number of causes, including normal maturation and development, particularly for learners at typical ages for puberty. Similarly, physical symptoms can mimic a variety of non-TBI medical illnesses and disorders, including sleep disorders, intoxication, and even somatization of emotional dysregulation.

In order to better facilitate accurate identification of TBI etiology, knowledge of prior functioning and interviews are important tools. Knowledge of the learner's baseline level of functioning and comparison of that baseline to current functioning, and symptom presentation is an important first clue that a TBI may have occurred. The second tool is perhaps the easiest to use – simply asking the student or the caregiver regarding any recent or past injuries sustained to the head, including sports, motor vehicle collisions, or hard falls at home or play that may have coincided with a change in functioning in any of the aforementioned domains. Obtaining this abbreviated psychosocial history can provide a multidisciplinary team of educators the critical information needed for the next step – evaluation and/or formal assessment.

Assessment

Strong Tier 1 assessments of baseline functioning (universal screenings) and regular progress monitoring are critical in all classrooms for all students as a core feature of typical response-to-intervention (RTI) problem-solving frameworks in schools (Shapiro, 2017). With this core framework in place, identifying students throughout the academic year that demonstrate marked differences in their performance is more easily facilitated. Similarly, for learners who demonstrate deficits at the beginning of the year, comparisons to prior years' academic performance may also be useful if injury occurred over the summer months.

Further assessments of observed deficits including screenings, psychosocial history interviews, behavioral checklists, observational assessments, and "Can't Do/Won't Do" (VanDerHeyden & Witt, 2008) assessments may all provide critical information to the multidisciplinary team of educators that handle referrals for further evaluation. The multidisciplinary team may be called different things in different areas such as a problem-solving team, child study team, school-based intervention team, etc. It is this team of educators that then often determines whether additional assessments of cognitive and academic functioning are warranted. This may or may not include specific neurocognitive testing by school-based or external professionals.

It is helpful during this formal individual evaluation to further query the history of head injuries; often caregivers or the learners themselves may recall incidents not previously reported. Documentation of a positive or negative history of head injuries and/or documented TBI can be valuable information to rule out any acquired injury etiology of observed deficits. Depending on whether the student meets the eligibility criteria for more formal services, educators have a several options to consider with regard to classification and mechanisms for service delivery.

Reintegration

Reintegration is a multisystemic process incorporating educators, learners, caregivers, medical staff, and the multidisciplinary team. Reintegration is best facilitated when there is ongoing communication between the systems. As one of the often-cited key barriers to service delivery for learners with TBI (Canto et al., 2014), lack of communication hinders successful reintegration for all levels of severity. Reintegration includes facilitation of the learner's return to full educational participation at the appropriate pace for the needs of the learner's physical and psychosocial recovery. Protocols for this process are needed at the school and district levels to provide educators with the guidance and process details needed to support successful transition and reintegration, even if that simply means a concussion on the football field during practice Tuesday night and transition to education (with observation) the following school day.

When a child is returning to school after sustaining a TBI, a "return to learn" (Baker et al., 2014) protocol is recommended. While there is not a one-size-fits-all approach to concussion and TBI recovery and each student should be assessed individually, the protocol can be consistent across cases in terms of: documentation, gathering of data regarding baseline functioning, observation, communication with caregivers and medical staff as needed, assessment, and progress monitoring. The return to learn team can mimic the multidisciplinary problem-solving team and be comprised of several members including teachers, school nurses, school psychologists, and athletic trainers. Depending on the school and district, different school personnel may be responsible for monitoring students' progress in regards to cognitive functioning. It may be appropriate to ease the student back into school, with a reduced workload or by offering frequent breaks from doing work. Similarly, depending on the severity, the student may not be able to immediately return to school for multiple days and may require partial days at school (Bradley-Klug et al., 2015).

In addition to observation by educators and family, it is often suggested that the student participate in self-monitoring, specifically monitoring their level of cognitive function (Halstead et al., 2013). Students can self-monitor their cognitive function by keeping track of how long they work for without increased symptoms and requesting breaks as needed. Self-monitoring of symptoms may be a more common tactic with older students, as they are likely better able to keep track of the progression of their symptoms, and notify the multidisciplinary team if they worsen. Like with other types of injuries, physical rest is important, and cognitive rest should be viewed with equal importance. The role of cognitive rest on TBI recovery is supported by several organizations (National Association of School Nurses, American Academy of Pediatrics) and researchers (Bradley-Klug et al., 2015; Lewandowski & Reiger, 2009; Olympia, Ritter, Brady & Bramley, 2016).

In general, a return to learn protocol should have several key educator roles including assessment, intervention, progress monitoring, and adjustments as needed (Bradley-Klug et al., 2015). Again, the emphasis should be on multisystemic collaboration and communication between medical and academic teams (Olympia et al., 2016).

Disability Classification and Mechanisms for Service Delivery

Depending on whether the student meets the eligibility criteria for more formal services, educators have several options to consider with regard to classification and mechanisms for service delivery (Canto, Crisp, Larach, Blankenship, 2016; Chesire et al., 2015), extending to hospital and home-based educational services to service delivery within the general education classroom. Of these options, the decision will often depend upon the presenting symptoms (persistence and severity), the acuteness of need for intervention, and the particular school-based intervention framework (e.g., RTI). The role of educators in this process is in the consideration and implementation of these options.

For moderate-to-severe TBI, the development of a formal Individualized Education Program (IEP) may be the most appropriate as outlined in the 2004 Individuals with Disabilities Education Improvement Act (IDEIA). As one of 13 disability classification categories, TBI is defined in IDEIA (2004) as follows:

> an acquired injury to the brain caused by an external force, resulting in total or partial functional disability or psychosocial impairment, or both, that adversely affects a child's educational performance. Traumatic brain injury applies to open or closed head injuries resulting in impairments in one or more areas, such as cognition; language; memory; attention; reasoning; abstract thinking; judgment; problem-solving; sensory, perceptual, and motor abilities; psychosocial behavior; physical functions; information processing; and speech. Traumatic brain injury does not apply to brain injuries that are congenital or degenerative, or to brain injuries induced by birth trauma.

For the latter types of brain injury (e.g., congenital or injuries due to birth trauma), learners may be served within the other health impairment (OHI) classification. Within both classifications, students are eligible for IEPs, developed collaboratively within the multidisciplinary team (which also includes caregivers and learners as team members). In summary, a formal IEP includes all of the following:

(1) statement of present level of functioning;
(2) measureable goal statements (both academic and functional) if learner will participate in regular districtwide/statewide assessments;
(3) statement of how and when progress will be measured and reported;
(4) description of the intervention supports and aids that will be provided within general or special education, using empirically supported interventions where possible;
(5) statement regarding the student's participation with nondisabled peers;
(6) statement of any testing accommodations or explanations why the student cannot participate in the regular assessment;
(7) start date, frequency, duration, and location of service delivery;
(8) statement on appropriate postsecondary goals for first IEP after student turns 16 (or younger if elected by IEP team); and
(9) statement about the transfer of rights at age of majority (if applicable in that state) no less than one year before age of majority (IDEIA, 2004; Jacob, Decker, & Hartshorne, 2011).

Other options for service delivery include school-based problem-solving teams, "504 plans", and nursing plans (Canto et al., 2016; Chesire et al., 2015). Using a multitiered system of support, problem-solving teams can begin to monitor responsiveness to designated interventions with very little delay between assessment, intervention, and review of responsiveness due the high frequency of these meetings. A primary benefit of this type of approach, especially for mTBIs is the ability to document early symptom presentation, resolution, and sleeper effects (those effects that become more pronounced over time).

The phrase "504 plans" is an abbreviation of educational plans with basis in Section 504 of the Rehabilitation Act of 1973, which provides equal access to school for students with TBI. In contrast to IEPs where content and goals can be restructured according to the needs of the disability, this anti-discrimination law prevents altering the content complexity or delivery, but does allow modifications and accommodations to promote equal access. While likely more often used in shorter duration (e.g., six months), these plans can follow the students through postsecondary and workplace settings (Chesire et al., 2015). If identified as the appropriate vehicle, 504 plans serve as a guide for educators in providing recommended accommodations and modifications and become part of the learner's permanent academic record.

Lastly, nursing plans may be useful for students with TBI presenting with physical symptomology. Coordinated by the school nurse, the benefit of nursing plans is to have trained medical personnel follow up the symptom presentation over time and provide recommendations for continued physical recovery. Educators then work with the nurse to ensure delivery is consistent with the idiosyncratic physical needs and constraints imposed by the TBI.

Intervention Implementation

Educators are clearly the primary individuals identifying, designing, and implementing interventions for learners in the school-based environment. Interventions should be thoughtfully considered with consideration of the empirical-basis for their support when available (IDEIA, 2004) and suitability for the idiosyncratic symptom presentation. Inherent in intervention implementation is the timeframe for regular progress review, or systematic progress monitoring. Many symptoms resolve and present at different rates depending on the speed of healing, severity of injury, and the cognitive, physical, and sensory demands placed on the learner with TBI.

For example, symptoms of mTBIs often resolve within three weeks from injury (Halstead et al., 2013). However, an increase in the sensory environment of the fast-paced and stimulating school environment (or perhaps even within video game activities at home) may increase headaches experienced by the learner with TBI. Interventions may or may not fall into the categories of adaptations or modifications.

Adaptations versus Modifications. The definition of an accommodation, from various sources, is a change made to instruction/assessment intended to help students fully access the general education curriculum without changing the instructional content (e.g., Smith & Canto, 2015). These in-class and on-campus accommodations are considered by the multidisciplinary team and adopted and documented if deemed appropriate, with appropriate regular progress monitoring review points specified. If necessary, similar accommodations could also be made at home (Halstead et al., 2013). Common accommodations identified by multidisciplinary teams include extended time on tests or assignments, frequent breaks, alternate/small group test settings, restrictions in physical education, and providing notes for the student (Eftaxas & Canto, 2017; Smith & Canto, 2015).

Modifications are defined as alterations made to instruction and/or assessment that change, lower, or reduce learning or assessment expectations (Smith & Canto, 2015). The major difference between accommodations and modifications is the level of expectation from the student, changes that often require a specified IEP. Modifications within an IEP alter what is required or expected of the student, whereas accommodations (504 Plans) are supports that assist the student in obtaining the work expected of all students (Halstead et al., 2013).

Identification of appropriate modifications often include the input of a school-based team, as an IEP is developed based on that students specific and unique needs. Modifications identified by multidisciplinary problem-solving team members as being commonly implemented include reducing or modifying the students' workload, differentiated instruction, altering academic goals, consideration of special education placement, and the use of assistive technology (Eftaxas & Canto, 2017).

Progress Monitoring

Finally, educators are key in the progress monitoring of learners with TBI. Progress monitoring is needed to evaluate the unique symptoms experienced by the learner after TBI, the rehabilitation and recovery from injury, as well as the RTIs. Additionally, progress monitoring is needed for ongoing classification and the identification of potentially more suitable interventions, accommodations, or modifications as symptoms abate or present themselves over time. Progress monitoring tools should be sensitive to short-term changes in functioning including curriculum-based measures and symptom checklists. Medical re-evaluations may also be needed to effectively monitor the recovery from injury. Likely unsuitable progress monitoring measures would include annual summative state or districtwide assessments of proficiency. While those assessments may serve other valuable purposes, they are not sensitive or frequent enough to measure small changes in recovery for the better or worse.

Interventions for TBI

Given the unique constellation of symptom presentation for learners with TBI, it is imperative that interventions are selected with careful consideration of observed or reported domain area deficits (in lieu of a manualized or one-size-fits-all) approach. As lamented by Jantz et al. (2014), the literature identifying interventions specifically targeting emotional, social, and behavior interventions experienced by learners with TBI is limited.

That said, many of the recommended interventions are those that, regardless of etiology, focus on *key deficit skills or processes*. For example, many interventions targeting impaired executive functioning for learners with ADHD and other disability groups (such as learning disabilities) are similarly recommended for learners with TBI exhibiting the same skill or performance deficits (e.g., use of advanced organizers and empathic redirection of off-task behavior). Thus, it is recommended that empirically supported interventions are selected for specific observed deficits across all domains listed in Fig. 1 based on the need as determined by the multidisciplinary intervention team given observed and reported symptoms.

Conclusion

Historically, a neglected population in the broad education literature and in the broader social context, the attention on learners with TBI has thankfully increased very recently. Given the vast numbers of school-aged children and adolescents sustaining a TBI each year, it is surprising that this area is still considered a low-incidence disability. That said, it is highly likely that educators across schools will interact with one or more learners with TBI each year in classrooms.

In this chapter, a primer on TBI and its effect on learners was presented with emphasis on the idiosyncratic nature of the injury and, thus, the need for individualized reintegration and educational plans. The role of educators in the identification, assessment, reintegration, disability classification, intervention delivery, and progress monitoring was described. Lastly, specific intervention options were discussed with cautions that interventions should not be simply picked from a menu, but rather targeting key observations and reported deficits in the physical, cognitive, emotional, social, and behavioral domains.

We are optimistic that the future may be brighter for learners with TBI, given increased attention to the social significance of this problem, especially when educators focus on the individualized needs of these students over time.

References

Baker, J. G., Rieger, B. P., McAvoy, K., Leddy, J. J., Master, C. L., Lana, S. J., & Willer, B. S. (2014). Principles for return to learn after concussion. *International Journal of Clinical Practice, 68*(11), 1286–1288.

Bradley-Klug, K. L., Fundman, A. N., Nadeau, J., Cunningham, J., & Ogg, J. (2010). Communication and collaboration with schools: Pediatricians' perspectives. *Journal of Applied School Psychology, 26*(4), 263–281. doi:10.1080/15377903.2010.518583

Bradley-Klug, K. L., Garofano, J., Lynn, C., DeLoatche, K. J., & Lam, G. Y. H. (2015). Returning to school after a concussion: Facilitating problem solving through effective communication. *School Psychology Forum, 9*(3), 184–198.

Canto, A. I., Chesire, D. J., Buckley, V. A., Andrews, T. W., & Roehrig, A. D. (2014). Barriers to meeting the needs of students with traumatic brain injury. *Educational Psychology in Practice: Theory, Research and Practice in Educational Psychology, 30*(1), 88–103. doi:10.1080/20667363.2014.883498

Canto, A. I., Crisp, M. A., Larach, H., & Blankenship, A. P. (2016). Inclusion and Students with Traumatic Brain Injuries. In General and Special Education Inclusion in an Age of Change: Impact on Students with Disabilities (pp. 157–177). Emerald Group Publishing Limited..

Centers for Disease Control and Prevention. (2010). *Traumatic brain injury in the United States: Emergency department visits, hospitalizations and deaths, 2002–2006.* Retrieved from http://www.cdc.gov/traumaticbraininjury.

Chesire, D. J., Canto, A. I., & Buckley, V. A. (2011). Hospital–school collaboration to serve the needs of children with traumatic brain injury (TBI). *Journal of Applied School Psychology, 27*(1), 60–76.

Chesire, D. J., Buckley, V. A., Leach, S. L., Scott, R. A., & Scott, K. K. (2015). Navigating the terrain in the identification and program development for children with mild traumatic brain injuries. *School Psychology Forum*, 9(3), 199–213.

Davies, S. C., Trunk, D. J., & Kramer, M. M. (2014). Traumatic brain injury and the transition to postsecondary education: Recommendations for student success. *School Psychology Forum*, *3*(8), 168–181.

Eftaxas, D. M., & Canto, A. I. (2017). *School psychologists' knowledge of traumatic brain injuries and willingness to lead a concussion team.* Unpublished manuscript. Department of Educational Psychology and Learning Systems, Florida State University, Tallahassee, FL.

Halstead, M. E., McAvoy, K., Devore, C. D., Carl, R., Lee, M., & Logan, K. (2013). Returning to learning following a concussion. *Pediatrics*, *132*(5), 948–957. doi:10.1542/peds.2013-2867

Jantz, P. B., Davies, S. C., & Bigler, E. D. (2014). *Working with traumatic brain injury in schools: Transition, assessment, and intervention.* New York, NY: Routledge.

Jantz, P. B., Comerchero, V. A., Canto, A., & Pierson, E. (2015). Traumatic brain injury and grief: Considerations and practical strategies for school psychologists. *Contemporary School Psychology*, 19, 218-229. doi: 10.1007/s40688-015-0047-9

Laurer, L. L., Meaney, D. F., Margulies, S. S., Mcintosh, T. K. (2002). Modeling brain injury/trauma. In V. S. Ramachandran (Ed.), *Encyclopedia of the human brain.* Oxford: Elsevier Science & Technology.

Lewandowski, L. J., & Rieger, B. (2009). The role of a school psychologist in concussion. *Journal of Applied School Psychology*, 25(1), 95–110. doi:10.1080/15377900802484547

Mayo Foundation for Medical Education and Research. (2014). *Traumatic brain injury.* Retrieved from http://www.mayoclinic.org/diseases-conditions/traumatic-brain- injury/basics/symptoms/con-20029302

Olympia, R. P., Ritter, J. T., Brady, J., & Bramley, H. (2016). Return to learning after a concussion and compliance with recommendations for cognitive rest. *Clinical Journal of Sport Medicine*, *26*(2), 115–119. doi.org/10.1097/JSM.0000000000000208

Shapiro, E. S. (2017). *Tiered instruction and intervention in a response-to-intervention model.* National Center for Learning Disabilities. Retrieved from http://www.rtinetwork.org/essential/tieredinstruction/tiered-instruction-and-intervention-rti-model

Smith, S. M., & Canto, A. I. (2015). Trends in traumatic brain injury research in school psychology journals 1985–2014. *School Psychology Forum*, *9*(3), 165–183.

VanDerHeyden, A. M., & Witt, J. C. (2008). Best practices in can't do/won't do assessment. In A. Thomas & J. Grimes (Eds.). *Best practices in school psychology* (5th ed., pp. 131–140). Bethesda, MD: National Association of School Psychologists.

Chapter 9

An Overview of Classroom-based Speech-Language Pathology Services

Rita L. Bailey

Abstract

Speech pathology services have not been traditionally provided within school classroom settings. This chapter will describe the service-delivery options for provision of speech pathology services in classroom settings. A review of select research related to the efficacy of these services is included as applied examples for educators.

Keywords: Classroom-based; speech pathology; inclusive; service-delivery models; visual supports

This chapter is intended to share evidence-based methods for provision of speech pathology services in classroom settings. Speech-language pathologists (SLPs), special educators, and other school personnel who teach children with disabilities will find information regarding available options for provision of speech pathology services within school classroom settings with specific examples taken from recent peer-reviewed research.

Speech, language, hearing, and swallowing disorders are an educational priority because they threaten the academic, social, and emotional well-being of children with disabilities. These disorders can have an effect on the ability to fully engage with instruction and participate in learning processes in and out of school. The purpose of this chapter is to provide

Viewpoints on Interventions for Learners with Disabilities
Advances in Special Education, Volume 33, 183–196
Copyright © 2018 by Emerald Publishing Limited
All rights of reproduction in any form reserved
ISSN: 0270-4013/doi:10.1108/S0270-401320180000033009

practical and research-based techniques and strategies for provision of classroom-based speech pathology services in inclusive educational environments. Provision of speech pathology services within public school classrooms has been described as "nontraditional" (Nippold, 2011), and it is one of many models for service delivery that should be considered as a part of a wide continuum of service-delivery options. Great care was taken to provide descriptions of this service-delivery model that are mindful of the realities of school environments, taking into consideration the time and resource constraints of school personnel, and have at least the beginnings of an evidence-base. Therefore, although the strategies described in this chapter provide the reader with ideas for provision of speech pathology services in the school environment, it is not meant to be an all-inclusive guide for practitioners.

While classroom-based speech pathology services are the focus of this chapter, it is important to note that a wide variety of options exist for delivery of speech-language pathology services for students with communication disorders in the public schools. Decisions regarding intervention and service-delivery are determined by many factors. According to the American Speech-Language-Hearing Association's (ASHA, 2000) *Guidelines for the Roles and Responsibilities of the School-Based Speech-Language Pathologist* document, the following principles must guide SLPs as they determine treatment plans for school-based services:

(a) "Disability is a natural part of the human experience and in no way diminishes the right of individuals to participate in or contribute to society. Improving educational results for children with disabilities is an essential element of our national policy of ensuring equality of opportunity, full participation, independent living, and economic self-sufficiency for individuals with disabilities." (U.S. Congress, 1997 [Sec. 601(c)])

(b) Society's trends and challenges affect the role of SLPs.

(c) Educational success leads to productive citizens.

(d) Language is the foundation for learning within all academic subjects.

(e) School-based SLPs help students maximize their communication skills to support learning.

(f) The school-based SLP's goal is to remediate, ameliorate, or alleviate student communication problems within the educational environment.

(g) A student-centered focus drives team decision-making.

    (h) Comprehensive assessment and thorough evaluation provide information for appropriate eligibility, intervention, and dismissal decisions.

    (i) Intervention focuses on the student's abilities, rather than disabilities.

    (j) Intervention plans are consistent with current research and practice.

    (k) Address the need for the specific service provider and the relation to the "team" of members involved in instruction of a child receiving this service. (p. 2)

SLPs should follow these guidelines to best determine appropriate services and service-delivery methods for students with speech, language, hearing, and/or swallowing impairments.

School-Based Speech Pathology Services

SLPs generally assess, diagnose, treat, and help to improve development of delayed or impaired speech, language, literacy, cognitive-communicative, voice, swallowing, and fluency skills that may negatively impact students' abilities to learn and participate fully in school environments. As school-based professionals, SLPs provide individualized instruction and training for students with a wide range of speech sound disorders. They work with students who stutter or exhibit other fluency disorders. They also provide therapy for students with voice problems, such as abnormal vocal pitch or impaired voice quality. Students who experience cognitive-communicative impairments, such as decreased attention, memory, and executive functioning are provided speech pathology services with the goal of minimizing the educational impact of these deficits and/or to improve skills in these areas. SLPs also provide therapy services for students with difficulties understanding and producing language in all forms, and students who use augmentative and/or alternative forms of communication (ASHA, 2016; see Table 1).

Students with swallowing impairments, known as dysphagia, may also receive speech therapy services from school-based SLPs (Bailey, Stoner, Angell, & Fetzer, 2008). Through their work with students, SLPs gain knowledge about students and the unique communication comprehension and production skills and deficit areas that need to be addressed. With the common goal of the public schools focusing on educating all children, SLPs may find that the specialized information they possess is most

Table 1: SLP Practice Areas.

1. Fluency disorders	Stuttering
	Cluttering
2. Disorders of motor planning and execution	Articulation
	Phonological
3. Language-spoken and written	Listening
	Speaking
	Processing
	Reading
	Writing
	Pragmatics
	Phonology
	Morphology
	Syntax
	Semantics
	Pragmatics
4. Cognition	Attention
	Memory
	Problem-solving
	Executive functioning
5. Voice	Phonation
	Quality
	Pitch
	Loudness
	Alaryngeal voice
6. Feeding and swallowing	Oral phase
	Pharyngeal phase
	Atypical eating
7. Auditory habilitation or rehabilitation	Language, communication and listening skills impacted by hearing loss, deafness

effectively shared with other school personnel to be implemented within classrooms, rather than individually providing the interventions. This must be done in a way that facilitates knowledge and skill development so that children can become proficient communicators. That is why it is so important to measure the effect of classroom-based interventions.

In order to provide the most comprehensive SLP services then, it is optimal that they be provided in partnership with other school professionals. Nippold (2012) stated that:

> to maximize the chances of effective remediation, SLPs must work closely with other school professionals, such as special educators, who often have considerable expertise in remediating reading deficits, and with counselors who can help students learn positive strategies for coping with frustration. (p. 117)

Nippold (2011) also specifically suggested that "...it is critical that the SLP work cooperatively with other school-based professionals, especially with classroom teachers, special education teachers, and principals" (p. 393).

Classroom-Based Models

Several types of classroom-based service models have been suggested for use in the field of education (Friend & Cook, 2010). With the convergence of both the inclusive education movement and the more recent response to intervention initiative, an increased number of individualized educational services currently must be provided to students with and without disabilities in general education classrooms. An obvious response to this need is the use of co-teaching education models. In co-teaching, two or more school-based professionals take collective responsibility for their students. Typically, a co-teaching model involves a general education teacher paired with a special education teacher or other specialist, such as a SLP. Together they work to deliver instruction to a classroom of students with mixed abilities.

Several variations of a co-teaching model exist. These include a one-teach, one-assist model, station teaching, parallel teaching, alternative or small group teaching, and team teaching. The use of these general approaches may be static or change according to the instructional applications or needs of individual students and classrooms (Gregory & Kuzmich, 2005). Although a single co-teaching model may be adopted for use across schools, classrooms, and lessons, in order to best individualize education for student needs, SLPs who serve students in this way should choose to use certain models for specific instructional, classroom, or student reasons. Therefore, it is important that general and special educators have a working understanding of a variety of models of co-teaching that are available for use. Friend and Cook (2010) described the following service delivery options as options for co-teaching models:

(a) One teach, one observe – SLP either serves as a classroom instructor or an observer, while the classroom teacher provides instruction.
Example: While a general or special educator leads a class language lesson, an SLP attends to each student with identified language deficits who receives speech pathology services.
(b) One teach, one "drift" – one professional assumes primary teaching responsibilities, while the other assists individual students.
Example: While an SLP leads a class lesson on listening skills, the general or special educator ensures that the classroom remains quiet by attending to those who are disrupting and assisting them in the task(s).
(c) Station teaching – each teaches at a separate center.
Example: Both the classroom teacher and an SLP develop stations within the classroom where smaller groups come to work on specific vocabulary skills.
(d) Parallel teaching – each instructs half the class using the same material.
Example: Students are split into two groups and a classroom instructor each teach the unit. While the same materials may be used, the SLP may individualize instructional strategies to match the skills and attributes of the students' in the classroom who receive speech pathology services.
(e) Remedial teaching – one presents material, while the other re-teaches previously taught material.
Example: An SLP re-teaches material for students who have language delays or disorders, while the classroom teacher moves to new material.
(f) Supplemental teaching – one presents the lesson in a standard format while the other adapts the lesson.
Example: The classroom instructor presents the lesson in a standard format, while the SLP adapts the lesson for particular students and their learning needs.

While description of these commonly used co-teaching service delivery options may be helpful, unfortunately, there is not a lot of data available about the efficacy of these models and their use in the field of speech pathology. A cursory understanding of the effectiveness of these methods was ascertained with the completion of a metasynthesis of qualitative research related to co-teaching with special and general educators in inclusive classrooms (Scruggs, Mastropieri, & McDuffie, 2007). The researchers evaluated 32 qualitative investigations completed from 1989 to 2005. Their purpose was to summarize and integrate the findings of the available qualitative research in a systematic way in order to "shed light on the perspectives of co-teaching from the perspectives of relevant research" (p. 394). The results of their metasynthesis found that professionals using the co-teaching models reported that for co-teaching to be effective, there was a consistent need for administrative support, cooperation/voluntary participation from teachers in the co-teaching model, compatibility between co-teachers, and a need for planning time, and training. For this to be used effectively, at a minimum, administrative support for common planning time and scheduling would be required. Additionally, it may be important to allow those who wish to co-teach have a role in how they are paired for instructional periods to facilitate increased compatibility. Specific professional development requests included training in peer mediation, strategy instruction, self-advocacy, and self-monitoring skills.

Clearly, the use and effectiveness of co-teaching service-delivery models has not been agreed-upon within the field of speech-language pathology. As in all cases, the appropriate education plan for students with disabilities is one that is individualized for the needs of each student. Co-teaching models are just one type of classroom-based intervention.

Classroom-Based Interventions

In this chapter, the author will provide an overview of select published examples of speech pathology services delivered within classrooms in cases where researchers reported measuring a positive therapeutic effect of these interventions. An overview of published research involving speech pathology interventions provided within classroom-based environments will be summarized and these descriptions of classroom-based interventions that have indicated a positive therapeutic result will be shared as examples of classroom-based speech pathology services for school-based professionals.

Several published research reports have described speech pathology services provided within general education classrooms. Examples that involve classroom-based interventions for a wide variety of *language delays and impairments* were among those cited most often in published reports. Therapists and other school-based professionals may find these examples useful when determining for themselves the best approaches for individual students.

Overview of Classroom-Based Approaches

Recently, a large classroom-based investigation was conducted with 104 children in 39 pre-kindergarten classrooms in Florida, Ohio, and Kansas to examine the impact of two phonemic awareness interventions on measures of phonological awareness including skills such as alphabet knowledge and other measures of early literacy skills (Goldstein et al., 2017). Children included in this investigation had been found not to be responsive to prior whole classroom instruction called "core" instruction. In this case, classroom teachers and teacher aides were trained by SLPs to provide interventions in small groups of children within their classrooms and then were observed and supported in these activities by the researchers. Intervention sessions followed one of the two curricula for phonological awareness, and groups of children were advanced through the lessons as they demonstrated acquisition of early literacy skills at each level. While not all pre- to posttest measures showed significant improvement, the vast majority of students included in the interventions were found to benefit from these additional classroom-based lessons on phonemic awareness.

Gillam, Olszewski, Fargo, and Gillam (2014) completed an investigation to determine the impact of a narrative and vocabulary instruction program provided by an SLP in a regular first-grade classroom when compared to a similar classroom without the additional instruction. In this study, the SLP provided the intervention targeting skills needed to produce narratives in just one of two Title 1 classrooms that were similar in student demographics and pre-project skill levels. Each classroom had seven bilingual children. Lessons involved skills such as story retelling, story generation, and listening and reading comprehension skills in the SLP-administered program along with additional instruction on targeted vocabulary. The SLP provided the instruction for 30 minutes, three times per week for 6 weeks as the instructor for the class during the intervention, while an undergraduate student provided assistance to the SLP as needed. This maintained the same teacher to student ratio for both classrooms. The other classroom received instruction provided by a general education teacher from the standard, district-approved curriculum (with no specific instruction on narration). Following this classroom-based intervention, the children in the experimental group exhibited more complex narratives than the other group as well as showing greater improvements in measures of vocabulary at post-test. The instructional set up in this investigation appears to be roughly similar to the "one teach, one drift" co-teaching model described by Friend and Cook (2010).

Kouri (2016) reported on the impact of implementation of three different types of feedback cueing strategies for children ranging from age 7 years to 9 years who had been identified to have reading and language delays. Guided reading sessions were implemented once per week in three grade school classrooms and a university speech and hearing clinic. The interventions were provided by graduate students in their fourth semester of graduate training in a university program in speech pathology. Interventions included three feedback strategies. The first strategy was graphophonemic feedback. This includes a hierarchy of prompts and cues based on skills such as letter-sound identifications, vowel corrections, segmenting, blending, and chunking orthographic units. The second strategy was feedback related to meaning. This includes providing various semantic, syntactic, and visual context cues. The third strategy was a mix of both graphophonemic and meaning feedback cues. In this study, positive results were indicated for the feedback strategies used, with the mixed feedback strategies reported as more effective for facilitating word error corrections than the other two interventions. Unfortunately, additional information about the classroom and clinical settings was not provided, so it is not clear whether the students' classroom teachers were present for the intervention or not.

Conversely, Starling, Munro, Togher, and Arciuli (2012) described a classroom-based intervention where an SLP-trained inclusive secondary schoolteacher makes modifications to their oral and written instructional language for the purpose of providing classroom-based support to adolescent students with language impairments. In this project, the researchers measured the impact of a training program for classroom teachers that taught them to provide specific language supports to a classroom of students with language impairments. Forty-three students in two schools were divided into a control group (16 males, 6 females) and an experimental group (17 males, 4 females) with similar pre-project assessment levels. Classroom teachers were taught to modify their written and oral language and were provided training in facilitating information processing and direct vocabulary instruction within the existing classroom curriculum. A total of ten 50-minute instructional sessions were provided to the classroom teachers. The teachers were taught modifying written language by breaking large amounts of written language into smaller, visually distinct sections, adding graphics and visual icons, providing descriptions for vocabulary, and making sure that questions were listed on the same page as the text being read. Teachers were also taught to modify their oral language by using explicit instructions rather than inferred, allowing additional time for students to respond, repeating and rephrasing key information, and facing the class when delivering important information. Teachers were taught to facilitate information processing by deconstructing complex texts through the use of a mind map, identifying key facts, providing a visual planner, providing sequencing aids, and involving the whole class in creating visual aids for the lesson. Finally, teachers were taught to use instruction techniques that included prioritizing vocabulary for each new curricular topic, embedding vocabulary in activities such as creation of visual symbols, and conducting whole-class lessons on morphemic analysis. Results of this randomized controlled study indicated that teachers significantly increased their use of the language modification techniques in the experimental group. Further, students in the experimental group showed significant improvement in written expression and listening comprehensive relative to the control group. This example is in agreement with Nippold's (2012) recommendation that "SLPs be able to share with teachers their expertise in language development, language disorders, and language intervention techniques – information that can benefit many students in a typical classroom" (p. 394).

A trained and teacher-implemented intervention model has also been used successfully with younger children to encourage improved literacy development. In Carson, Gillon, and Bousted's (2013) a quasi-experimental design investigation was employed in classroom settings to measure the impact of training teachers to implement a programmed intervention for phonological awareness, reading, and spelling development. The investigation included 129 5-year-old children in several classrooms. The phonological awareness instruction was delivered by teachers in addition to their regular literacy instruction in classrooms of children with and without spoken language impairment (SLI) for 10-weeks. An additional 95 children received the regular literacy instruction, which included phonics instruction, but did not specifically target phonological awareness training only for the same 10-weeks of the semester. The effects of the intervention were measured in both groups and results indicated that children with SLI showed significant improvements in phonological awareness, reading, and spelling skills. In addition, only 6% of the children who received the intervention were found to have word decoding difficulties as compared to 26% of the children who received only the regular literacy instruction.

Interventions for children with greater communication support needs have long been classroom-based, such as the use of visual language supports and strategies. Low-tech visual communication supports include options such as printable picture cards, social stories, visual schedules, and picture exchange systems. These systems are often integrated in classrooms of children with speech difficulties, language impairments, and social communication disorders (Wellington & Stackhouse, 2011). Wellington and Stackhouse measured the results of a specific training in use of visual support strategies provided by speech pathologists for classroom teachers and teacher assistants (TA) followed by a period of direct mentoring. The training involved a group training session followed by a mentoring sessions with the SLP and SLP assistant. Training consisted of demonstration of a variety of visual support techniques through case examples, video materials, and handouts. Specifically, a description was provided of speech, language, and communication needs and examples of each type was provided. The impact of these disabilities to access the curriculum was discussed. Next, differentiation of the curriculum for children with speech, language, and communication impairments was explained along with visual support techniques and strategies for differentiating the curriculum through their use. Finally, visual support materials were demonstrated. These included supports such as color-coded sentence makers, labeling, communication books, vocabulary books, gesture, signing, and sequence strips. The researchers measured the impact of this training program on the teachers' and TAs' knowledge and skills as well as their implementation of strategies in their classrooms after the training. The results indicated that targeted training with mentoring positively changed teacher and TA practice in the use of visual support strategies. In addition, participants reported increased confidence in their ability to use visual communication supports within their classrooms and also felt more confident in differentiating the use of these supports within the classroom for individual children. This is incredibly important, as children with significant communication impairments must be adequately supported in order to effectively communicate in all settings throughout their school day.

Today's school system places many demands on the educators. It is important to note that in this and in several of the classroom-based intervention studies described, training and education by SLPs followed by mentoring and/or consistent observation were included as a component of the intervention. This may be a critical component to correct implementation of the intervention. In addition, consistent measurement of the impact of classroom-based interventions is needed to ensure they are meeting student needs.

As a final example of classroom-based provision of speech pathology services, students have also been incorporated as peer-tutors who join with SLPs to deliver speech pathology services in a classroom setting. Grunke, Janning, and Sperling (2016) used a peer-tutoring intervention and measured the impact on text production of students with learning and speech disorders. In this case study, the researchers chose three children who "produced texts with the fewest number of [written] words" and paired them with three children who wrote the highest number of [written] words during a class-wide screening assessment. The peer-tutors were provided with training in the use of an intervention that involved direct instruction and the use of story maps. Specifically, the training was described as a "two hour briefing by the second author on how to implement the training along with a card summarizing the strategy" (p. 228). They were advised to follow a sequence for direct instruction where the peer mentor demonstrated use of story maps, the peer mentor and the participant completed the story map together, and finally, the participant completed the story mapping task as independently as possible. From baseline through intervention phases in a multiple baseline design investigation, all three participants markedly increased their performance on the discrete task that was tested. The results indicated that the intervention was highly effective across all students. The use of peer-tutors who were supervised by SLP professionals was described as "easy to implement and carry out, and this arrangement can provide opportunities for total participation by all students" (p. 233). The many limitations of this case report do not allow generalizability of the findings.

Conclusion

To facilitate successful outcomes in classroom-based service delivery, it is clear that SLPs must be exceptional team members as well as leaders and collaborators. These skills are needed to provide collaborative consultation or training skillfully and efficiently. SLPs must be willing to provide both specialized information and training as well as be open and willing to learn from other professionals in school settings.

It is evident that the role of SLPs in classroom-based delivery of speech pathology services must include at a minimum the ability to establish rapport with classroom personnel, providing training, modeling, and measurement of intervention techniques. Specifically, carving out time for providing professional development for other school-based professionals is needed for services to be provided with integrity. The review of published research related to classroom-based delivery of speech pathology services has underscored the significance of laying the foundation for intervention with team members who may partner with SLPs in the classroom. SLPs must create a climate where students' speech-language and classroom communication needs are maintained as a central classroom focus for all who interact with students with communication disabilities. The establishment of that central paradigm will be critical to effective classroom-based service delivery of speech pathology services.

References

American Speech-Language-Hearing Association. (2000). *Guidelines for the roles and responsibilities of school-based speech-language pathologist.* Rockville, MD: Author.

American Speech-Language-Hearing Association. (2016). *Scope of practice in speech-language pathology* [*Scope of practice*]. Retrieved from www.asha.org/policy.

Bailey, R. L., Stoner, J. B., Angell, M. E., & Fetzer, A. (2008). School-based speech-language pathologists' perspectives on feeding/swallowing management in the schools. *Language, Speech, and Hearing Services in Schools, 39,* 441–450.

Carson, K. L., Gillon, G. T., & Boustead, T. M. (2013). Classroom phonological awareness instruction and literacy outcomes in the first year of school. *Language, Speech, and Hearing Services in Schools, 44,* 147–160.

Friend, M., & Cook, L. (2010). *Interactions: Collaboration skills for school professionals* (6th ed.). Boston, MA: Allyn & Bacon.

Gillam, S. L., Olszewski, A., Fargo, J., & Gillam, R. B. (2014). Classroom-based narrative and vocabulary instruction: Results of an early-stage, nonrandomized comparison study. *Language, Speech, and Hearing Services in Schools, 45,* 204–219.

Goldstein, H., Olszewski, A., Haring, C., Greenwood, C. A., McCune, L., Carta, J., … Kelley, E.S. (2017). Efficacy of a supplemental phonemic awareness curriculum to instruct preschoolers with delays in early literacy development. *Journal of Speech, Language, and Hearing Research, 60,* 89–103.

Gregory, G., & Kuzmich, L. (2005). *Differentiated literacy strategies.* Thousand Oaks, CA: Corwin.

Grunke, M., Janning, A. M., & Sperling, M. (2016). The effects of a peer-tutoring intervention on the text production of students with learning and speech problems: A case report. *Learning Disabilities: A Contemporary Journal, 14*(2), 225–235.

Kouri, T. A. (2016). Comparison of feedback strategies during guided reading instruction with children with language impairment. *Contemporary Issues in Communication Science and Disorders, 43,* 268–284.

Nippold, M. A. (2011). From the Editor…Language intervention in the classroom: What it looks like. *Language, Speech, and Hearing Services in Schools, 42,* 393–394.

Nippold, M. A. (2012). From the Editor…Different service delivery models for different communication disorders. *Language, Speech, and Hearing Services in Schools, 43*(2), 117–120.

Scruggs, T. E., Mastropieri, M. A., & McDuffie, K. A. (2007). Co-teaching in inclusive classrooms: A metasynthesis of qualitative research. *Exceptional Children, 73,* 392–416.

Starling, J., Munro, N., Togher, L., & Arciuli, J. (2012). Training secondary school teachers in instructional language modification techniques to support adolescents with language impairment: A randomized controlled trial. *Language, Speech, and Hearing Services in Schools, 43,* 474–495.

Wellington, W., & Stackhouse, J. (2011). Using visual support for language and learning in children with SLCN: A training programme for teachers and teaching assistants. *Child Language Teaching and Therapy, 27*(2), 183–201.

Chapter 10

Interventions for Students with Physical Disabilities and Other Health Impairments

Sunday O. Obi

Abstract

Students with physical and health impairments represent a small but growing group of individuals with diverse educational needs. They are those students whose physical limitations or health problems interfere with school attendance or learning to such an extent that special services, training, equipment, materials, or facilities are required. Therefore, the purpose of this chapter is to discuss some of these impairments and acquaint both general and special educators with interventions for helping students with physical and health impairments succeed.

Keywords: Cerebral palsy; orthopedic impairment; neuromotor impairment; chronic conditions; hypoxia; paraplegia; choreoathetoid; atonic; spina bifida; scoliosis

Students with physical and health impairments are an extremely heterogeneous group with a wide variety of conditions and diseases. Disabilities that fall within the category of physical and health impairments may range from cerebral palsy, paralysis, epilepsy, asthma, diabetes, hyperactivity disorder, human immunodeficiency virus (HIV)/acquired immune deficiency syndrome (AIDS) infection, a terminal illness, and allergies are just a few. Some physical and health impairments are congenital, that is, present at birth; others are acquired after birth through disease

Viewpoints on Interventions for Learners with Disabilities
Advances in Special Education, Volume 33, 197–220
Copyright © 2018 by Emerald Publishing Limited
All rights of reproduction in any form reserved
ISSN: 0270-4013/doi:10.1108/S0270-401320180000033010

or injury. Physical and health problems can have grave, little, or no effect on school performance.

With so many different conditions under the category of physical and health impairments, there are also a lots of diverse causes. Cerebral palsy and spina bifida can be caused by abnormal brain growth. Some other disorders are caused genetically, the result of an injury, poisoning, hormonal abnormalities, while some are still unknown. Many students with physical disabilities utilize wheelchairs and other prosthetics for mobility and assistive technology to facilitate communication and participation in everyday life activities. Others with physical and health impairments may require ongoing medical treatment and may be hospitalized, frequently. Most students with physical and health impairments qualify for special education services under the Individuals with Disabilities Education Act (IDEA) categories of multiple disabilities, orthopedically impaired, or other health impaired. IDEA defines physical disabilities and health impairments as follows:

> Children with health conditions and physical disabilities who require special education are served under two IDEA categories: other health impairments (OHI) and orthopedic impairments.
>
> **Other health impairment** means having limited strength, vitality, or alertness, including a heightened alertness to environmental stimuli, that results in limited alertness with respect to the education environment, that –
>
> Is due to chronic or acute health problems such as asthma, attention deficit disorder or attention deficit hyperactivity disorder, diabetes, epilepsy, a heart condition, hemophilia, lead poisoning, leukemia, nephritis, rheumatic fever, sickle cell anemia, or Tourette syndrome; and
>
> i. Adversely affects academic performance. (§1401 [2004], 20 *CFR* §300.8[c][9])
>
> A severe **orthopedic impairment** adversely affects a child's educational performance. The term includes impairments caused by a congenital anomaly (e.g., clubfoot, absence of some member, etc.), impairments caused by disease (e.g., poliomyelitis, bone tuberculosis), and impairments from other causes (e.g., cerebral palsy, amputations, and fractures or burns that cause contractures). (20 USC §1401 [2004], 20 *CFR* §300.8[c][8])

Although IDEA uses the term *orthopedic impairment*, children with physical disabilities may have orthopedic impairments or neuromotor impairments. An orthopedic impairment involves the skeletal system – bones, joints, limbs, and associated muscles. A *neuromotor impairment* involves the central nervous system, affecting the ability to move, use, feel, or control certain parts of the body. Although orthopedic and neuromotor impairments are two distinct and separate types of disabilities, they may cause similar limitations in movement. Many of the same educational, therapeutic, and recreational activities are appropriate for students with orthopedic and neuromotor impairments (Best, Heller, & Bigge, 2010). And a close relationship exists between the two types, for example, a child who cannot move his legs because of damage to the central nervous system (neuromotor impairment) may develop disorders in the bones and muscles of the legs (orthopedic impairment), especially if he does not receive proper therapy and equipment.

Note in each IDEA disability definition the common clause: *that adversely affects a child's educational performance.* A child is entitled to special education services if his/her educational performance is adversely affected by a health-related condition or a physical disability. Most health impairments and physical disabilities that result in special education are *chronic conditions* – that is, they are long-lasting and most often permanent (e.g., cerebral palsy is a permanent disability that will affect a child throughout his/her life). By contrast, an *acute condition*, although it may produce severe and debilitating symptoms, is of limited duration (e.g., a child with pneumonia will experience symptoms, but the disease itself is not permanent). Some children with chronic health conditions or physical disabilities experience flare-ups or episodes of acute symptoms (e.g., a child with cystic fibrosis may experience periods of acute respiratory difficulties).

Studies of the number of children with health impairments and physical disabilities have produced hugely diverse findings. One review of prevalence studies found estimates of chronic health conditions in childhood ranging from as low as 0.22% to as high as 44% depending on the researchers' concepts and definitions (van der Lee, Mokkink, Grootenhuis, Heymans, & Offringa, 2007). In the middle of that range is Sexson and Dingle's (2001) estimate that chronic medical conditions affect up to 20% (approximately 12 million) of school-age children in the United States. Whatever the actual number, researchers widely accept that the incidence of chronic health conditions has increased considerably in recent decades. In 1960, data showed that just 1.8% of American children and adolescents had a chronic health condition that limited their activities compared with 7% in 2004 (Perrin, Bloom, & Gortmaker, 2007).

Clearly, a great many children's lives are affected by health impairments and physical disabilities. During the 2012 and 2013 school year, however, only around 59,000 children between the ages of 3 and 21 years received special education services under the orthopedic impairments disability category compared with approximately 779,000 children served under OHI (U.S. Department of Education, 2014). These two disability categories represent approximately 1% and 12% of all children receiving special education services, respectively.

Two factors make the actual number of children with health conditions and physical disabilities much higher than the number of children receiving special education services under these two IDEA categories. First, numerous children have chronic health conditions or physical impairments that do not adversely affect their educational performance sufficiently to warrant special education. Second, because physical and health impairments often occur with other disabilities, children may be counted under other categories, such as multiple disabilities, speech impairment, or intellectual disabilities. For example, for special education eligibility, a diagnosis of intellectual disabilities may take precedence over a diagnosis of physical impairment.

Therefore, the purpose of this chapter is to examine historical legislative perspectives on providing services to children with physical disabilities and other health impairments (OHIs) and acquaint general and special educators with methods for helping students with physical and health impairments succeed in school and beyond. Special education of children with physical disabilities and health impairments in the United States has a history of more than 100 years as illustrated in Table 1.

Defining Children with Physical Disabilities or OHIs

Children with physical disabilities or OHIs are those whose physical limitations or health problems interfere with school attendance or learning to such an extent that they require special services, training, equipment, materials, or facilities. Here we address those encountered most frequently in school-age children.

Epilepsy

Whether we are awake or asleep, our brains are continually astir with electrical activity. When abnormal electrical discharges in the brain cause a

Table 1: Historical Events in the Education of Children with Physical Disabilities and Health Impairments.

Date	Historical Event	Educational Implications
1893	Industrial School for Crippled and Deformed Children is established in Boston.	This was the first special institution for children with physical disabilities in the United States (Eberle, 1922).
Circa 1900	The first special classes for children with physical impairments begin in Chicago.	This was the first time children with physical disabilities were educated in public schools (La Vor, 1976).
Early 1900s	Serious outbreaks of tuberculosis and polio occur in the United States.	This led to increasing numbers of children with physical impairments being educated by local schools in special classes for the "crippled" or "delicate."
Early 20th century	Winthrop Phelps demonstrates that children can be helped through physical therapy and the effective use of braces. Earl Carlson (who himself had cerebral palsy) was a strong advocate of developing the intellectual potential of children with physical disabilities through appropriate education.	The efforts of these two American physicians contributed to increased understanding and acceptance of children with physical disabilities, and to recognition that physical impairment did not preclude potential for educational achievement and self-sufficiency.
Early 20th century to 1970s	Decisions to "ignore, isolate, and institutionalize these children are often based on mental incompetence presumed because of physical disabilities, especially those involving communication and use of upper extremities" (Conner, Scandary, & Tullock, 1988, p. 6).	Increasing numbers of children with mild physical disabilities and health conditions were educated in public schools. Most children with severe physical disabilities were educated in special schools or community agencies (e.g., the United Cerebral Palsy Association).

Table 1: (*Continued*)

Date	Historical Event	Educational Implications
1975	PL 94-142 mandates a free appropriate public education for all children with disabilities and requires schools to provide related services (e.g., transportation services, physical therapy, school health services) necessary for students to be educated in the least restrictive environment.	No longer could a child be denied the right to attend the local public school because there was a flight of stairs at the entrance, bathrooms were not accessible, or school buses were not equipped to transport wheelchairs. The related services provision of IDEA transformed schools from "solely scholastic institutions into therapeutic agencies" (Palfrey, 1995, p. 265).
1984	The Supreme Court rules in *Independent School District v. Tatro* that schools must provide intermittent catheterization as a supportive or related service if necessary to enable a student with disabilities to receive a public education.	The *Tatro* ruling expanded the range of related services that schools are required to provide and clarified the differences between school health services, which can be performed by a nonphysician, and medical services, which are provided by physicians for diagnostic or eligibility purposes.
1984	The World Institute on Disability is cofounded by Ed Roberts, an inspirational leader for self-advocacy by people with disabilities.	This was a major milestone in the civil rights and self-advocacy movement by people with disabilities.
1990	Americans with Disabilities Act (ADA; PL 101-336) is passed.	The ADA provides civil rights protections to all people with disabilities in private sector employment and mandates access to all public services, accommodations, transportation, and telecommunications.

1990	Traumatic brain injury (TBI) is added as a new disability category in the reauthorization of IDEA (PL 101-476).	This addition raised teachers' awareness of the educational needs of children with TBI and led to increased services and research dedicated to meeting those needs.
1999	The U.S. Supreme Court rules in *Cedar Rapids v. Garret F.* that a local school district must pay for the one-on-one nursing care for a medically fragile student who required continuous monitoring of his ventilator and other health-maintenance routines.	The decision reaffirmed and extended the Court's ruling in the 1984 *Tatro* case that schools must provide any and all health services needed for students with disabilities to attend school, as long as performance of those services does not require a licensed physician.
2004	The Improving Access to Assistive Technology Act of 2004 (PL 108-364) is signed into law. Third time Congress amends and extends provisions of the Technology-Related Assistance for IDEA of 1988.	Congress funds an Assistive Technology Act Project (ATAP) in each state to assist people with disabilities in obtaining AT services throughout their entire life spans. ATAP activities include product demonstrations; AT device loan programs; financing assistance; and public awareness regarding the availability, benefits, and costs of AT. For more info, go to www.resna.org/taproject.

Source: Heward (2017).

disturbance of movement, sensation, behavior, or consciousness, a *seizure* has occurred. Some have compared the event to "an engine misfiring or to a power surge in a computer" (Hill, 1999, p. 231). Anyone can have a seizure. It is common for a seizure to occur when someone has a high fever, drinks excessive alcohol, or experiences a blow to the head. When seizures occur chronically and repeatedly, the condition is known as a *seizure disorder* or, more commonly, epilepsy. Epilepsy is not a disease, and it constitutes a disorder only while a seizure is actually in progress. It is estimated that 3% of the population is prone to seizures and about 3 million Americans have epilepsy (Epilepsy Foundation of America, 2013a; National Dissemination Center for Children with Disabilities, 2010). There are several types of seizures.

The *generalized tonic-clonic seizure* (formerly called *grand mal*) is the most conspicuous and serious type of seizure. The affected child usually has little or no warning that a seizure is about to occur; the muscles become stiff, and the child loses consciousness and falls to the floor. Then the entire body shakes violently as the muscles alternately contract and relax. Saliva may exude from the mouth, the legs and arms may jerk, and the bladder and bowels may be emptied. In most cases, contractions diminish in 2–3 minutes, and the child either goes to sleep or regains consciousness in a confused or drowsy state. Generalized tonic-clonic seizures may occur as often as several times a day or as seldom as once a year. They are more likely to occur during the day than at night.

An *absence seizure* (previously called *petit mal*) is far less severe than the generalized tonic-clonic type but may occur much more frequently – as often as 100 times per day in some children. Usually, a brief loss of consciousness occurs, lasting from a few seconds to half a minute or so. The child may stare blankly, flutter or blink his/her eyes, grow pale, and drop whatever he/she is holding. He/she may be mistakenly viewed as daydreaming or not listening. The child may or may not be aware he/she has had a seizure, and no special first aid is necessary.

A *complex partial seizure* (also called *psychomotor*) may appear as a brief period of inappropriate or purposeless activity. The child may smack his/her lips, walk about aimlessly, or shout. Although he/she may appear to be conscious and even respond to spoken directions, the child is unaware of her unusual behavior. A complex partial seizure usually lasts 2–5 minutes, after which the child has amnesia about the entire episode.

A *simple partial seizure* is characterized by sudden jerking motions with no loss of consciousness. Partial seizures may occur weekly, monthly, or just once or twice a year. During seizures, the teacher should keep dangerous objects out of the child's way and, except in emergencies, should not try to physically restrain him/her. Many children experience a warning sensation, called an *aura*, a short time before a seizure. The aura takes various forms: distinctive feelings, sights, sounds, tastes, and even smells. The aura can be a useful safety valve enabling the child to leave the class or group before the seizure occurs. Some children report that the warning provided by the aura helps them feel more secure and comfortable.

Diabetes

Diabetes is a chronic disorder of metabolism that affects an estimated 29.1 million children and adults in the United States, or 9.3% of the population (Centers for Disease Control and Prevention [CDC], 2014a). Without a proper medical management, a child with diabetes cannot obtain and retain adequate energy from food. Not only does the child lack energy, but also many important body parts (particularly the eyes and the kidneys) are affected by untreated diabetes. Early symptoms include thirst, headaches, weight loss (despite a good appetite), frequent urination, and cuts that are slow to heal.

Children with Type 1 diabetes (formerly called *juvenile diabetes* or *early-onset diabetes*) have insufficient insulin, a hormone normally produced by the pancreas and necessary for the metabolism of glucose, a form of sugar produced when food is digested. Children with diabetes must follow a specific diet prescribed by a physician and receive daily injections of insulin under the skin. Most children with diabetes learn to inject their own insulin – in some cases as frequently as four times per day.

The most common form of diabetes, Type 2 diabetes, results from insulin resistance (the body failing to properly use insulin), combined with relative insulin deficiency. Type 2 diabetes occurs most often in adults who are overweight, but the recent increase in childhood obesity has led to a dramatic rise in the incidence of Type 2 diabetes in children (Hannon, Rao, & Arslanian, 2005).

Teachers who have a student with diabetes in their classroom should learn to recognize symptoms of both too little and too much sugar in the child's bloodstream and ensure the child receives the appropriate treatment for each condition (Gretch, Bhukhanwala, & Neuharth-Pritchett, 2007). *Hypoglycemia* (low blood sugar), also called *insulin reaction* or *diabetic shock*, can result from taking too much insulin, usually strenuous exercise, or a missed or delayed meal (the blood sugar level is lowered by insulin and exercise and raised by food). Symptoms of hypoglycemia include faintness, dizziness, blurred vision, drowsiness, and nausea. The child may appear irritable or have a marked personality change. In most cases, giving the child some form of concentrated sugar (e.g., sugar cube, fruit juice, or a candy bar) ends the insulin reaction within a few minutes. The child's doctor or parents should inform the teacher and school health personnel of the appropriate foods to give in case of insulin reaction.

Hyperglycemia (high blood sugar) is more serious; it indicates that too little insulin is present and the diabetes is not under control. Its onset is gradual rather than sudden. Symptoms of hyperglycemia, sometimes called *diabetic coma*, include fatigue; thirst; dry, hot skin; deep, labored breathing; excessive urination; and fruity-smelling breath. A doctor or nurse should be contacted immediately if a child displays such symptoms.

Asthma

Asthma is a chronic lung disease characterized by episodic bouts of wheezing, coughing, and difficulty breathing. An asthmatic attack is usually triggered by allergens (e.g., pollen, certain foods, or pets), irritants (e.g., cigarette smoke or smog), exercise, or emotional stress. The result is a narrowing of the airways in the lungs, which increases resistance to the airflow in and out of the lungs and makes it harder for the individual to breathe. The severity of asthma varies greatly, from mild coughing to extreme difficulty breathing that requires emergency treatment. Many children with asthma experience normal lung functioning between episodes.

Asthma is the most common lung disease of children; estimates of its prevalence range from 7% to as high as 10% of school-age children (Asthma and Allergy Foundation of American, 2011; CDC, 2014b). The causes of asthma are not completely known, but most consider it the result of an interaction of heredity and environment.

Primary treatment for asthma begins with a systematic effort to identify stimuli and environmental situations that trigger attacks. Asthma can be controlled effectively in most children with a combination of medications and limiting exposure to known allergens. Most children whose breathing attacks are induced by physical exercise can still enjoy physical exercise and sports though careful selection of activities (e.g., swimming generally provokes less exercise-induced asthma than running) and/or taking certain medications before rigorous exercise.

Cystic Fibrosis

Cystic fibrosis is a disease in which the body's exocrine glands excrete thick mucus that blocks the lungs and parts of the digestive system. Cystic fibrosis occurs predominantly in white people, but it can affect all races. Children with cystic fibrosis often have difficulty breathing and are susceptible to pulmonary disease (lung infections). Malnutrition and poor growth are common characteristics of children with cystic fibrosis because of pancreatic insufficiency that causes inadequate digestion and malabsorption of nutrients, especially fats. Affected children often have large and frequent bowel movements because food is only partially digested. Getting children with cystic fibrosis to consume enough calories is critical to their health and development.

Medications prescribed for cystic fibrosis include enzymes to facilitate digestion and solutions to thin and loosen the mucus in the lungs. Children with cystic fibrosis undergo daily physiotherapy in which the chest is vigorously thumped and vibrated to dislodge mucus followed by positioning the body to drain loosened secretions. During vigorous physical exercises, some children may need help from teachers, aides, or classmates to clear their lungs and air passages.

Sickle Cell Disease

Sickle cell disease affects the red blood cells' ability to carry oxygen; the sickle-shaped cells do not easily move through the blood, causing blockages that lead to several complications. Sickle cell disease is most common in African Americans, but may affect people of other races as well. Children with sickle cell disease are at risk for episodes of severe pain, serious infections, organ damage, acute chest syndrome (a condition similar to pneumonia), and stroke.

Treatments for children with sickle cell disease vary according to their symptoms (CDC, 2014c). Common treatments include blood transfusions, medication, and increasing fluid intake. For children with sickle cell disease, there is a lot of emphasis on prevention of various symptoms. For instance, pain crises may be prevented or lessened by avoiding high altitudes or extreme (too hot or too cold) temperatures. Preventive measures for helping children avoid infection are particularly important, including following food safety guidelines, practicing thorough hand washing, and vaccinating on schedule.

HIV and AIDS

HIV can lead to AIDS. A person with AIDS cannot resist and fight off infections because of a breakdown in the immune system. Opportunistic infections such as tuberculosis, pneumonia, and cancerous skin lesions attack the person's body, grow in severity, and ultimately result in death. Although no vaccine or cure exists for AIDS, advances in antiretroviral drug treatment have dramatically reduced mortality rates.

HIV, which is found in an infected person's bodily fluids (blood, semen, vaginal secretions, and breast milk), is transmitted from one person to another through sexual contact and blood-to-blood contact (e.g., intravenous drug use with shared needles and transfusions of unscreened contaminated blood). Women can transmit HIV to their children during pregnancy, birth, or breastfeeding (CDC, 2015).

Because of fear generated by misconceptions about the spread of the disease, some school districts have barred children with HIV/AIDS from attending school in defiance of the IDEA principle of zero reject. However, saliva, nasal secretions, sweat, tears, urine, and vomit do not transmit HIV unless those fluids contain blood (CDC, 2015). A child with HIV/AIDS in the classroom presents no undue health risks to other children. Children with HIV/AIDS cannot legally be excluded from attending school unless they are deemed a direct health risk to other children (e.g., exhibit biting behavior and have open lesions).

Cerebral Palsy

Cerebral palsy – a disorder of movement and posture – is the most prevalent physical disability in school-age children. Cerebral palsy is a permanent condition resulting from a lesion to the brain or an abnormality of brain growth. Many diseases can affect the developing brain and lead to cerebral palsy. Children with cerebral palsy experience disturbances of voluntary motor functions that may include paralysis, extreme weakness, lack of coordination, involuntary convulsions, and other motor disorders. They may have little or no control over their arms legs, or speech, depending on the type and degree of impairment. More severe forms of cerebral palsy are often diagnosed in the first few months of life. In many cases, however, cerebral palsy is not detected until the child is 2–3 years old, when parents notice that their child is having difficulty balancing or standing. The motor dysfunction usually does not get progressively worse as a child ages. Cerebral palsy can be treated but not cured. It is not a disease; not fatal; not contagious; and in the great majority of cases, not inherited.

The causes of cerebral palsy are varied and not clearly known. It has most often been attributed to the occurrence of injuries, accidents, or illnesses that are *prenatal* (before birth), *perinatal* (at or near the time of birth), or *postnatal* (soon after birth) and that result in decreased oxygen to low-birth-weight newborns. Recent improvements in obstetrical delivery and neonatal care, however, have not decreased the incidence of cerebral palsy: about 3 children per 1,000 live births (United Cerebral Palsy, 2015). Factors most often associated with cerebral palsy are intellectual disabilities of the mother, premature birth (gestational age of 32 weeks or less), low birth weight, and a delay of 5 minutes or more before the newborn's first cry.

Because the location and extent of brain damage are so variable in individuals with cerebral palsy, a diagnosis of the condition is not descriptive of its effects. Cerebral palsy is classified in terms of the affected parts of the body and by the nature of its effects on muscle tone and movement (Best & Bigge, 2010). The term *plegia* (from the Greek "to strike") is used in combination with a prefix indicating the location of limb involvement:

- *Monoplegia* – only one limb (upper or lower) is affected.
- *Hemiplegia* – two limbs on same side of the body are involved.
- *Triplegia* – three limbs are affected.
- *Quadriplegia* – all four limbs (both arms and legs) are involved; movement of the trunk and face may also be impaired.
- *Paraplegia* – only legs are impaired.
- *Diplegia* – impairment primarily involves the legs, with less severe involvement of the arms.
- *Double hemiplegia* – impairment primarily involves the arms, with less severe involvement of the legs.

Cerebral palsy is also classified by its effects on muscle tone (hypertonia or hypotonia) and quality of movement (athetosis or ataxia) (Hoon & Tolley, 2013). Approximately 50–60% of all individuals with cerebral palsy have *spastic cerebral palsy* which is characterized by tense, contracted muscles (hypertonia).

Athetosis occurs in about 20% of all individuals with cerebral palsy. Children with *athetoid cerebral palsy* make large, irregular, twisting movements they cannot control. When they are at rest or asleep, little or no abnormal motion occurs. An effort to pick up a pencil, however, may result in wildly waiving arms, facial grimaces, and extension of the tongue.

These children may not be able to control the muscles of their lips, tongue, and throat and may drool. They may also seem to stumble and lurch awkwardly as they walk. At times, their muscles may be tense and rigid; at other times, they may be loose and flaccid. Extreme difficulty in expressive oral language, mobility, and activities of daily living often accompanies this form of cerebral palsy.

Ataxia is the primary type of involvement in 1–10% of the cases of cerebral palsy. Children with *ataxic cerebral palsy* have a poor sense of balance and hand use. They may appear to be dizzy while walking and may fall if not supported. Their movements tend to be jumpy and unsteady, with exaggerated motion patterns that often overshoot the intended objects. They seem to be constantly attempting to overcome the effect of gravity to stabilize their bodies.

Spina Bifida

Congenital malformations of the brain, spinal cord, or vertebrae are known as *neural tube defects*. The most common neural tube defect (4.1 in 10,000 live births in the United States per year) (Spina Bifida Association, 2015) is spina bifida, a condition in which the vertebrae do not enclose the spinal cord. As a result, a portion of the spinal cord and the nerves that control muscles and feeling in the lower part of the body fails to develop normally. Of the three types of spina bifida, the mildest form in spina bifida occulta, in which only a few vertebrae are malformed, usually in the lower spine. The defect is usually not visible externally. Approximately 10–20% of Americans have spina bifida occulta, but because they experience few or no symptoms, very few ever know they have it (National Institutes of Neurological Disorders and Stroke, 2013). If the flexible casing (meninges) that surrounds the spinal cord bulges through an opening in the infant's back at birth, the condition is called meningocele. These two forms do not usually cause any loss of function for the child.

Muscular Dystrophy

Muscular dystrophy refers to a group of about 40 inherited diseases marked by progressive *atrophy* (wasting away) of the body's muscles. Duchenne muscular dystrophy (DMD) is the most common and most severe type. DMD affects only boys (1 in 3,500 male births), but about one-third of cases is the result of genetic mutation in families with no history of the disease (Best, 2010a). Muscle weakness is usually evident between the ages of 2 and 6 years, when the child begins to experience difficulty in running or climbing stairs. The child may walk with an unusual gait, showing a protruding stomach and hollow back. The calf muscles of a child with muscular dystrophy may appear unusually large because the degenerated muscle has been replaced by fatty tissue.

Educational Approaches

Academic Interventions

Judicial rulings and legislative actions have made dramatic changes in the ways in which children with physical or health impairments are educated today. Intervention begins as soon as the impairment is diagnosed. Special educational services, as well as medical services, may be initiated at birth. Preschools now provide multidisciplinary services to children with physical or health impairments. Public schools must provide access to all facilities. They must also supply equal opportunities for children with disabilities to participate in school activities, transitional services, and free and appropriate education. The reform and restructuring of special education, mandated by the courts, has opened public school doors to many physically and/or health impaired children who were formerly taught at home, in hospitals, in residential institutions, in special schools, or in special classes.

Children with physical disabilities may be given an education in any one of several settings, depending on the type and severity of the condition, the services available in the community, and the medical prognosis for the condition. If such children ordinarily attend regular public school classes but must be hospitalized for more than a few days, they may be included in a class in the hospital itself. If they must be confined to their homes for a time, a visiting or homebound teacher may provide tutoring until they can return to regular classes. In these cases, which usually involve accident victims or conditions that are not permanently and severely disabling, relatively minor, commonsense adjustments are required to continue the children's education and keep them from falling behind their classmates.

It is not possible to prescribe educational goals and curricula for children with physical disabilities as a group because their limitations vary so greatly from child to child. Even among children with the same condition, goals and curricula must be determined after assessing the individual child's intellectual, physical, sensory, and emotional characteristics.

A physical disability, especially a severe and chronic one that limits mobility, may have two implications for education. The child may be deprived of the experiences that nondisabled children have, and the child may find it impossible to manipulate educational materials and respond to educational tasks the way most children do. For example, a child with severe cerebral palsy cannot take part in most outdoor play activities and travel experiences and may not be able to hold and turn pages in books, write, explore objects manually, or use a typewriter without a special equipment.

For children with impairment that is only physical, curriculum and educational goals should ordinarily be the same as for nondisabled children: reading, writing, arithmetic, and experiences designed to familiarize them with the world about them. In addition, special instruction may be needed in mobility skills, daily living skills, and occupational skills. That is, because of their physical impairments, these children may need special, individualized instruction in the use of mechanical devices that will help them perform tasks that are much simpler for those without disabilities. For children with other disabilities in addition to physical limitations, curricula will need to be further adapted (Biggs, 1991; Hanson & Harris, 1986).

Educational goals for students with severe or profound disabilities must be related to their functioning in everyday community environments. Only recently have educators begun to address the problems of analyzing community tasks (e.g., crossing streets, using money, riding public transportation, and greeting neighbors) and planning efficient instruction for individuals with severe disabilities (Bigge, 1991; Snell & Browder, 1986). Efficient instruction in such skills requires that teaching occur in the community environment itself.

The range of educational objectives and curricula for children with physical disabilities is often extended beyond the objectives and curricula typically provided for other students in school. For example, very young children and those with severe neuromuscular problems may need objectives and curricula focusing on the most basic self-care skills (e.g., swallowing, chewing, and self-feeding). Older students may need not only to explore possible careers in the way all students should but also to consider the special accommodations their physical limitations demand for successful performance.

Nonacademic Interventions – Team Approach

One of the main considerations is the use of the team approach in developing and carrying out a child's educational program. The team generally includes the parents, teachers, medical professionals, and health-related professionals such as physical therapist (PT). Parents are critical members of the team and should be involved in all educational decisions. The team should design a program that meets the needs of the student in five basic goal areas: (a) physical independence, including mastery of daily living skills; (b) self-awareness and social maturation; (c) communication; (d) academic growth, and (e) life skills training. They often need an interdisciplinary team of professionals to aid in all of their special needs. For example, a student may need a PT to work on their gross motor goals, an occupational therapist (OT) to work on fine motor and self-help skills, a speech therapist to work on any difficulty with language. To help the students become more self-competent, the teachers and therapist(s) can help the child learn to take care of their own special needs.

Although some students can fully access and benefit from education with minimal accommodations, the intensive health and learning needs of other students require a complex and coordinated array of specialized instruction, therapy, and related services. In addition to progressing in the general education curriculum to the maximum extent possible, many students with health impairments or physical disabilities also need intensive instruction in a "parallel curriculum" on "coping with their disabilities" (Bowe, 2000, p. 75). Similar in function to the "expanded core curriculum" for students with visual impairments, the parallel curriculum for students with health impairments and physical disabilities includes increasing independence by self-administering special health care routines; using adaptive methods and assistive technologies for mobility, communication, and daily-living tasks; and learning self-determination and self-advocacy skills.

The transdisciplinary team approach has special relevance for students with health impairments and physical disabilities. No other group of exceptional children comes into contact, both in and out of school, with as many different teachers, physicians, therapists, and other specialists. Because the medical, educational, therapeutic, vocational, and social needs of these students are often complex, educational and health care personnel must openly communicate and cooperate with one another. Two particularly important members of the team for many children are the PT and the OT. Each is a licensed health professional who has completed a specialized training program. Other specialists who frequently provide instruction and related services to children with physical disabilities and health impairments include the following:

- *Speech-language pathologists* provide speech therapy, language interventions, oral motor coordination (e.g., chewing and swallowing), and augmentative and alternative communication services.
- *Adapted physical educators* who provide physical education activities designed to meet the individual needs of students and disabilities.
- *Recreation therapists* provide instruction in leisure activities and therapeutic recreation.
- *School nurses* provide specific health care services to students, monitor students' health, and inform individualized education program (IEP) teams about the effects of medical conditions on students' educational programs.
- *Prosthetists* make and fit artificial limbs.
- *Orthotists* design and fit braces and other assistive devices.
- *Orientation and mobility specialists* teach students to navigate their environment as effectively and independently as possible.
- *Biomedical engineers* develop or adapt technology to meet a students' specialized needs.
- *Health aides* carry out medical procedures and health-care services in the classroom.
- *Counselors and medical social workers* help students and families adjust to disabilities.

Environmental Modifications. Environmental modifications are frequently necessary to enable a student with health or physical impairments to participate more fully and independently in school. Environmental modifications include adaptations to provide increased access to a task or an activity, changing the way in which instruction is delivered, and changing the manner in which the task is done (Best, Heller, et al., 2010; Heller, Dangel, & Sweatman, 1995). Although barrier-free architecture is the most publicly visible type of environmental modification for making community buildings and services more accessible, some of the most functional adaptations require little or no cost:

- Install paper-cup dispensers near water fountains so students in wheelchairs can use them.
- Move a class or an activity to an accessible part of a school building so that a student with a physical impairment can participate.

- Provide soft-tip pens that require less pressure for writing.
- Provide a head-mounted pointer stick and keyboard guard that enable a student with limited fine-motor control to strike one computer key at a time.
- Change desks and tabletops to appropriate heights for students who are very short or who use wheelchairs.
- Provide a wooden pointer to enable a student to reach the upper buttons on an elevator control panel.

Assistive Technology. Individuals with physical disabilities use both low-tech assistive devices (e.g., adapted eating utensils, a "grabber" or "reacher" that enables a person in a wheelchair to reach items on a shelf) and high-tech assistive devices (e.g., computerized synthetic speech devices, electronic switches activated by eye movements) for a wide variety of purposes, including mobility, performance of daily life skills, improved environmental manipulation and control, better communication, access to computers, recreation and leisure, and enhanced learning (Best, Reed, & Bigge, 2010; Dell, Newton, & Petroff, 2008). IEP team members should not view a student's acquisition and use of assistive technology as an educational outcome in itself but as a means of increasing the student's independence and access to various activities and opportunities.

New technological aids for communication are used increasingly by children whose physical impairments prevent them from speaking clearly. For students who can speak but have limited motor function, voice input/output products enable them to access computers. Such developments allow students with physical impairments to communicate expressively and receptively with others and take part in a wide range of instructional programs. Many individuals with physical disabilities use telecommunications technologies to expand their world, gain access to information and services, and meet new people. Many children and adults with disabilities use email, Facebook, and other social media to communicate with others, make new friends, and build and maintain relationships.

Mobility Devices. Some students cannot move freely from place to place without the assistance of a mobility device. Many children as young as 3–5 years old can learn to explore their environment with freedom and independence in "energy efficient, creative, wheeled scooter boards and wheeled go-carts that provide mobility without restricting upper or lower extremity functions" (Evans & Smith, 1993, p. 1418). Adapted bicycles enable children with disabilities to enjoy the thrill of bicycle riding and reap the health benefits (Klein, McHugh, Harrington, Davis, & Lieberman, 2005).

Advances in wheelchair design have made manual chairs lighter and stronger, powered chairs have been adapted for use in rural areas, and new environmental controls have put wheelchair users into contact with both immediate and distant parts of their world. A student should not be described as being "confined to a wheelchair." This expression suggests that the person is restrained or even imprisoned. Most students who use wheelchairs leave them from time to time to exercise, travel in an automobile, or lie down. The preferred language is "has a wheelchair" or "uses a wheelchair to get around."

Animals. Animals can help children and adults with physical disabilities in many ways. Nearly everyone is familiar with guide dogs, which can help people who are blind travel independently. Another recent and promising approach to the use of animals by people with disabilities is the helper or service dog. Depending on a person's needs, dogs can be trained to carry books and other objects (in saddlebags), pick up telephone receivers, turn light switches on or off, and open doors. Dogs can also assist with balance and support – for example, to help a person propel a wheelchair up a steep ramp or stand up from a seated position. Additionally, dogs can be trained to contact family members or neighbors in an emergency. Monkeys also have been trained to serve as personal care attendants for people with disabilities.

Seating and Positioning. To prevent the development of pressure sores and help students maintain proper seating and positioning, teachers must know how to move and transfer students with physical disabilities. Teachers should follow routines for lifting and transferring a child with disabilities that entail standard procedures for each child for (a) making contact with the child, (b) communicating what is going to happen in a manner the child can understand, (c) preparing the child physically for the transfer, and (d) requiring the child to participate in the routine as much as possible.

Medications. Many students with health or physical impairments require specialized procedures such as taking prescribed medication or self-administering insulin shots, tracheotomy care, ventilator or respirator care, and managing special nutrition and dietary needs. These special health-related needs are prescribed in an individualized health care plan (IHCP), which is included as part of the student's IEP. In addition to the condition, the IHCP "includes precise information about how to handle routine health-care procedures, physical management techniques, and medical emergencies that may arise while the child is at school" (Getch, Bhukhanwala, & Neuharth-Pritchett, 2007, p. 48). Teachers and school personnel must be trained to safely administer the health care procedures they are expected to perform (Heller, Fredrick, Best, Dykes, & Cohen, 2000).

For no group of exceptional children is the continuum of educational services and placement options more relevant than for students with special health needs and physical impairments. Most children with health or physical impairments spend at least part of the school day in regular classrooms. From 2012 to 2013, 64% of students with OHIs and about 55% of those who received special education services under the category of orthopedic impairment were educated in regular classrooms (U.S. Department of Education, 2014). The percentage of students in each disability category served in resource rooms was 22% and 16%, respectively.

Conclusion

In this chapter, we have addressed the issues surrounding the delivery of special education programs to students with physical and health impairments. For example, several decades ago, these students rarely attended their neighborhood schools with their same-aged peers. In recent years, however, advances in the medical field have extended the lives of children with physical and health impairments. Additionally, federal legislation has mandated that children with disabilities receive a free and appropriate education and that they be educated with their nondisabled peers to the maximum extent possible. The purpose of this chapter was to provide an overview of some interventions that have demonstrated effectiveness in providing assistance to these students. The chapter also discussed the more common conditions of physical and health impairments affecting school-age children. Specific characteristics of these physical and health impairments were provided along with suggestions for meeting the educational and medical needs of students with such impairments in inclusive settings. Stressed throughout the chapter was the need for professionals to understand that each individual with physical and health impairment needs to be taken on a case by case basis to decide on the most appropriate inclusive placement and which educational and treatment techniques to employ.

References

Asthma and Allergy Foundation of America. (2011). *Asthma facts and figures*. Washington, DC: Author. Retrieved from http://www.aafa.org/display.clm?d=8&sub=42. Accessed on February 10, 2015.

Best, S. J. (2010a). Physical disabilities. In S. J. Best, K. W. Heller, & J. L. Bigge (Eds.), *Teaching individuals with physical or multiple disabilities* (6th ed., pp. 32–58). Upper Saddle River, NJ: Merrill/Pearson.

Best, S. J., Heller, K. W., & Bigge, J. L. (2010). *Teaching individuals with physical or multiple disabilities* (6th ed.). Upper Saddle River, NJ: Merrill/Pearson.

Best, S. J., Reed, P., & Bigge, J. L. (2010). Assistive technology. In S. J. Best, K. W. Heller, & J. L. Bigge (Eds.), *Teaching individuals with physical or multiple disabilities* (6th ed., pp. 175–220). Upper Saddle River, NJ: Merrill/Pearson.

Bigge, J. L. (1991). *Teaching individuals with physical and multiple disabilities* (3rd ed.). Columbus, OH: Merrill/Macmillan.

Bowe, F. (2000). *Teaching individuals with physical and multiple disabilities* (4th ed.). Upper Saddle River, NJ: Merrill/Pearson.

Centers for Disease Control and Prevention. (2014a). *National Diabetes Statistics Report: Estimates of diabetes and its burden in the United States, 2014.* Atlanta, GA: U. S. Department of Health and Human Services. Retrieved from http://www.cdc.gov/diabetes/pubs/statsreport14/national-diabetes-report-web.pdf. Accessed on February 10, 2015.

Centers for Disease Control and Prevention. (2014b). *Asthma data, statistics, and surveillance.* Atlanta, GA: U. S. Department of Health and Human Services. Retrieved from http//www.cdc.gov/ncbddd/sicklecell/treatments.html. Accessed on February 10, 2015.

Centers for Disease Control and Prevention. (2014c). *Sickle cell disease: Complications and treatment.* Retrieved from http//www.cdc.gov/ncbddd/sicklecell/treatments.html. Accessed on February 26, 2015.

Centers for Disease Control and Prevention. (2015). *HIV transmission.* Retrieved from http://www.cdc.gov/hiv/basics/transmission.html. Accessed on February 26, 2015.

Conner, E. P., Scandary, J., & Tullock, D. (1988). Education of physically handicapped and health impaired individuals: A commitment to the future. *DPH Journal, 10*(1), 5–24.

Dias, M. S. (2003). *Hydrocephalus and shunts in the person with spina bifida.* Washington, DC: Spina Bifida Association. Retrieved from http://www.sbaa.org/atf/cf/(99DD789C-904D-467E-A2E4-DF1D36E381C0)/fs_hydrocephalus.pdf.

Eberle, L. (1922). The maimed, the halt and the race. Reprinted in R. H. Bremner (Ed.), *Children and youth in America: A documentary history, Vol. 2: 1866–1932* (pp. 1026–1028). Cambridge, MA: Harvard University Press.

Epilepsy Foundation of America. (2013a). *Epilepsy statistics.* Landover, MD: Author. Retrieved from http://www.epilepsy.com/learn/epilepsy-statistics. Accessed on February 25, 2015.

Evans, J. C., & Smith, J. (1993). Nursing planning, intervention, and evaluation for altered neurologic function. In D. B. Jackson & R. B. Saunders (Eds.), *Child health nursing: A comprehensive approach to the care of children and their health* (pp. 1353–1430). Philadelphia, PA: Lippincott.

Getch, Y., Bhukhanwala, F., & Neuharth-Pritchett, S. (2007). Strategies for helping children with diabetes in elementary and middle schools. *Teaching Exceptional Children, 39*(3), 46–51.

Hanson, M. J., & Harris, S. R. (1986). *Teaching the young child with motor delays.* Austin, TX: Pro-Ed.

Hannon, T. S., Rao, G., & Arslanian, S. A. (2005). Childhood obesity and Type 2 diabetes mellitus. *Pediatrics, 116,* 473–480.

Heller, K. W., Dangel, H., & Sweatman, L. (1995). Systematic selection of adaptations for students with muscular dystrophy. *Journal of Developmental and Physical Disabilities, 7,* 253–265.

Heller, K. W., Fredrick, L. D., Best, S., Dykes, M. K., & Cohen, E. T. (2000). Specialized health care procedures in the schools: Training and service delivery. *Exceptional Children, 66,* 173–186.

Hill, J. L. (1999). *Meeting the needs of students with special physical and health care needs.* Upper Saddle River, NJ: Merrill/Pearson.

Klein, R. E., McHugh, E., Harrington, S. L., Davis, T., & Lieberman, L. J. (2005). Adapted bicycles for teaching riding skills. *Teaching Exceptional Children, 37*(6), 50–56.

La Vor, J. L. (1976). Federal legislation for exceptional persons: A history. In F. J. Weintraub, A. Abeson, J. Ballard, & M. L. La Vor (Eds.) *Public policy and the education of exceptional children* (pp. 96–111). Reston, VA: Council for Exceptional Children.

National Dissemination Center for Children with Disabilities. (2010, June). *Epilepsy, disability fact sheet #6.* Washington, DC: Author. Retrieved from http://www.parentcenerhub.org/wp-content/uploads/repo_items/fs6.pdf. Accessed on February 8, 2015.

National Institutes of Neurological Disorders and Stroke. (2013, June). *Spina bifida fact sheet.* Bethesda, MD: Author. Retrieved from http://www.ninds.nih.gov/disorders/spina_bifida/detail_spina_bifida.htm#261953258. Accessed on February 25, 2015.

Palfrey, J. S. (1995). Amber, Katie, and Ryan: Lessons from children with complex medical conditions. *Journal of School Health, 65,* 265–267.

Perrin, J. M., Bloom, S. R., & Gortmaker, S. L. (2007). The increase of childhood chronic conditions in the United States. *Journal of the American Medical Association, 297,* 2755–2759.

Sexson, S. B., & Dingle, A. D. (2001). Medical disorders. In F. M. Kline, L. B. Silver, & S. C. Russell (Eds.), *The educator's guide to medical issues in the classroom* (pp. 29–48). Baltimore, MD: Brookes.

Snell, M. E., & Browder, D. M. (1986). Community-referenced instruction: Research and issues. *Journal of the Association for Severely Handicapped, 11,* 1–11.

Spina Bifida Association. (2014). *What is spina bifida?* Retrieved from http://www.spinabifidaassociation.org/site/c.evKRI-70X1oJ8H/b.8277225/k.5A79/What_is_Spina_Bifida.htm. Accessed on February 25, 2015.

Spina Bifida Association. (2015). *State rate fact sheets.* Retrieved from http://www.spinabifidaassociation.org/site/c.evKRI-70X1oJ8H/b.8095657/k.5D77/State_Rate_Fact_Sheets.htm. Accessed on February 25, 2015.

United Cerebral Palsy. (2015). *What is cerebral palsy?* Washington, DC: Author. Retrieved from http://cerebralpalsy.org/about-cerebral-palsy/. Accessed on February 25, 2015.

U.S. Department of Education (2014). *Thirty-sixth annual report to Congress on the Implementation of the Individuals with Disabilities Education Act.* Washington, DC: Author.

Van der Lee, J. H., Mokkink, L. B., Grootenhuis, M. A., Heymans, H. S., & Offringa, M. (2007). Definitions and measurement of chronic health conditions in childhood: A systematic review. *Journal of the American Medical Association, 297,* 2741–2751.

Chapter 11

Viewpoints on Interventions for Learners with Disabilities: Beyond Tradition

Festus E. Obiakor, Jeffrey P. Bakken and Jessica Graves

Abstract

Changes are occuring at a startling fillip in our society and our world. One of the changes is the need to revamp how persons with disabilities are treated and educated. In the United States of America, laws have been pulmulgated to reduce the plight of learners with disabilties. As a result, myriad intervention strategies have been instituted to identify, assess, label, place, and educate these learners. However, some interventions continue to be very traditional. To go beyond tradition and adequately maximize the fullest potential of learners with disabilties, we must value the "specialness" of special education as a powerful intervention program, listen to new voices with new ideas, and debunk deficit thinking that are prejudicial, especially in helping people with disabilities to survive in our competitive society. Interestingly, the chapters in this book have exposed the different intervention options for learners with disabilities. Clearly, without innovative interventions for these learners, special education will be a failure.

Keywords: Intervention; learners with disabilities; "specialness" of special education; new voices; new thinking

Viewpoints on Interventions for Learners with Disabilities
Advances in Special Education, Volume 33, 221–234
ISSN: 0270-4013/doi:10.1108/S0270-401320180000033011

People with disabilities are no more strangers in our midst today. They can no longer be ignored, downplayed, or demeaned. While many countries such as the United States of America have made frantic efforts to design innovative intervention programs for these individuals, some countries still do not have appropriate laws to protect them. In addition, many general and special education professionals continue to "scotch the snake but not kill it" in the retrogressive ways that they have viewed people with disabilities and programs designed to assist them. Sadly, instead of viewing special education as an intervention or remediation program for persons with disabilities, some poorly prepared or misinformed professionals view special education as a "placement" or "setting." The logical extension is that in many cases special education is not doing what it is supposed to do as an indispensable educational intervention program. And many scholars (e.g., Obiakor & Gibson, in press; Obiakor & Smith, 2012; Smith & Tyler, 2010; Tetzloff & Obiakor, 2015) now wonder why it does not seriously bother or shame general and special educators, school leaders, community leaders, and government agencies that some learners in our classrooms are misidentified, misassessed, mislabeled, misplaced, and misinstructed because of their disabilities. Instead of enjoying the benefits of special education as an important intervention program, many learners with disabilities are still placed and instructed in very restrictive environments.

The chapters in this book have addressed multidimensional intervention strategies for different learners with disabilities. To a large extent, these intervention strategies are tied to special education principles and priorities. Some years ago, Blackhurst and Berdine (1993) argued that special education must always be aimed at providing intervention services different from, supplementary with, and additional to those provided in a regular classroom with a systematic modification and adaptation of instruction, equipment, and materials. Based on this thorough definition, special education is a much-needed intervention service for all learners struggling to succeed in academic arenas. In other words, if done authentically right, at-risk, disadvantaged, disenfranchised, urban, suburban, rural, poor, homeless, and culturally and linguistically diverse (CLD) students would benefit from special education. It is unconscionable that these atypical learners continue to endure problems and crisis in today's general and special education programs that are supposed to help them to maximize their fullest potential. The question then is, what can we do to remediate or eliminate these socio-educational problems? In this chapter, we share our viewpoints on interventions for learners with disabilities that go beyond tradition.

Frameworks for Special Education Interventions

To understand the societal efforts that have been undertaken to assist learners with disabilities, it is important to expose the historical contexts and frameworks of these efforts. Yes, individuals with disabilities have existed and participated in societal functions in one way or another. For instance, the Jewish Talmud, Moslem Koran, and Christian Bible made particular references on persons with disabilities. As a result, two questions come to mind. First, what kind of intervention techniques have been used to work with them? And second, have these intervention techniques helped them to maximize their fullest potential? In fact, all societies, including the United States have continued to focus on how to take care of their less fortunate, less powerful, disenfranchised, and disadvantaged (Obiakor & Algozzine, 1995). Interestingly, people with disabilities fall under this less fortunate, less powerful, disenfranchised, disadvantaged, and vulnerable group. And, for many CLD learners with disabilities, their problems become doubly troublesome. From these historical contexts, it appears that efforts have concentrated on how to tolerate and/or victimize these individuals rather than on making functional intervention efforts to truly educate them with *real pedagogical power*. Earlier, Hilliard (1992) observed that real pedagogical power means that "all children who may have disabilities receive sophisticated, valid services that cause them to do better than they would have done if they had not received special services at all" (p. 168).

In the late 18th century, Jean Marc Itard, a French physician believed in real pedagogical power when he decided to take on the task of educating Victor, the "wild boy" of Aveyron, France. Even this "wild boy" was able to acquire some skills, an indication that special education works as an intervention tool when done right. In the early parts of the 20th century, Dr. Alfred Binet, the brain behind the current Stanford–Binet Intelligence Scale, noted that human knowledge and/or intelligence can be assessed and improved. Using his experiences with his special class, Binet (1909) warned against the over reliance on his intelligence quotient tool. As he remarked:

> It is in this parochial sense, the only one accessible to us, that we say that intelligence of these children has been increased.

> We have increased what constitutes the intelligence of a pupil: the capacity to learn and to assimilate instruction. (p. 104)

This means that no brain is a *tabula rasa* (blank slate) and that all children can learn when provided with adequate intervention strategy. Put another way, intervention works!

More than three decades ago, Gould (1981) decried the mismeasure of persons with and without disabilities and argued that "if Binet's principles had been followed, and his tests consistently used as he intended, we would have been spared a major misuse of science in our century" (p. 155). In addition, he warned against the blind use of the theory of biological determinism – that is, the belief that human attributes are only genetically based. Goodlad (1993) corroborated Gould's premise and noted that:

> We appear incapable of getting beyond individuals as the units of assessment with the accompanying allocation of responsibility for success and failure. We must adopt as standard practice the kind of contextual appraisal that tells whether schools have in place the curriculum, materials, pedagogy, and other conditions necessary to the good education of individuals. The absence of these exposes and brings inequities that are the moral responsibility of a caring people in a just society to correct. (p. 2)

The Relationship Between Legal Principles and Special Education Interventions

It is a natural instinct for people to associate or deal with those who behave, look, speak, and act like them. Anyone who does not fall in that norm is traditionally misperceived, misanalyzed, mistreated, and miseducated (James, 1958; Obiakor, 2008, 2009). As a result, innovative interventions especially those that go beyond tradition are needed for learners with disabilities since they do not fit into the norm. It should be no surprise that those with disabilities continue to be discriminated against, ostracized, labeled, and called demeaning names (e.g., stupid and retarded). Today, advocates of these learners have pressed for innovative ways to positively respond to their unique needs in quantifiable ways (Obiakor, Harris, & Beachum, 2009).

In the United States, it is impossible to divorce the education of learners with disabilities from the Civil Rights Movement and the subsequent events that followed. To a great extent, educational intervention programs for these learners have been historically influenced by social developments and court decisions in the 1950s and 1960s. For example, the landmark *Brown v. Board of Education of Topeka* (1954) case was a civil rights case that declared separate education as unequal education and unconstitutional (Obiakor, 2009). The ruling of this case became a catalyst that prompted parents and professionals to lobby for equitable education for learners with disabilities. The *Brown* ruling, in the United States, led to more landmark cases that have had historical and educational impacts. For example, the P*ennsylvania Association for Retarded Children v. Commonwealth of Pennsylvania (1971)* case held that children could not be denied access to public schools, and entitled them to a free and appropriate public education. In the *Mills v. Board of Education* 1972 case, a class action lawsuit was filed on behalf of 18,000 children with varied special needs in the Washington, DC schools. In this case, the court ordered the district to educate all learners with disabilities and further clarified that specific procedures had to be followed to determine whether a student should receive special services. Generally, these cases and other subsequent cases formed the framework for the laws that currently guide the field of special education (Yell, 2004). The question is: What have we learned from these court cases regarding intervention programs for learners with disabilities?

In the United States, many laws have historically impacted the fields of general and special education. For instance, the 1964 *Civil Rights Act* (PL 88-352) provided legal rights to equality in education and other sectors of human interactions. In 1973, Section 504 of the Vocational Rehabilitation Act (PL 93-112) was passed to provide learners with disabilities with (a) free and appropriate public education, (b) civil rights, (c) accessibility of programs, and (d) employability rights. In 1975, the Education of All Handicapped Children's Act (PL 94-142) was passed with the following fundamental ingredients: (a) education for students from 3 to 21 years, (b) free and appropriate public education, (c) identification of students, (d) nondiscriminatory assessments, (e) placement in the least restrictive environment (LRE), (f) confidentiality of information, (g) procedural safeguards, and (h) development of individualized education plans (IEPs). In 1986, PL 94-142 was amended to accommodate young children from birth to three years. This law (PL 99-457) was enacted to provide not just IEPs for children but also individual family support programs for parents and guardians.

PL 94-142 was renamed as the Individuals with Disabilities Education Act (IDEA, 1990; PL 101-476). This act involved funding for states to provide educational services to students from birth through 21, and ensured procedural safeguards for parents that guarantee meaningful participation in the evaluation process (Katisyannis, Yell, & Bradley, 2001). Additionally, IDEA guaranteed improvement in the education of students with special needs through research training, technical supports, and transitional supports for students. To challenge the private sectors, the 1990 American with Disabilities Act (PL 101-336) was passed to provide more societal opportunities for persons with special needs. IDEA (1997) was reauthorized as PL 105-17 to facilitate disciplinary procedures and reduce litigation costs. The No Child Left Behind Act (2001; PL 107-110) was passed to educate all learners and quantifiably account for their progress at all levels. Later, IDEA (2004) was again reauthorized as the Individuals with Disabilities Education Improvement Act (PL 108-446). This law mandated that teachers of students with special needs be highly qualified, meaning they must be certified in the content areas that they are teaching (Smith, 2005). Recently, in December, the Every Student Succeeds Act (2015; PL 114-95) was passed to reauthorize the 1965 Elementary Secondary Education Act. Clearly, these governmental efforts have defined laudable special education steps that are tied to strategic intervention plans for learners with disabilities.

Interventions Beyond Tradition

For innovative interventions to work, general and special education professionals working with learners with disabilities must (a) understand the "specialness" of special education, (b) value new voices, and (c) discourage deficit thinking.

Understanding the "Specialness" of Special Education

The goal of any educational intervention program is to maximize the fullest potential of its students. The critical question remains, Do we stay the course, resist change, or move forward in the education of learners with disabilities. More than a decade ago, Schrag (1993) confirmed that "the proportion of students being served within special education programs today and in the future is changing, which requires closer integration and coordination of services within the educational system and with a broader array of health and social services" (p. 208). The response of the federal government with regard to these imperatives has been "accountability without accountability." Sadly, some accountability measures have continued to hurt the spirit of special education for students who need it (Kauffman, 2003, 2004; Obiakor, 2007; Utley & Obiakor, 2001). In his piece titled, "The Death of Special Education," Lieberman (2001) argued that:

> Special education has been swallowed by the beast: the school system, with its mandated curriculum, mandated tests, and mandated standards. Now, children with disabilities are entitled – no, are practically required – to have the same education as every other child, regardless of whether or not that education is of high quality or is appropriate for a child with a disability. (p. 39)

While it is iconoclastic to believe special education "has been swallowed by the beast" because of accountability challenges that are forced upon it, it is equally unrealistic to assume that we should just "stay the course" in special education. Any field or profession that does not believe in positive change is dead. Clearly, recent demographic changes in our society have challenged general and special educators and leaders to look for innovative ways to maximize the potential of all their students (Obiakor, 2007; Rueda, 2007). As Rueda (2007) argued, "given the longstanding but continuing controversy over the issue of overrepresentation of diverse students in special education, the future implications for identification, referral, assessment, and instructions are abundant" (p. 292). Kauffman (2003, 2004) and Mostert, Kauffman, and Kavale (2003) have been critical of new voices in special education. Without these new voices, how can we advance innovative interventive strategies for learners with disabilities. As they noted, it is wrong to criticize the current system of special education because such criticisms are anti-special education.

Valuing New Voices

The chapters in this book have exposed voices, ideas, and intervention techniques that have been known to work for learners with disabilities. They also have exposed readers to new voices, ideas, and intervention techniques that are beyond tradition. Clearly, *new voices are needed to advance the historical importance of special education and the central idea that intervention must be differentiated and individualized.* The whole process of special education must be appropriately targeted to reach all learners with disabilities. For example, innovative intervention efforts must be made to (a) provide an appropriate education, (b) identify learners who truly need educational modifications at every level, (c) follow procedural safeguards, (d) educate learners in LREs, (e) maintain confidentiality of information of learners, (f) collaborate and consult with parents and guardians, and (g) work with multidisciplinary team members and professionals (Obiakor, 1999, 2001). To a large measure, innovative intervention strategies are always successful for these learners with disabilities, when general and special educators and school leaders continue to

1. Develop and use identification, assessment, and instructional strategies that function within the context of cultural competence.
2. Create a collaborative system of community support that focuses on eradicating social stereotyping based on disability, race, ethnicity, national origin, gender, and socio-economic status.
3. Develop an awareness and appreciation for the many family forms that value individual differences and strengths.
4. Thwart conditions that lead to violence in the home or community and cultivate a sense of safety for children and families.
5. Advocate economic policies and human services that are profamily and prohuman by virtue of proven outcomes.
6. Promote culturally competent practices in schools and in the larger society to respect differences in worldviews and learning styles among all individuals, including those with disabilities.
7. Advocate expanded services that provide for affordable quality childcare to meet the varied needs of all families and children.
8. Develop collaborative community approaches to problem-solving that involve students, parents, schools, and community leaders.
9. Recognize that institutional barriers in the environment can impede learning.
10. Embrace new technologies that will improve the lives of persons and learners with disabilities and narrow the gaps of communications among peoples and communities.
11. Reconfigure curricula that incorporate culturally and disability sensitive variables.
12. Reinstitute service opportunities that cultivate a sense of belonging and resiliency in all youth, including those with disabilities.
13. Broaden visions in educational reform that include health care reform, economic reform, and the investment in human capital.

Discouraging Deficit Thinking

For innovative interventions to work, special education professionals avoid deficit thinking. For example, these professionals must go beyond the archaic theory of biological determinism and the myth of socio-economic dissonance (Gould, 1981; Obiakor & Martinez, 2016; Obiakor & Smith, 2012; Weikart, 1977). For instance, more than 40 years ago, Weikart (1977) warned that the deficit model of thinking, when applied to a certain population (in this case, learners with disabilities), "seems to limit potential assistance to that group because it channels thinking in ways that emphasize weaknesses rather than strengths, and it interprets differences from the norm as individual deficits" (p. 175). The logical extension is that:

> We cannot limit ourselves to the identification of trait dimensions or typological classifications across individuals without also considering the characteristics of the environments within which individuals function. Nor can we limit ourselves to an analysis of the environmental determinants of human differences without also considering the hereditary determinants. Finally, we have to ask ourselves what kind of society is most desirable for the expression of human diversity – for the opportunity for each of us to grow as individuals and at the same time not infringe on the rights of others to develop their own individuality. (Minton & Schneider, 1985, p. 489)

Minton and Schneider's (1985) statements above have far-reaching implications for research, policy, and practice in the general and special education of all learners. For instance, first, research that focuses on behavior problems of children and youth needs to address measures that will help to understand them. When we understand them, we assist them to be functional, goal-directed decision-makers in our complex society. Put another way, research that focuses on underlying pathological attributes of learners needs to be valued with caution because such a research is deficit-oriented and lacks measurable, observable, and intervention-based attributes. Second, research, policy, and practice ought to go hand-in-glove. About two decades ago, Keogh (1990) noted that "from this perspective, policy should follow research, and change should be found in evidence" (p. 186). It is apparent that something is wrong with traditional intervention strategies for learners with disabilities. Third, research that divorces itself from the fundamental principles of individualized instructional programming for these learners fails to appreciate or value their unique styles and differences.

In the end, research studies that is not tied to intervention and with skewed divisive, emotionally loaded, and political underpinnings must be discouraged in special education. Any research that does not lend itself to common-sense problem-solving interpretation and intervention must be viewed with caution. Fortunately today, most scholarly publications (e.g., *Behavior Disorders, Exceptional Children, Intervention in School and Clinic, Journal of Special Education, Multicultural Learning and Teaching, Multiple Voices, Remedial and Special Education, Teacher Education and Special Education*) are demanding pedagogical and practical implications. Consequently, scholars, educators, and leaders must begin to broaden their definitions, theories, and intervention models to reduce illusory conclusions, perceptual assumptions, and prejudicial generalizations (Obiakor, 2007).

It has become very apparent that educator preparation programs have roles to play in fostering new interventions in schools and classrooms. Clearly, poorly prepared teachers teach learners with disabilities poorly. It is important that teacher educators and leaders practice what they preach – they must use divergent techniques to prepare future educators who will, in turn, use divergent techniques to teach learners who exhibit different styles, skills, and needs. To look for the "magic pill" that can cure educational problems of all learners is not realistic. However, the key is for teacher educators and leaders to prepare those who value individual differences and cultural needs of these learners (Wilder, Obiakor, & Algozzine, 2003). By so doing, they become aware of emotional first-aids needed to address disruptions and crises confronting their learners (Obiakor, Mehring& Schwenn, 1997). Clearly, teacher educators and leaders must embrace and not bemoan new socio-emotional and multicultural paradigms that incorporate quality and equity in general and special educational intervention programs (Obiakor, in press; Obiakor & Gibson, in press; Obiakor & Smith, 2012). In the end, they must avoid any kind of multiculturalism that tends to project "goodness" with underlying negative intentions and phony sense of community. This kind of goodness hampers ways to increase the knowledge about the interactions between human behaviors and cultural styles.

Conclusion

The United States has tried to institute historical policies and legal mandates to protect learners with disabilities. In addition, it has tried to provide them with equitable public education. However, the interpretation and implementation of pertinent laws have garnered many loopholes that need to be sealed for learners with disabilities. Our intervention techniques must be beyond tradition. If these learners get misidentified, misassessed, mislabeled, misplaced, and misinstructed, it means that their educational intervention needs cannot be met. Appropriate educational programming should be in the LREs that help these learners to maximize their fullest potential. We believe the heart and soul of quality service delivery for these learners must include nonrestrictive environments and settings that maximize their potential. Clearly, such environments must be disability, racially, culturally, linguistically, and socio-economically accepting.

Finally, for some strange reason, we seem to be unprepared for changes in general and special education. While we do advocate for iconoclastic behaviors in education, it is critical that we embrace change, not necessarily as a natural phenomenon as it sometimes happens, but as something that is made to happen. Our learners need innovative intervention strategies that could make them to grow. That is why we urge the readers of this book to be a part of change just as the contributors of this book have posited. In fact, all of us must be collaboratively, consultatively, and cooperatively involved in change to meet the unique needs of our learners with and without disabilities, advance our profession, and uplift fellow humans.

References

Americans with Disabilities Act. (1980). Pub. L. No. 101-336.

Binet, A. (1909). *Les ideas modernes sur les enfants [Modern ideas for children]*. Paris, France: Hammarion.

Blackhurst, A. E., & Berdine, W. H. (1993). *An introduction to special education* (3rd ed.). New York, NY: Harper Collins.

Brown v. Board of Education of Topeka Kansas. (1954). 347 U.S. 483, 745-ct-686, 98 L. Ed. 873, 530. 0. 326.

Civil Rights Act. (1964). Pub. L. No. 88-352.

Education of All Handicapped Children Act. (1975). Pub. L. No. 94-142.

Education of All Handicapped Children Act Amendments. (1986). Pub. L. No. 99-457.

Every Student Succeeds Act. (2015). Pub. L. No. 114-95.

Goodlad, J. I. (1983). Access to knowledge. In J. I. Goodlad & T. L. Lovitt (Eds.), *Integrating general and special education* (pp. 1–22). New York, NY: Merrill.

Gould, S. J. (1981). *The mismeasure of man.* New York, NY: W. W. Morton.

Hilliard, A. G. (1992, October/November). The pitfalls and practices of special education practice. *Exceptional Children, 59,* 168–172.

Individuals with Disabilities Education Act. (1990). Pub. L. No. 101-476.

Individuals with Disabilities Education Act. (1997). Pub. L. No. 105-17.

Individuals with Disabilities Education Improvement Act. (2004). Pub. L. No. 108-446.

James, W. (1958). *Talk to teachers on psychology, and to students on life's ideas.* New York, NY: W. W. Norton.

Kauffman, J. M. (2003, July/August). Appearances, stigma, and prevention. *Remedial and Special Education, 24,* 195–198.

Kauffman, J. M. (2004). The President's commission and the devaluation of special education. *Education and Treatment of Children, 27,* 307–324.

Keogh, B. K. (1990, October/November). Narrowing the gap between policy and practice. *Exceptional Children, 57*(2), 186–190.

Lieberman, L. M. (2001). The death of special education. *Education Week,* January 17, pp. 39–41.

Mills v. *Board of Education of the District of Columbia.* (1992). 348 f. Supp. 866 (D.D.C.1972).

Minton, H., & Schneider, F. (1985). *Differential psychology.* Prospect Heights, IL: Waveland Press.

Mostert, M. P., Kauffman, J. M., & Kavale, K. A. (2003, August). Truth and consequences. *Behavioral Disorders, 28,* 333–347.

No Child Left Behind Act. (2001). Pub. L. No. 107-110.

Obiakor, F. E. (1999). Teacher expectations of minority exceptional learners: Impact on "accuracy" of self-concepts. *Exceptional Children, 66,* 39–53.

Obiakor, F. E. (2001a). Developing emotional intelligence in learners with behavioral problems: Refocusing special education. *Behavior Disorders, 26,* 321–331.

Obiakor, F. E. (2001b). *It even happens in good schools: Responding to cultural diversity in today's classrooms.* Thousand Oaks, CA: Corwin Press.

Obiakor, F. E. (2007). *Multicultural special education: Culturally responsive teaching.* Upper Saddle River, NJ: Pearson/Merrill Prentice Hall.

Obiakor, F. E. (2008). *The eight-step approach to multicultural learning and teaching* (3rd ed.). Dubuque, IA: Kendall/Hunt.

Obiakor, F. E. (2009). Educating African American urban learners: Brown in context. In M. C. Brown, II & R. D. Bartee (Eds.), *The broken cisterns of African American education* (pp. 61–72). Charlotte, NC: Information Age.

Obiakor, F. E. (in press). *Powerful multicultrual essays for innovative educators and leaders: Optomizing "hearty" conversations.* Charlotte, NC: Inormation Age.

Obiakor, F. E., & Algozzine, B. (1995). Educating learners with problem behaviors: An unresolved issue for general and special educators. In F. E. Obiakor & B. Algozzine, B. (Eds.), *Managing problem behaviors: Perspectives for general and special educators* (pp. 1–19). Dubuque, IA: Kendall/Hunt.

Obiakor, F. E., & Gibson, L. (in press). Reversing the use of Hobson's choice: Unworkable intervention choice for culturally and linguistically diverse learners with problem behaviors. *Journal of the International Association of Special Education (JIASE)*.

Obiakor, F. E., Harris, M. K., & Beachum, F. D. (2009). The state of special education for African American learners in Milwaukee. In G. Williams & F. E. Obiakor (Eds.). *The state of education of urban learners and possible solutions: The Milwaukee experience* (pp. 31–48). Dubuque, IA: Kendall/Hunt.

Obiakor, F. E., & Martinez, J. (2016). *Latin@ voices in multicutural education: From invisibility to visibility in higher education.* New York, NY: Nova Science Publishers.

Obiakor, F. E., Mehring, T. A., & Schwenn, J. O. (1997). *Disruption, disaster, and death: Helping students deal with crises.* Arlington, VA: Council for Exceptional Children.

Obiakor, F. E., & Smith, R. (2012). *Special education practices: personal naraatives of African American scholars, educators, and related professionals.* New York, NY: Nova Science Publishers.

Obiakor, F. E., Utley, C. A., & Rotatori, A. F. (2003). *Advances in special education: Effective education for learners with exceptionalities* (Vol. 15). Oxford: Elsevier Science/JAI Press.

Pennsylvania Association for Retarded Children v. Commonwealth of Pennsylvania. (1971). 343 F. Supp. 279 (D. C. Pa 1971).

Rueda, R. (2007). Multicultural special education: Future perspectives. In F. E. Obiakor (Ed.), *Multicultural special education: Culturally responsive teaching* (pp. 290–297). Upper Saddle River, NJ: Pearson/Merrill Prentice Hall.

Schrag, J. A. (1993). Restructuring schools for better alignment of general and special education. In J. I. Goolad & T. C. Lovitt (Eds.), *Integrating general and special education* (pp. 203–227). New York, NY: Merrill.

Smith, D. D., & Tyler, N.C. (2010). *Introduction to special education: Making a difference* (7th ed.). Upper Saddle River, NJ: Merrill.

Tetzloff, L., & Obiakor, F. E. (2015). James M. Kauffman's ideas about special education: Implications for educating culturally and linguistically diverse students. *International Journal of Special Education, 30*(2), 1–13.

Utley, C. A., & Obiakor, F. E. (2001). *Special education, multicultural education, and school reform: Components of quality education for learners with mild disabilities.* Springfield, IL: Charles C. Thomas.

Vocational Rehabilitation Act. (1973). Pub. L. No. 93-112.

Weikart, D. P. (1977). Preschool intervention for the disadvantaged child: A challenge for special education. In H. H. Spicker, K. J. Anastasiow, & W. L. Hodges (Eds.), *Children with special needs: Early development and education* (pp. 73–89). Minneapolis, MN: Leadership Training Institute/Special Education, University of Minnesota.

Wilder, L. K., Obiakor, F. E., & Algozzine, B. (2003, Summer). Homeless students in special education: Beyond the myth of socioeconomic dissonance. *The Journal of At-Risk Issues, 9*, 9–16.

Yell, M. L. (2004). *The law and special education* (2nd ed.). Upper Saddle River, NJ: Prentice Hall.

Index

NOTE: Page numbers followed by '*f*' and '*t*' refers to figures and tables in the text.